THE HELL-FI

CW00540347

Evelyn Lord, an expert in Local 1
works of history including *The Knig*
Stuart Secret Army.

The
Hell-Fire Clubs

SEX, SATANISM AND SECRET SOCIETIES

EVELYN LORD

YALE UNIVERSITY PRESS
NEW HAVEN AND LONDON

Published with assistance from the Annie Burr Lewis Fund

First printed in paperback 2010

For information about this and other Yale University Press publications, please contact:

U.S. Office: sales.press@yale.edu   yalebooks.com
Europe Office: sales@yaleup.co.uk   yalebooks.co.uk

Set in Caslon Regular by J&L Composition Ltd, Filey, North Yorkshire
Printed in Great Britain by Hobbs the Printers Ltd, Totton, Hampshire

Library of Congress Cataloging-in-Publication Data

Lord, Evelyn.
    The Hell-Fire clubs: sex, Satanism and secret societies / Evelyn Lord.
        p. cm.
    Includes bibliographical references and index.
    ISBN 978–0–300–11667–0 (ci: alk. paper)
    1. Hell Fire Club (Medmenham, England). 2. England–Social life and customs–18th century. I. Title.
    DA485.L67 2008
    366–dc22

                                                                        2008016696

A catalogue record for this book is available from the British Library.

ISBN 978–0–300–16402–2 (pbk)

10 9 8 7 6 5 4 3

Contents

Acknowledgements   vii

List of Illustrations   ix

The Hell-Fire Clubs Time Line   xi

Introduction   xix

Chapter 1 Prelude to the Fires of Hell   1

Chapter 2 Gentlemen's Clubs, Journalistic Hacks,
           the Mohocks and Change   19

Chapter 3 The Hell-Fire Clubs   45

Chapter 4 Interlude Abroad: the Grand Tour, Dilettanti
           and Divans   75

Chapter 5 The Medmenham Friars   97

Chapter 6 *Essay on Woman*: the Friars Exposed   115

Chapter 7 Public Men and Private Vices   131

Chapter 8 Scotland and the Fires of Hell   157

Chapter 9 Beefsteaks, Demoniacs, Dalkey and
           Colonial America   187

           Conclusion   211

           Notes   215

           Bibliography   233

           Index   243

Acknowledgements

Thanks for their help to Cambridge University Library, especially Rare Books, Special Collections of Edinburgh University, Special Collections St Andrews University, the Scottish National Archives, the Scottish National Library, Matthew Bailey of the National Portrait Gallery, Emma Whinton-Brown of the National Monuments Record, Jennifer Adams of the British Museum Department of Coins and Medals, Jennifer Ramkaloon of the British Museum Department of Prints and Drawings, Philip Judge for drawing maps, Heather McCallum of Yale University Press, Dr Rosemary Sweet of University of Leicester for sound advice, Alec and Joyce Tait for chocolate, pork pies and beer, Gabriel Lord for putting up with me in Edinburgh and exploring Fife with me, Edward Lord for being Edward Lord.

Illustrations

1. *Philip, Duke of Wharton*, John Simon, after Charles Jervas (early eighteenth century), National Portrait Gallery, London

2. *John Wilmot, 2nd Earl of Rochester*, unknown artist (*c.*1665–1670), National Portrait Gallery, London

3. *He and His Drunken Companions Raise a Riot in Covent Garden*, after William Hogarth (1735), © The Trustees of the British Museum

4. *The Diabolical Maskquerade* (1721), © The Trustees of the British Museum

5. *Sir Francis Dashwood*, attributed to Nathaniel Dance (1776), National Portrait Gallery, London

6. Unknown man, formerly known as Paul Whitehead, John Downman (1770), National Portrait Gallery, London

7. Charles Churchill, by J.S.C. Schaak (*c.* 1763–1764), National Portrait Gallery, London

8. *John Wilkes*, unknown artist (*c.* 1769), National Portrait Gallery, London

9. West Wycombe Park, Temple of Venus, reproduced by permission of English Heritage.NMR

10. West Wycombe Mausoleum, reproduced by permission of English Heritage.NMR

11. West Wycombe Church, reproduced by permission of English Heritage.NMR

12. West Wycombe House as remodelled by Sir Francis Dashwood, reproduced by permission of English Heritage.NMR

13. *The Earl of Sandwich*, by Joseph Highmore (1740), National Portrait Gallery, London

14. Map of the Firth of Forth, Scotland, drawn by Philip Judge
    Map of the East Neuk of Fife, home of the Beggar's Benison, drawn by Philip Judge

15. Beggar's Benison medal, © the Trustees of The British Museum

16. Beggar's Benison Testing Platter, reproduced courtesy of the University of St Andrews

17. Wig Club Wig Stand, reproduced courtesy of the University of St Andrews

18. Beggar's Benison Wine Glass, photograph reproduced courtesy of John de T. Vischer

19. Wig Club Phallic Glass, reproduced courtesy of the University of St Andrews

20. Beggar's Benison Bible, photograph reproduced courtesy of Larry Hutchison

21. Castle Dreel at Anstruther in Fife, photograph by Gabriel Lord

22. The author at Anstruther in Fife, photograph by Gabriel Lord

The Hell-Fire Clubs Time Line

Date	National	Cultural	Hell-Fire
1602			Damned Crew
1603	Accession of James I		
1605	Gunpowder Plot		
1609			Society of Boys
1616		Death of Shakespeare	
1623		First Folio published	Tityre Tues
1647			Earl of Rochester born
1649	Execution of Charles I; Commonwealth		
1653			Term Rake-Hell coined
1660	Restoration	John Evelyn and Samuel Pepys active	
1665	Great Plague		
1666	Fire of London		
1676			Rochester at Epsom

Date	National	Cultural	Hell-Fire
1679			Rochester dies
1688	Glorious Revolution		
1689	Mary's letter to the Magistrates		
1690		John Locke, *Essay on Human Understanding*	
1691	Foundation of Societies for Reformation of Manners		George Bubb born
1696	Jacobite Assassination Plot		
1697		Daniel Defoe, *Essay upon Projects*	
1698			Duke of Wharton born
1700	Edinburgh Society for Reformation of Manners		
1701	Act of Settlement	Yale College founded	
1702	Accession of Queen Anne; War of Spanish Succession		
1704	Battle of Blenheim	Isaac Newton, *Optics*	
1706	Battle of Ramillies		

Date	National	Cultural	Hell-Fire
1707	Union with Scotland		
1708			Sir Francis Dashwood and John Cleland born
1709			Ned Ward's *Secret History of Clubs* published
1710	Visit of Iroquois chiefs		Paul Whitehead born
1711	South Sea Fund started	*The Spectator* founded	
1712	Trial of Jane Wenham		The Mohock Scare
1713	Treaty of Utrecht		
1714	Accession of George I		
1715	Jacobite Rebellion; Riot Act passed		
1716		*The Ladies Physical Directory*	
1717		Horace Walpole born	
1718	First silk mill in production, at Derby	Society of Antiquaries founded	Earl of Sandwich born
1719	Attempted Jacobite landing in Scotland	Daniel Defoe, *Robinson Crusoe*	
1720	South Sea Bubble		

Date	National	Cultural	Hell-Fire
1721	Robert Walpole becomes first minister		The Hell-Fire Club
1722	Atterbury Plot	Daniel Defoe, *Moll Flanders*	
1724	Black Acts adding many capital offences	Daniel Defoe, *Tour through Great Britain*	Schemers Club
1725			John Wilkes born
1726			Sir Francis Dashwood's first Grand Tour
1727	Accession of George II		
1728		John Gay, *Beggar's Opera*	
1731	Treaty of Vienna		
1732			Duke of Wharton dies; Beggar's Benison founded; Society of Dilettanti founded
1733		Pope, *Essay on Man*	Dashwood in Russia; Society of Beefsteaks founded
1735		Hogarth, *Rake's Progress*	Irish Hell-Fire Club
1736	Repeal of the Witchcraft Act		

Date	National	Cultural	Hell-Fire
1739	War of Jenkins's Ear	Wesley starts preaching	Trial of Lord Santry for murder
1740	War of Austrian Succession		
1741		David Hume, *Essays: Moral and Political*	
1742	Walpole resigns		
1744	Broadbottom Ministry	*The School of Venus* published	Divan Club founded
1745	Jacobite Invasion		
1746	Battle of Culloden		End of Divan Club
1749		Henry Fielding, *Tom Jones* published; John Cleland, *Memoirs of a Woman of Pleasure* published	
1751	Julian Calendar Act; Pelham's Ministry		Medmenham Friars founded; Norwich Hell-Fire Club
1752	Pitt's Ministry		
1753	Last Jacobite execution	*Essay on Woman* written by John Wilkes and Thomas Potter	
1754	Newcastle's Ministry		
1756	Seven Years War		

Date	National	Cultural	Hell-Fire
1762	Bute's Ministry; Dashwood Chancellor	*North Briton* 45	Horace Walpole visits Medmenham Abbey; Knights of the Cape
1763	Treaty of Paris		Expulsion of Wilkes from the Friars
1767		Dashwood and Franklin meet	Demoniacs founded
1771			Dublin Hell-Fire refounded
1773			Mohawks reappear
1774			Wig Club founded; Paul Whitehead dies
1775	War of American Independence		Dashwood dies
1776		Adam Smith, *Wealth of Nations*	
1781			Phoenix Club in Oxford
1783	American Independence		
1787	Societies for the Suppression of Vice founded		
1789		William Blake, *Songs of Innocence*	

Date	National	Cultural	Hell-Fire
1791	United Irishmen founded	Tom Paine, *Rights of Man* published	John Cleland dies
1792			Earl of Sandwich dies
1793	French War starts		
1795	Orange Society founded		
1797			John Wilkes dies; Kingdom of Dalkey

Introduction

The scene is the House of Lords, the date is May 1721. A peer, with a bible in his pocket and an expression of piety on his face, stands up to speak. He is a handsome fellow, young and upright; his voice is clear and rings out with sincerity, or so it seems to some of his listeners. He says he is glad of the chance to justify himself 'by declaring that he is far from being a patron of blasphemy or an enemy of religion', but he could not support a bill which he considered to be repugnant to Holy Scripture. Taking the family bible from his pocket, he treats his listeners to several passages from the Epistles of Saints Peter and Paul, and concludes that the bill should be thrown out.[1]

The bill he was arguing about was the Bill to Prevent Blasphemy and Profaneness, and it was aimed at suppressing a 'scandalous society with the name of the Hell-Fire Club'. The speaker was the twenty-three-year-old Philip, Duke of Wharton, the alleged founder and patron of the club.

London in the spring of 1721 was abuzz with rumours of high-born Devil-worshippers who mocked the established Church and religion, and allegedly supped with Satan – rumours which went as far as the ears of the King, George I, and resulted in a royal proclamation against such clubs, and the aforesaid bill being put into Parliament. What did the hell-fire clubs represent, and why was there such an outcry against these organisations?

The hell-fire clubs represented an enduring fascination with the forbidden fruit offered by the Devil, and a continuing flirtation with danger and the unknown. These clubs issued a challenge to Satan to make himself known, and a challenge to the Church and the ethics of society to prevent this. The members of such clubs were on a mission for excitement; they wanted sensual delights, sexual pleasure, and an alternative to religion. They hit out at the moral code of Christian society, and questioned the conventional teachings of the established Church. But the members of these clubs faced a dilemma: if they believed in Satan and hell-fire, did they by implication believe in a supernatural being called God, and a place called Heaven? The Hell-Fire Club members of 1721 denied that they were atheists, but were they, in fact, reaffirming Christian theology by mocking outdated superstitions? They belonged to an age that sought to demystify death and challenge the superstitions surrounding death. For hell-fire club members Hell was a mere invention designed to frighten sinners and send them down the paths of righteousness. However, for most members of these clubs their aims were neither intellectual nor theological. Instead they were seeking to shock society, cause havoc and, first and foremost, have a good time.

The eighteenth century, in which these clubs flourished, has been called the Enlightenment, but it was also an age when pleasure was seen as a right for everyone,[2] and the members of the hell-fire clubs were definitely seeking pleasure, the more extreme the better. Unfortunately, the sources that tell us about what went on at club meetings are few and unreliable. These clubs were, after all, secret societies, but what their contemporaries did not know about them they were happy to make up. Fact and fiction are intertwined in writing about the hell-fire clubs.

Books on the subject have always tended towards the sensational, with lurid covers of monks or naked women set against a background of flames. The latest edition of Geoffrey Ashe's book on the clubs is an example, with a simpering nude beauty on the cover who bears no relation to the scholarly and serious text inside the book.[3] Many books on the hell-fire clubs are based on the false supposition that Sir Francis Dashwood of West Wycombe was the founder of a hell-fire club. The highly imaginative accounts of what Sir Francis and his friends did at Medmenham Abbey in Buckinghamshire have been treated by twentieth- and twenty-first-century writers as historical fact. Undoubtedly there was some sort of secret society that met under Sir Francis's auspices at Medmenham Abbey, and certainly the grounds at West Wycombe were remodelled in a way which suggested the female form, but it is a leap from there to contemporary claims that the Medmenham club specialised in sex.[4] Our contemporary obsession with sex has caused this element of the clubs to be over-emphasised.[5]

In his books on the hell-fire clubs Ashe suggests that Sir Francis Dashwood was trying to recreate the Abbey of Thélème. The Abbey of Thélème appeared in *The History of Gargantua and Pantagruel* written by the French monk François Rabelais, who forsook the monastery and went on his travels throughout Europe. In the book the giant *Gargantua* gives Friar John, a renegade monk, an estate on which to found a new abbey. This abbey was to be the converse of the usual enclosed religious orders as instead of being based on obedience to a set of rules, Thélème was to allow its occupants individual free will, without recourse to civil or moral laws (*thelema* is Greek for will). They were hand-picked, and all were young and beautiful. They lived a life of cultured luxury, cut off from the outside world. Thélème's motto was *Fay ce que vouldras*, or 'Do what you will'. Sir Francis Dashwood placed this motto over the front door of Medmenham Abbey. As in Thélème, the members of the club that met at Medmenham were hand-picked, but there the similarity ended: they were not all young and beautiful, and Sir Francis's interpretation of 'Do what you will' was within the confines of the club rules and general social acceptability.

In the latest edition of his book Ashe includes a discussion on the Manson family, Hell's Angels and the Oz trial and asks if these can be linked in any way to the eighteenth-century hell-fire clubs. He suggests that the latter give a context to the Manson family, a view articulated in the *Daily Telegraph* on 27 January 1971. The radical magazine *Oz* included an article searching for extenuating circumstances for the Manson family, but faced trial on a charge of obscenity. Ashe shows that the editors of the magazine stated later that the trial had brought together political and sexual revolutionaries, and suggests that this links back to the hell-fire clubs. The Hell's Angels, Ashe writes, are the Mohock gangs of the early eighteenth century reborn, performing ritualised urban terrorist acts.

Ashe also brings in the Marquis de Sade and his unsavoury activities, which he sees as an offshoot of the hell-fire clubs. Ashe claims that he will take us on a journey that is unsettling, showing us scenes of horror and introducing the reader to the natural, the supernatural, and magic, black and otherwise.[6] I will argue that there is virtually no evidence for scenes of horror in the accounts of the hell-fire clubs; rather, hedonism ruled in a mix of sociability and rampant sexuality that led to excess.

Although not all the clubs to be discussed were known at the time as hell-fire clubs, they all have many elements in common. Members were invariably male, usually young and from the leisured class (the exception to this is the Scottish Beggar's Benison). The youths of the lower classes might make havoc in the streets, but they lacked the organisation of the hell-fire clubs, which were clubs in every sense of the word, with formal meetings, subscriptions and initiation ceremonies.

There were three strands of clubs within the hell-fire genre. All of these acted collectively in a socially subversive manner, denying the moral and ethical teaching of society and the Church. One strand was the public face of the clubs. They attacked innocent passers-by at night, just for the hell of it; the early eighteenth-century club the Mohocks was an example of this. A second strand mocked religion: one example is the Duke of Wharton's club; and the third strand was preoccupied with sex, for example Medmenham Friars and the Scottish Beggar's Benison.

The earliest of the clubs emerged in the seventeenth century; but the hell-fire clubs were definitely an eighteenth-century phenomenon. The eighteenth century was the great age of clubs, and this was due to an institution that we in the twenty-first century are very familiar with – the coffee-house. The eighteenth-century coffee-house was a place where like-minded men could meet, read the newspapers and discuss the affairs of the day. It provided a space away from home and the hurly-burly of the tavern, the Houses of Parliament or the Stock Exchange. Certain coffee-houses became favoured by certain groups, political or otherwise, and from there it was but a short step to form an exclusive club which had a recognised membership and barred outsiders. Roy Porter has argued that the Enlightenment was born in the coffee-house, and he quotes Samuel Johnson's view that 'Solitude is an obstacle to pleasure and improvement.'[7] Sociability was one of the tenets of the Enlightenment and it involved friendship, which the *Spectator* described as the 'elixir of life'. Pleasure and happiness were key words of this era; sociability was another. The rational enlightened man was clubbable. This was the age of gentlemen's clubs, Masonic lodges, and friendly societies promoting good fellowship. Porter describes these as 'outposts of the Enlightenment and free republics of a rational society'.[8]

THE ENLIGHTENMENT

There is no single definition of the 'Enlightenment', and it might more usefully be called 'enlightenments'. Its many meanings have been contested from the eighteenth century onwards. J.W. Yolton suggests that the term is 'a name or label that has become affixed to a cluster of ideas and attitudes; indeterminate and fluctuating', but these had one common element: 'the demolition of old myths' and, although it was not the Age of Reason, it used reason to solve and explore human life and its activities.[9] Many historians would disagree with this definition, and the historiography of the Enlightenment has been through many phases, each reflecting the time in which it was written. These need not concern us here, except to note that the word 'Enlightenment', redolent of light breaking through, encourages a Whig perception of history as moving forward towards perfection. However, many artists and philosophers saw the Enlightenment as a break with the past, and many twentieth- and twenty-first-century philosophers and historians see it as the dawn of modernity.

In practical terms the Enlightenment refers to the period *c.* 1688–*c.* 1789, when critical attitudes were taken to inherited authority in all spheres of human life. Enlightenment ideals saw happiness as a virtue, and virtue as integral to the psychology of pleasure. The natural world and Mankind were no longer a mystery, but could be dissected by scientific study; thus old superstitions and myths could be blown away. France was central to Enlightenment thinking, and some historians, for example Peter Gay, have denied the existence of an English Enlightenment.[10] This is not reflected in the evidence.

An example of the use of the term in the eighteenth century can be found in the words of Immanuel Kant: 'If someone asks are we living in an enlightened age today? The answer would be we are living in an Age of Enlightenment.'[11] The fundamental work that articulated the ideas behind the intellectual changes of the eighteenth century in English – John Locke's *An Essay concerning Human Understanding* of 1690 – suggests that a different term might be used:

Let us then suppose the mind to be, as we say, a white paper void of all characters, without any ideas; how comes it to be furnished?

Whence comes it by that vast store which the busy and bound-less fancy of man has painted upon it, with an endless variety? Whence has it all the materials of reason and knowledge? To this I answer in one word, from experience, in that is all our knowledge founded . . .[12]

The Enlightenment was also the Age of Experience, and the hell-fire clubs in all their disguises were out to grab experience by the neck, shake it and see what fell out. By day the club members might be courtiers, Members of Parliament and respectable members of the community. By night they broke social rules to experience forbidden pleasure. Hedonism ruled the night and social constraints were thrown out. By day business could be transacted in the open, the towns bustling with people going on their way, but by night the secret dispossessed and depraved came out on the streets. In the seventeenth and eighteenth centuries as the light failed so night began, and this was night without streetlights, so it could be very dark indeed, the only lights being those of the link-boys with their flaming torches to guide travellers. Streets that by day were familiar became strange and dangerous places by night.[13] This allowed the gangs or clubs to indulge in street violence on an epic scale. Pearson lists fifteen such clubs operating in late seventeenth- and early eighteenth-century London.[14]

Unalloyed hedonism could not go unchecked for long. Societies were formed to suppress vice and stop blasphemy, and to act as a counterbalance to what moral reformers saw as a crisis, with men fighting and fornicating excessively and the diabolical cavorting of the rake-hells.

The term 'rake-hell' was in common use between *c.* 1550 and *c.* 1725 to describe someone who was a thorough knave, an utterly vile debauchee. In 1653, Henry More used the word to describe the dissolute men who endeavoured to extinguish memory by drink and sex.[15] Rake-hells disturbed the nights of innocent citizens and decent society, and decent society disapproved wholeheartedly of their activities. As the story of the rake-hells emerges, so will the story of those who tried to stop them.

Do the fires of hell fuelled by the figures of naked demons flicker through these pages? Or is this simply a story of wealthy men with too much time and licence on their hands, wanting to assert their masculinity?

SEXUALITY

Historians describe the eighteenth century as an age of sexual exuberance;[16] a time when sexuality was liberated and became central to the happiness of the individual. Sex was on public view as never before.[17] Sex, however, has always been with us, and what concentrates the minds of contemporary historians writing about sex and the eighteenth century is the print culture of the time (and the modern obsession with sex which means that works on sexuality sell).[18] In the eighteenth century sexual experiences, fantasies and fears were written down and distributed widely. These have helped the discourse on sexuality and gender to flourish, while the scientific discoveries of the era which led to a better understanding of the human body resulted in women's bodies becoming a legitimate area for research, as well as in a debate on women's libido and gender differences.

Eighteenth-century moralists wanted to promote clearly defined gender roles and to show that the physical differences between men and women affected their characters and the role they played in society. The ideal woman should be obedient, respectable and chaste, a domesticated person with no animal instincts. The ideal man was a virile figure who occupied the public space and domin-ated the home. Sexual prowess was a matter of pride, but violence was part of the construction of masculinity. Robert Shoemaker shows that in the late seventeenth and early eighteenth centuries violence reinforced gender identity, but as the eighteenth century progressed such aspects of masculinity became unacceptable, and were replaced by politeness and moderation.[19] This mirrors the three phases of the hell-fire clubs, which moved from public violence in the early decades of the eighteenth century to private meetings behind closed doors in the second half of the century.

Did the ideal gender-specific world of the eighteenth-century moralists exist? While the coffee-house might be a male preserve, taverns, theatres and streets were thronged with women, as Hogarth's paintings show. The interaction of women with the rest of society was determined by class, occupation and location; in the anonymity of the town women could have more freedom of action, and it is in the towns, some historians have argued, that 'modern standards of male and female gender identity developed'.[20]

Sex, drunkenness and the violence of the clubs go hand in hand with politics and polite society. We start in the early seventeenth century when secret societies and clubs were viewed with suspicion by the government simply as groups with the potential for conspiracy against authority. The Civil War and Commonwealth damped down some of the excesses of the early seventeenth century, and the fires of Hell burned low. The image of an all-consuming fire became a reality after the Restoration, when in 1666 London burned, and the Great Fire of London remained in many people's minds as an illustration of what Hell might be like. It served as a warning to sinners, a warning that was often ignored. Blasphemy, profanity and Sabbath-breaking were rife. Excessive drunkenness, gambling and promiscuity made a spectacle of the streets.

Clubs withdrew indoors, or moved to the country, where pleasure could be had in private and discussion of the existence of Heaven and Hell could not be overheard by prying churchmen. There Priapus became king, and Bacchus god; hell-fire took a classical turn that had to be reached by crossing the River Styx. Public and respected men became satyrs, and decency fled, to the delight of the hack writer and the gutter press, which like today sold itself on sensational exaggerated stories. This is the age when John Cleland's *Memoirs of a Woman of Pleasure* (alias *Fanny Hill*) and Hogarth's prints were published, nature was replaced by science, and the known world expanded, and as it expanded it took the hell-fire clubs with it.

AIMS OF THE HISTORIAN AND THIS BOOK

The aim of this book is to demythologise the hell-fire clubs, and to sift fact from fiction. Myths distort history, but leak into it with invidious results. In the case of the hell-fire clubs myth is all the more likely because there are so few reliable sources on them. Conclusions have to be drawn from very meagre evidence. This is not a search for the truth about the clubs. That can never be known. The old model of history that 'presupposes the existence of an objective historical truth that will uncover the past as it was' has been replaced by what Conrad Russell called a search for 'some approximation of the truth'.[21] My account of the hell-fire clubs is an approximation of the truth based on my interpretation of the available sources, but an interpretation influenced by modern vision.

I am by trade a local historian, investigating relationships within and between communities, and the interaction of people and place set within a wider social and economic context. Voluntary associations such as the hell-fire clubs were communities within communities. My second concern as a local historian is the relationship of people and place. Did place play a part in the hell-fire clubs? London and its teeming streets certainly did, and so did the sights and societies observed by travellers on the Grand Tour, while the landscape of West Wycombe reflects in physical features the mind-set of the Medmenham Friars.

My third concern as a local historian is the wider social and economic context that the hell-fire clubs operated within. The late seventeenth and eighteenth centuries were a period of flux, of increasing population, and of urbanisation. It was a politically unstable period, but a period of intellectual excitement, in which older certainties were challenged. Some contemporaries saw society as morally decayed. Were the hell-fire clubs a symptom of this? Antithetical to the hell-fire clubs were the societies that sought to reform manners and morals, a contrast that highlights the class divisions of eighteenth-century society. Hell-fire club members were usually from the upper class, whilst the reformation societies' members were drawn from the emerging middle class. Class is one element in a discussion of the hell-fire clubs; gender is another. The use of space also plays a part in the discourse.

The structure of the book is broadly chronological. This fits in with the different phases of the hell-fire clubs, and with changes in social attitudes as well. (The historian's business is to communicate, tell a story that is accessible to all.) This is the story of men who met together socially, to satisfy their intellectual and physical needs in ways that outsiders sometimes found shocking. Although historians have placed different constructions on these clubs, I think the key lies in the title to Mackie's paper, 'Boys will be boys'. The clubs were evidence of a universal assertion of masculinity that has existed in some form and will exist as long as the human race survives. They were symbols of the traditional importance of the body and its power, and examples of how this power could be exerted through violence and sexual activity. The clubs took the form they did because of the time in which they flourished: a time of intellectual challenge and scientific research, and of growing individual freedom, set against political and religious uncertainties.

CHAPTER 1

Prelude to the Fires of Hell

THE DAMNED CREW AND THE BUGLE BOYS

The story of the hell-fire clubs starts in the second year of the seventeenth century, as the elderly Queen Elizabeth I neared the end of her life. As she lay dying she secured the Protestant succession by bestowing the Crown of England on James VI of Scotland. Although the country felt relief that a Protestant king would follow a Protestant Queen, the fear of a return of Catholicism remained, as the memory of the brief but bloody reign of Queen Mary was still fresh in people's minds. The Gunpowder Plot showed that this fear was justified, and that there were fanatical papists who were willing to kill to restore the country to Rome.

In 1602 'A profane company . . . called the Damned Crew, men without fear or feeling either of Hell or Heaven, delighting in that title were shipped down the Thames and never seen again', John Manningham wrote in his diary in March 1602; 'there was a company of young gallants which called themselves the Damned Crew. They would meet together on nights, and vow amongst themselves to kill the next man they met whosoever; so divers murders were committed but not one punished.' The nineteenth-century editor of Manningham's diary suggested that the leader of the London Damned Crew was 'Sir Edward Bayham', a Catholic who was connected with Robert Catesby and the Gunpowder Plot.

He was sent to Rome by the plotters to inform the Pope of the plight of the English Catholics.[1] There was a Captain Edmund Baynham connected to the Gunpowder Plot, and Father Garnett, one of the plotters, did send him to Rome, but there is no evidence to link him with the Damned Crew. He had a reputation as a wild young man, imprisoned in 1603 for speaking against James I. The Damned Crew could have been a group of Catholics transported for the safety of the country, although Manningham's account suggests that this was a gang of young men, whose random violence disturbed the streets of London at night. Random street violence reappeared in the eighteenth century and it was then that the Damned Crew were rediscovered, as desperate London magistrates sought for legal precedents by which to curb the outbreak. As well as the Damned Crew the magistrates' trawl through the records revealed another seventeenth-century club, allegedly formed by Lord Vaux's regiment in the Low Countries and brought back to England by returning soldiers. They wore blue and yellow ribbons in their hats and had a 'prince' called Ottoman and nicknames such as Tityre. The club was called the Tityre Tues.

The King's council feared this club might be planning mischief.[2] Religion was at the bottom of this fear, as Lord Vaux, a Catholic, had been in the Spanish Netherlands fighting for Spain against the Protestant rebels. Secret societies frighten governments because they are potential agents for subversion and the destabilisation of society. They are portents of the unknown and forces for revolution. Clubs and societies demand loyalty from their members over and above loyalty to the Crown and the state, and James I was always suspicious of such organisations, especially as Vaux was a Catholic.

Edward, Lord Vaux, came from an ancient Catholic family. He had been made a ward of Elizabeth I but his mother purchased the wardship back in 1598 and brought him up as a good Catholic boy. He too was suspected of being implicated in the Gunpowder Plot, and spent several years in Italy as an exile. On his return he was arrested and sentenced to life imprisonment and the loss of all his lands for refusing to take an oath of allegiance to James I, but eventually he was pardoned and released on surety. He was in Flanders in 1622–24, and this is when the club known as the Tityre Tues was assumed to have been formed.

There is another origin suggested for the Tityre Tues, taken from an examination of a witness in 1623 who said that the club had a naval origin:

Five or six other gentlemen of the admiral went ashore in the Isle of Wight, to the town of Newport and lay at the sign of the Bugle [a tavern], where they did combine themselves into a league of amity; at that time the club had no name and no articles, but later we did call ourselves the Tittere Tues, alias the Bugle Boys

The witness said that the club wore orange ribbons and claimed that their only aim was to make merry, drink wine and take tobacco. They possessed the criteria for being a club: a treasurer, who collected £20 in subscriptions, and a password 'oatmeal', known only to members.[3] Not surprisingly, the government was deeply suspicious of this club and compiled a list of members and their status. They were found to be respectable citizens, knights and military men. Their aim was, as the witness stated, no more sinister than setting out to have a good time in congenial company. Lord Vaux's religion caused the government disquiet, but the list of Tityre members included Sir Richard Brooke, a staunch Protestant.

Where did they get their unusual name? One implausible suggestion is that it comes from Virgil's first eclogue, 'Tityre, you lie beneath the spreading beech',[4] which is a lament for land lost in Italy after the Battle of Philippi. Thus, the Tityres were classically educated gentlemen protesting about land lost to enclosure: a fanciful idea, for which there is no evidence. It is more likely that

the phrase either comes from a slang term for the female pudendum
'tittery whoppet', or is taken from the ballad 'The Tityre Tues' by
George Chambers, sung to the tune of 'Chevy Chase', published in
1568 and about Catholics executed for treason.[5] However, where
the words came from, or what they meant, is unknown.

The dominant concerns of the 1620s when the information
was collected about the Bugle Boys were the tension between the
court and the country parties, and an endemic fear of Catholics.
The court party represented the ever-more centralised bureau-
cracy concentrated around the King; the country party was
composed of the country gentry and the yeomen who opposed
the oppressive laws and harsh taxes. Whereas Elizabeth I had
contained the different parties by permitting them all to have
allies at court, the Stuarts allowed factions to develop and the
court excluded men from the Shires. The tensions of the 1620s
were to lead to the Civil War, and clubs such as the Bugle Boys
were seen as subversive anti-government elements in society.
Jacobean society thrived on suspicion. Neighbour was encouraged
to inform on neighbour, and government spies and secret agents
reported potential conspirators to the government. It was also a
superstitious age. James I came from Scotland with a reputation
for believing in and persecuting witches. Some time between
1591 and 1597 he wrote and published a dialogue called
Demonology. In this he describes witches as 'detestable slaves of
the Devil', and condemns magic, sorcery, necromancy, astrology
and many other superstitious manifestations. His aim was to
convince unbelievers of the existence and power of demoniacal
arts.[6] It is no coincidence that Shakespeare's Scottish play, first
performed by the King's Men in 1606,[7] included witches as
central to its plot. This is also the age of the theatre: by James's
reign there were six permanent theatres in London, and plays
were also performed in at least four inns.[8] Seventeenth-century

drama articulated the human condition, and the tension and problematic relationship between power and the sexes:[9] a relationship played out in the public and private dramas of the hell-fire clubs.

Street theatre also played a part in Jacobean London and other cities and towns. There were civic processions of livery companies and guilds, the colourful entourages of the nobility, royalty and the pageantry attending it, funeral processions, and in 1603 the doleful rumble of plague carts. The public face of the hell-fire clubs was an extension and an inversion of this street theatre, taking place at night rather than in the daytime and creating violence instead of spectacle.

The streets of Jacobean London were crammed and dirty; a contrast to the opulence of James's court which drew the nobility and gentry into town. The splendid court masques and New World exploration encouraged a taste for the exotic. *Othello* and *The Tempest* are this exoticism put into words. Perhaps a more prosaic example of this was another club discovered by the government.

In the section of the state papers that deals with the Tityre Tues and the Bugle Boys is a list of members of the Knights of the Blue. The Knights of the Blue's pseudonyms suggest that subversion was low on their list of objectives, and the consumption of alcohol high: Giants Drunkasadog and Drunkasarat meet with Giant Neversober and Giant Neverbegood: names that mask the identity of respectable citizens who met to carouse rather than to plot to overthrow the government.

Another pre-Restoration club was the Knights Errant, some-times known as the Hectors. A pamphlet of 1652 identifies them as discharged officers who had formed gangs and who lived by gaming, drinking and mugging passers-by. A year later they appeared as characters in a play by Edmund Gayton, a good example of how clubs and gangs frequently caught the literary imagination, and how drama is evident in the contemporaries' perception of these quasi-secret clubs.

The term 'hector' had long been used to describe a swaggerer, and 'swagger' was a word that could easily be applied to the behaviour of members of these seventeenth-century clubs. Often they came from the social elite and naturally swaggered their way through life. 'Hector' was probably a slang term for an erect penis, as this verse by the Earl of Rochester suggests:

> There's not a Petticoat goes by,
> But from my Cod-Piece out you fly
> Not to be held 'twixt hand and thigh
>
> I never felt a soft white hand
> But Hector-like you strutting stand,
> As if the world you would command.[10]

After the execution of Charles I, the Commonwealth government closed the theatres and places of public entertainment, and barred village customs like bringing in greenery at dawn to celebrate May Day, decorating ploughs and dragging them round the village for alms on Plough Monday, or Hoke Day celebrations when women bounced men in a blanket until they paid a ransom. Towns and villages were forced to remove their maypoles. Christmas was no longer a feast and a holiday, and the Sabbath had to be strictly observed. Stained glass and statues in parish churches were smashed, and wall paintings whitewashed over. Anything that smacked of ungodly superstition was severely punished. Britain in this period was a dour and colourless place.

It was the rakes that kept the fires of Hell flickering throughout the country until the flames burst joyfully into life at the restoration of Charles Stuart as Charles II in 1660 and colour returned to everyday life.

Restoration: 29 May 1660 annus mirabilis

'This day came in His Majestie Charles the 2nd to London after a sad and long Exile and Calamitous suffering both to the King and the Church', wrote John Evelyn in his diary after he stood in the Strand to watch the King's procession pass on 'so joyful a day, and so bright'. On 4 June he kissed the King's hand.[11] On 18 October those who had condemned Charles I to death were executed, and Oliver Cromwell's grave was opened and his remains violated. The old order was restored. Merry England recommenced. Christmas could be celebrated again, maypoles re-erected, theatres and public entertainment reopened.

At the same time as all this jollity, the Presbyterian Church was banned and the Episcopalian Church of England re-established as the national religion. Religious toleration was at an end. The output of the press was censored, and coffee-houses, those powerhouses of debate, needed a government licence before they could open; their owners were charged not to allow scandalous papers or libel on to their premises. Set against this increasing repression was the 'merry monarch' Charles II and his court of drinking, gambling and blaspheming rakes. Bursting on to the scene, like Satan himself, came John Wilmot, second Earl of Rochester (quoted above). He described himself thus:

> I've outswilled Bacchus, sworn of my own make
> Oaths that would fright Furies, and make Pluto quake
> I've swived more whores, more ways than Sodom's walls
> . . .
> Pox on't, why do I speak of these poor things?
> I have blasphemed my God, and libelled Kings![12]

Born in 1647, the son of an ardent Royalist, Rochester spent his early years in exile in Paris, returning to England with his mother in

1655. When his father died three years later he became the second Earl of Rochester. His debauch started at Oxford, where he was admitted to Wadham College in 1660 at the youthful and impressionable age of thirteen. Here he started to write poetry and also to drink heavily. By the time he left with his MA in September 1661 he was well versed in the ways of men. In the November of that year he departed on his Grand Tour of the continent. He returned to London in 1664 ready for mischief and fell in with a group of rakes already known in London for their outrageous behaviour: Henry Savile, Sir Charles Sedley and Henry Killigrew.

All three came from good families. Henry Killigrew (1652–1712) was the son of a clergyman, Henry Savile (1642–87) was the younger son of Sir William Savile of Rufford Abbey in Nottinghamshire, and Sir Charles Sedley (1639–1701) was the son of Sir John Sedley of Southfleet in Kent. Killigrew became a naval officer, and Savile also saw service in the navy with James, Duke of York. Sedley was a militia officer. All three served as MPs: Killigrew for Stockbridge and St Albans, Savile for Newark, and Sedley for New Romney, thus showing that scandal and public life could go hand in hand in the seventeenth century.

They entered into Restoration court life with gusto. Killigrew became known as a hard-drinking man whose claim to fame was sleeping with one of the King's former mistresses. Savile entered the Duke of York's household, and stayed there until he fell out with the Duke and was dismissed in 1675. Rumours claimed that this was because he was sexually involved with the Duchess of York. Sedley became the King's drinking companion.

Sedley's behaviour came to public notice on 16 June 1663 when he and his companions provoked a riot by standing naked on the balcony of the aptly named Cock Tavern in Bow Street, throwing bottles, into which they had pissed, on to the crowd below – a piece of explicit street theatre. Sedley was imprisoned for this escapade. Savile was known throughout London as a debauchee. As well as being involved with the Duchess of York, in 1671 he attempted to rape Elizabeth, the widow of the Earl of Northumberland, when they were both staying at Athorpe in Lincolnshire.

Duelling was banned in 1669, yet Savile was involved in two duels. In one he carried a challenge from his uncle Sir William Coventry to the Duke of Buckingham, and in the other he was the Earl of Rochester's second in a duel with John Mulgrave, Earl of Sheffield. Savile was lucky in that when he was in trouble with the law he had friends in high places to intercede on his behalf, and each time he was caught out he was sent to Paris as an envoy. He died in 1687 of liver disease and gangrene, the result of a venereal infection. These were the men who became the boon companions of the Earl of Rochester.

What caused their outrageous behaviour? They had political careers, literary acclaim and posts at court. But they were not satisfied. They needed more. Part of their behaviour was simply an outlet for masculine energy. Part was a response to the lean years of the Commonwealth, when their sort had no political voice, and they and their families had been robbed of their rightful position in society. Throwing bottles of piss at passers-by was an exercise in power over the people who may have helped to kill the King and deprive their families. It was a reassertion of their place in society. They acted in an anti-social way because in restored England they knew they could, and they knew from personal experience that social and religious certainties could be swept away. Life should be lived to the full while there was a chance. If life was uncertain, then life after death was equally uncertain. Many liberties were spurred on by the belief that death truly was the end. Rochester actually wrote that 'after death nothing is'.

Before his final illness Rochester's writings suggest that he believed in neither God nor the Devil, nor the afterlife of the soul. In a poem based on a line by Seneca he stated that 'Dead we become the lumber of the World'. He delighted in mocking the Church and flouting religion:

> For hell and the foul fiend that rules
> God's everlasting jails
> (Devised by rogues, dreaded by fools),
> Are senseless stories, idle tales,
> Dreams, whimsey, and no more.[13]

One of Rochester's first actions on returning to England was to abduct an heiress, Elizabeth Malet, an action for which he was sent to the Tower of London, but he was soon released and sent to serve in the navy. Eventually she married him, but marriage did not tame him, and he claimed that after a spell in the country with his wife, the Devil entered him as he crossed Brentford Common on his way back to London. In search of new experience Rochester disguised himself as a Dr Alexander Bendo and went about the city of London denouncing the King's mistresses and the city fathers: acts of sheer bravado which could have put him in the Tower once more. In the same disguise he handed out bills to passers-by advertising miraculous cures that were said to be especially good for the maladies of young women. The promise of these cures attracted large crowds, and he set up a laboratory where he examined young ladies' privy parts, dispensed quack medicines and interpreted omens. This is Rochester as an actor in his own personal drama.[14]

Samuel Pepys and John Evelyn were disgusted by the antics of Rochester and his cronies. Pepys describes in his diary for 30 May 1668 how he dined in an arbour, but was made miserable by the bawdy talk of Rochester and his companions: 'But what loose, cursed company was this that I was in tonight.' John Evelyn had a similar experience on 26 November 1670: 'Dined with the Lord Treasurer where was the Earl of Rochester, a very profane wit.'

Rochester's outrageous behaviour came to a head in June 1676 at Epsom when he was one of a party of men who amused themselves by tossing fiddlers in a blanket because they refused to play for them. A barber who came to see what was happening was attacked and only freed himself by promising to direct them to the house of the handsomest woman in Epsom. Instead he sent them to the constable's house, and when the constable came out to see who was trying to break his door down, he too was attacked and beaten. Rochester tried to draw his sword but was prevented from using it by Mr Downs, one of his companions. The constable's cries alerted the watch: they came up behind Downs and one of them hit him with a staff and broke his skull, an injury from which he died. Rochester and the rest of his companions ran away from the scene as fast as they could. Alcohol played a large part in this escapade, but underlying it was an assertion of power over those from a different class, and a disregard for authority. It was also a form of street theatre, and an inversion of the customary ritual of Hoke Day. Rochester was frequently involved in brawls and other violence; for example, he and his friends beat up the poet John Dryden who had insulted them.[15]

The elder statesman the Earl of Clarendon despaired of the young men of the Restoration court, claiming that they lacked judgement and compassion: 'the very mention of good nature was laughed at, and looked upon as the morals and character of a fool; and a roughness of manners or hard-heartedness and cruelty was affected'. Clarendon sums up the attitude of the rakes nicely.[16] It was true that the rakes were utterly oblivious to others and were single-minded in their pursuit of entertainment and debauchery. They might infect their wives and mistresses with syphilis (Rochester died of syphilis, so must have infected his wife), but they did not care. They might terrify and brutalise the ordinary citizen at night, but they had no remorse.

In the end, the past caught up with Rochester. In the summer of 1679 one of his former mistresses, Jane Roberts, died of syphilis and Rochester knew he would face a similar fate. Jane Roberts had received spiritual help in her last hours from Bishop Gilbert Burnet. Now Rochester sought him out and underwent a rapid conversion from atheist who mocked religion to passionate religious believer. He died, much wasted, on 26 July 1680. Burnet published an account of his deathbed as a warning to other young rakes, while an anonymous poet celebrated Rochester's conversion in the poem 'The Rake, or The Libertine's Religion'. The preface to this states that 'The libertine lives life at both ends'. His prayer is 'Give us this day our daily riot'. Stanza 5 describes the libertine's night out, and the poem ends with conscience, 'the fiend that cannot be denied', and the conversion and death of the libertine.[17] Rochester's last-minute conversion and the poem were used as propaganda by moralists to teach the next generation that a debauched life could be redeemed by admitting to sins and returning to the bosom of the established Church.

Rochester and his mates were rakes, atheists and debauchees but how do they fit in with the hell-fire clubs? As a group they belonged to a club that was known as 'the Ballers': young gentlemen who met in pursuit of pleasure and companionship.

THE BALLERS/BAWLERS

The Ballers Club was dedicated to drink and the pursuit of women. Members danced naked with prostitutes at 'Lady' Bennet's establishment (a brothel) but were on the whole harmless. They met at the Dog and Partridge Tavern in Fleet Street and were a club in the strict sense of the word. They charged members a subscription fee, and had an initiation oath that may have been written by Sir Charles Sedley.

The Oath of the Ballers at the Dog and Partridge by Sir C.S.

> We to this Order none receive
> That in his Glass a drop doth leave
> That will not turn and set and side it
> As long as Damsel can abide it,
> And eat and drink the best he can
> Like a true Dog and Partridge man
>
> Thou shalt no lady court whose Pride
> Will any tedious siege abide,
> Nor yet again descend so low
> 'Mongst those that know not to say No
> But when one proves truly kind
> As truly be thy love confined,
> Thou shalt no Observations heard
> To vent for wit and great man's board
> But whatsoever is said and done
> Must be forgotten by the next sun
> If thou would be thou installed
> And henceforth a Bawler called.[18]

Most of the Ballers' activities were innocent. They fell out with the authorities only once, when they attempted to import a box of leather dildoes from Holland, which were seized and burned by the customs officers. Rochester was in the country at the time, but was sent an account of what happened by Henry Savile: 'The dildoes were burnt without mercy, nothwithstanding Sedley and I made two journeys to the city in their defence, consider this my lord, you see what things are done in your absence and then pray consider whether it is fit for you to be blowing on coals in the country when there is revenge to be done to the ashes of these martyrs.'[19]

Were the Ballers one of the forerunners of the hell-fire clubs? Were they simply a lascivious club following in the wake of a dissolute court? Rochester's verse insulting the King refers to Charles's 'sceptre and prick of one length, she who plays with one may sway the other',[20] and is a good example of how the morals of Charles and his court were perceived.

In fact there are many links with clubs that were to follow. The exploits of the Ballers were in public, and the next phase of hell-fire clubbing also took place in public, on the streets of London. Rochester and his companions were young men living on unearned income, and with unlimited leisure time, which was a feature of many subsequent clubs. They drank to excess. They whored without mercy. They were profane, delighting in blasphemy and mocking religion. There are several references that liken Rochester to the Devil. Lord John Mulgrave described him as having a tail and cloven feet, while his masquerade as Dr Bendo has Rabelaisian overtones that resurfaced with the mid-eighteenth-century Medmenham Friars. But the links may be coincidental; the natural digressions of educated young men out to shock society. While the worthy Bishop Burnet believed that Rochester wished to reform society under a new system of intellectual and moral principles, and teach Mankind to face material reality through pleasure and pain, it is odd that this reforming zeal only surfaced on Rochester's deathbed, and his earlier escapades show that he failed to keep to his avowed maxims of doing nothing to hurt others or impair his health. But like the members of the later Enlightenment clubs, Rochester was living life by experimentation, flouting moral conventions. But the rakes' progress was far from unchallenged.

SOCIETIES FOR THE REFORMATION OF MANNERS

It was the blasphemous side of the rakes' activities that seized the attention of the authorities. In 1688 James II was replaced on the throne by his daughter Mary and his son-in-law William of Orange. James had been a man in the mould of his brother Charles II, but his daughter Mary was different – she was a God-fearing Protestant who was shocked by the licentiousness of London, its 'profane cursing, and profanation of the Lord's Day, the odious and loathsome sin of drunkenness, and all the houses of debauchery and evil fame'. In July 1689 she sent a letter to the magistrates of Middlesex and the City of London ordering them to put into action the laws against swearing, drunkenness and breaking the Sabbath. This was followed in 1691 by orders to the High Constables of Westminster, Holborn, Finsbury, Kensington and the Tower of London to issue warrants against those who cursed, profaned the Sabbath and indulged in excessive drinking and debauchery. The magistrates were flustered. How could they get information about these rakes? The public were not slow to respond, and a rash of illegal warrants were issued to informers out to catch their neighbours.

The magistrates were helped further in their work by the formation of voluntary societies for the reformation of manners, which can be seen as a reaction to the debauchery on show in the streets every day. They were not specifically aimed at the rake-hells and their clubs, but the rake-hells were a visible symptom of a dissolute society.

The societies for the reformation of manners were formed by groups of neighbours tired of the noise and drunkenness in the streets at nights, were organised by virtuous men and patronised by bishops and the clergy. They aimed to 'exchange drunkenness for good humour, lewdness for good breeding; and to stop houses from becoming stews for the entertainment of men and to stop herds of common women continually soliciting men, to stop God being publicly dishonoured and his laws trampled upon'.[21] It was not only London that was experiencing problems of street disorder. Such societies sprang up in Gloucester, Hereford, Buckingham and Bodmin in 1691, and within ten years towns as small as Wendover had a society, and counties as far apart as Shropshire and Surrey. The Nottingham society described 'great numbers of disorderly ale-houses in the town, to which many idle and dissolute persons frequently resort'. John Woodward noted that there were a number of unnecessary alehouses in market towns, leading young people into 'wicked confederacies'.[22]

The character of the reformation societies was the exact opposite of the rake-hell clubs in almost every way, most notably with regard to aims and membership. Reformation societies were formed by groups of respectable men rather than dissolute rakes. The reforma-tion societies wanted to suppress a specific nuisance. For example, the Tower Hamlets society founded in 1690 had the specific aim of suppressing the numerous brothels in that area. By 1694 London had sixteen societies with nearly 300 members.[23]

The Society for Reformation and Revival in Bristol is a good example of a provincial society, and one for which, unusually, a number of records have survived. The society had fifty-four founder members when it was formed in 1700; most of them were also members of the city council and the militia. Each paid a shilling subscription.[24]

The Bristol society had a number of aims. It observed that a great many lewd people harboured idle houses to debauch the youth of the city, and proposed to select people in each parish and report on the houses. It aimed to stop people profaning the Sabbath by visiting the hot wells, assembly room and spa, or tippling in alehouses on that day. They wanted to regulate the great number of single persons living disorderly lives in the city, and told the consta-bles to make a list of all such persons, their ages and trades. They also wanted to censor stage performances, music houses, lotteries, gaming and other disorderly practices. These repressive measures were countered by a real concern for the education and welfare of poor children.[25] Like the rake-hell clubs, the reformation societies were male dominated, but they drew their membership from the middle rank of society: from professional men, tradesmen and craftsmen who were anxious to restore some semblance of respectability to their neighbourhoods. The members of reformation societies believed sin to be the result of a struggle between God and the Devil that the Devil had won. Atheism, swearing, blasphemy and drunkenness were the marks of Satan's kingdom, and in the towns and cities of late seventeenth-century England it was obvious that the Devil was gaining the upper hand. They saw the Devil as instigating the debauchery in the streets, and wanted to counteract this by good example, which included informing on wrongdoers to the magistrates and 'naming and shaming' them publicly by issuing a blacklist of wrongdoers picked up in the streets at night.

Just as Rochester and his rake-hells were a reaction against the repression of the Commonwealth that got out of hand, so the societies for the reformation of manners were a reaction against what they perceived as a sinful society endangering its corporate soul. Both the rake-hells and the reformation societies believed in Mankind as communal and clubbable, and in fact the societies had no qualms about private vice as long as it did not impinge on the lives of others. But the Ballers and their like brought their vices into the public space, and the reformation societies wanted them shamed in public. Rake-hells' activities were seen as part of a wider national crime wave in the 1690s and one which was endangering civic society and the general good. 'National sins bring national disasters', wrote John Woodward in 1701, and national sins needed national remedies.[26] Social deviance had to be stopped for the public good.

These trends have to be seen against the background of the political situation of the 1690s. Although William and Mary had been offered the Crown by Parliament and a Bill of Rights had established a constitutional monarchy, James II had fled into exile but had not abdicated, and his supporters still believed he was the rightful king and plotted to restore him to the throne. The country was rent by conspiracies, suspicion and uncertainty. William III narrowly escaped assassination and a stream of traitors went to the gallows and the block. The prostitutes and villains and the clubs of rake-hells added to the feeling of unease and the perception that the streets of any town were dangerous after dark, a feeling that continued into the first decades of the eighteenth century thanks to gangs of young men who spent their nights terrorising innocent citizens.

CHAPTER 2

Gentlemen's Clubs, Journalistic Hacks, the Mohocks and Change

GENTLEMEN'S CLUBS

Sociability was one of the tenets of the Enlightenment, and representatives of sociability in the eighteenth century were gentlemen's clubs. Samuel Johnson described the club as 'an assembly of good fellows, meeting under certain conditions'.[1] On his visits to the Ivy Lane Club he had 'a disposition to please and be pleased', and could pass 'those hours in a free and unstrained interchange of sentiments, which otherwise would have been spent at home'.[2] Roy Porter defines clubs as 'republics of the Enlightenment',[3] which could describe Johnson's free unrestrained sentiments.

Gentlemen's clubs could cater for all tastes. They provided an opportunity for male friendships, a refuge from home and married life and a place to withdraw from the clamour of the streets, the court, Parliament or the Stock Exchange. In the club the hours could be idled away, alcohol could be taken in the company of fellows and gossip and dirty talk exchanged. Although they were almost exclusively male, there was the occasional club for women, and a few clubs admitted both men and women.

Eighteenth-century clubs were an urban phenomenon, and were related to the growth of leisure and consumerism. The

Enlightenment doctrine that happiness was a virtue and pleasure added to happiness found fulfilment in the club, while the eighteenth century's changing attitudes to social interaction that made sensibility and politeness desirable were cultivated through the club. New social discourse could be formulated in some clubs, but conversely clubs could reinforce the traditional patriarchal hierarchy.

Clubs operated in private enclosed spaces and were open only to members. This means that the evidence about them tends to be 'sparse and external'.[4] Their nature reflected the new respect for private and informal activities mediated through voluntary associations.[5]

The criterion for what constitutes a club, rather than a meeting of friends, is to have some sort of formal organisation, and rules to settle differences between members and create stability. New members have to be approved by the existing membership, and membership is confirmed by the payment of a subscription. The historiography of clubs and voluntary associations has tended to be dominated by urban historians. R.J. Morris describes critical links between clubs and class. Clubs, Morris suggests, were part of the power nexus of capitalism, and essential to the continuity of elite dominance of society.[6] The role of the elite in urban society and its development is further articulated by Clark:

> Arguably, landowners were the most crucial determinant of the social and cultural development of European cities in the pre-Industrial era. This was certainly true of Britain during the later Stuart and Hanoverian period as the influx of landowners in towns stimulated local consumption, the building industry, leisure and cultural activities.[7]

Clubs were an essential part of leisure and cultural activities, and part of the urban renaissance of the eighteenth century, and there was a fundamental link between voluntary associations, urbanisation and consumerism.[8] In his definitive book on British clubs, Clark emphasises the educational and reforming aspects of clubs such as the Spalding Gentlemen's Society and similar learned societies. He argues that such clubs offered a way of overcoming or alleviating urban problems and of transforming differences into harmony.[9]

Vic Gatrell implies that Clark's rather earnest description – preoccupied with the literary, philosophical and antiquarian clubs – ignores the part that alcohol and conviviality played in even the more sober societies. Gatrell stresses the satiric qualities of many eighteenth-century clubs, and the indignity of their initiation ceremonies and activities.[10] Humiliation at the initiation and a concentration on bodily functions at club meetings helped the club members to bond, and added to their enjoyment and participation.

Many of the hell-fire clubs belonged more to Gatrell's satiric clubs than to Clark's sober societies. Some were caricatures of literary and philosophic societies. Where the philosophic society discussed theology, the hell-fire members blasphemed and denied God. Where the antiquarians collected and catalogued artefacts, the hell-fire clubs collected images of the female form. While literary societies read learned tomes, the hell-fire clubs wrote lewd verses, and when the scientific societies experimented with laboratory apparatus, the hell-fire clubs experimented with their own bodies.

NED WARD AND THE WORLD OF LONDON CLUBS

In 1709 a book was published in London by a hack journalist Ned Ward: it was called *The Secret History of Clubs*. In the introduction Ward claimed that the book would discuss the clubs that were an excuse for the promotion of vice, faction and folly, and would describe the ritual and regalia of these clubs, their white wands, badges and their bacchanalian drinking.[11]

Ned Ward was one of a growing band of writers trying to make a living from journalism. Not much is known about his background, except that he was born in 1667 in the Midlands and claimed to be the son of a landed family, although the latter could not be proved. At the age of twenty-four he came to London to make his fortune by his pen. Six years later he sailed to Jamaica to try his luck there, but was soon back in England writing about his adventures in the West Indies, both real and imaginary.

In pursuit of a regular readership, in 1698 he came up with an idea, probably borrowed from the French, of a serial publication. The *London Spy* ran for eighteen monthly issues. It gave descriptions of trips round London and its taverns, coffee-houses, bagnios and bordellos, interspersed with poems. It was a work of fiction sprinkled with facts, and it is often difficult to see where fiction stopped and facts started. This means that *The Secret History of Clubs* has to be treated with caution, as not all the clubs that Ward described actually existed. Many were satiric inventions of his fertile imagination. Did, for example, the 'No Nose Club', consisting of members who had lost their noses through syphilis, and met at the Dog Tavern to dine on pigs' heads with the snouts removed, really exist? Or was the 'Farting Club', at pains to make a stink in the noses of the public and 'tune their arses with ale and juniper water', an actual group of men dedicated to anally retentive occupations, or was this a product of Ward's fertile imagination? Even if such a club did not exist, Ward's description of it is part of the bawdy humour of the early eighteenth century, with its emphasis on bodily functions and fluids. Farts, excreta and bums were part of the stock in trade of the caricaturist, often used to represent the contempt of the ruling class for the people.

The anal theme is continued in Ward's description of the Knights of the Golden Fleece, stock-jobbers who became aldermen, who met in Kent Street to smoke and drink, talk politics and tell bawdy stories. The club's motto was:

> Let honour still be due to Jason's Knights
> Tho' Tom-Turd's-Arms, the Golden Fleece beshites.[12]

The more respectable-sounding 'Broken Shopkeepers' Club' is surely satiric. According to Ward they met at 'Tumbledown Dick's' in the Mint to curse their creditors and 'drink confusion to the bailiffs'.[13]

We are on safer ground with some of the other clubs described by Ward, as we know they existed. The Yorkshire Club of Northern Tykes who met in Smithfield on market day 'to better their cunning against the Southern Air and run down the cockneys who have never travelled further north than Barnet or St. Albans' is one example.[14] The Mollies Club where transvestites could go to cross-dress is also known to have existed, as is the more socially acceptable Kit-Kat Club where Whigs could meet to discuss the politics of the day.[15] Ward himself was a high Tory, and some of his writings had political intent, such as his book on the Calves' Head Club, a club of alleged republicans.[16] Ward's political writings sometimes got him into trouble, and in 1706 he spent an hour in the pillory being pelted with dung. If many of the clubs in his *Secret History* were inventions, the taverns where they allegedly met were not, so that the book gives the location of London drinking houses which otherwise might be missed. Ward was, of course, very familiar with these places; in 1712 he opened his own alehouse in Clerkenwell in east London, moving to the Bacchus Tavern in Moorfields in 1717, and ended up opening a coffee-house in Gray's Inn. He died in 1731.

Moorfields was in close proximity to Grub Street, which by the eighteenth century was synonymous with sensational and not always truthful journalism. Ward's publications could be seen as forerunners of the satirical journal *Private Eye*.

The Secret History of Clubs went through many editions, and although Ward wrote it to make money, he also wanted to bring attention to groups of people he thought worth drawing to public notice. 'The Man Hunters Club' of wild young men who met in Chancery Lane near the Tennis Court Playhouse at the back of Lincoln's Inn was an example of this. Ward claimed that they chased innocent passers-by who were walking across Lincoln's Inn Fields at night, pretending they were pursuing someone who had done them wrong, shouting, 'That's he! Bloody wounds that's he.' Once caught, the victim was severely beaten. The rival to this club was 'The Man Killing Club', which Ward suggested was founded in the reign of Charles II, and which would only admit members who had already killed a man. Ward also described a club of direct relevance to the Hell-Fire Club, 'the Atheistical Club' which met at a tavern in Westminster 'to assert the Devil's cause: And to argue that the frame of Nature is an accident of Atoms'.[17]

Even if these last three clubs only existed in Ward's mind he was describing a dangerous trend in society of blasphemy and of random attacks on strangers. Put together, these suggested that society was on a downward spiral. The picture of London in the first decade of the eighteenth century painted by Ward was one of increasing crime, and especially crime directed at persons and property.

NED WARD'S LONDON

By the end of the seventeenth century London was one of the largest cities in Europe and its population was increasing rapidly. Estimates put the population at about 200,000 in 1600, which amounted to 7 per cent of the total population of England, 575,000 in 1700, and 675,000 in 1750, or 11 per cent of the total population of England. This was an annual increase of 2,750 souls, but since the crude death rate was higher than the crude birth rate the actual population turnover was more in the region of 8,000 a year. In the late seventeenth century one in six English adults had experienced life in London. Many of them came to the capital as economic migrants, young adults travelling alone: these migrants tended to be male. This was reversed in the early eighteenth century when female migrants predominated, coming to work as domestic servants in the houses of the nobility and the growing numbers of the middle class.[18]

In order to house its ever increasing population London spread its tentacles over the city walls and into the countryside beyond. The city itself was rebuilt after the Great Fire of London, and the 1667 Rebuilding Act stipulated that all new houses in the city had to be built of brick with tile roofs, to prevent further conflagration. The city was replanned, with wide boulevards replacing the narrow and curving pre-Fire streets and lanes. Cornhill and Cheapside were the shopping and business areas, and where the burgeoning middle class lived. The city of Westminster boasted the fine town houses of the nobility and gentry, but the east of the city of London was a poor area where the streets 'were narrow and incommodious for carriages and passengers and prejudicial to trade and the health of its inhabitants'.[19] Here the houses were crammed together in narrow streets and unsavoury courts. Smithfield, Cripplegate and Shoreditch were three such areas, and across the River Thames on the south bank Deptford, Bermondsey and Rotherhithe were also notably poor. Other poor areas, known as rookeries, perched on the land between the city of London and Westminster in St Giles, Holborn and Seven Dials (what is now Shaftesbury Avenue and the heart of theatre land). Even in the eighteenth century Drury Lane was known for its theatres; in the new piazza of Covent Garden prostitutes and robbers mingled and it was a place where meetings could take place without being observed.[20]

Trying to keep order and protect people and their property were a force of volunteers: the constable, the night watch, the beadles and the city marshals. The constables were the main law enforcers. They were ordinary people (usually but not always men) who served without payment or training for a year at a time. After being elected each constable had to take an oath to keep the peace and 'protect the innocent from the hands of violence and to bring offenders to justice'.[21] With the night watchmen they formed the night patrol, and this brought them into close contact with the gangs of young men who roamed the city looking for mischief. Constables were often the gangs' targets, and these unfortunate men were the butt of numerous assaults and indignities. Not surprisingly, many were reluctant to take up this unpaid post and would willingly pay a fine to avoid it.

Justice was enforced in the city of London by city magistrates chosen from the aldermen. Westminster had its own justices, and beyond the city walls, but still in close proximity to London and Westminster, the counties of Middlesex and Surrey also had benches of justices of the peace. The whole law and order process was a ramshackle organisation based on volunteers with little or no professional help. Night was a frightening time, as it was in most provincial cities and towns. Until the Improvement Acts of the late eighteenth century the streets were dark. By-laws required house-holders to light the area around their own houses, but few did so. After the Restoration and the reopening of the theatres and other places of entertainment Londoners began to go out at night more often, and crimes against people increased. Zacharias Conrad von Uffenbach, a German visitor to London in 1710, remarked upon the noise in the streets from 'crowds all shouting at each other'. He went to a place called Cupid's Gardens where 'countless whores were to be found' and 'disgraceful goings on took place. Near a tavern where men drink and find occasion for the devil's own work.'[22]

However, it was in the spring of 1712 that the Devil's own work manifested itself in earnest when a club of young men called the Mohocks prowled the streets.

THE MOHOCKS

London, March 1712. Panic gripped the city as a gang of young gentlemen made random attacks on passers-by, beat up the watch and insulted the constables. Good men feared to go out at night, but neither were they safe behind locked doors as the Mohocks smashed windows, pulled door-bells and assaulted the servants who answered them. These unprecedented attacks were shocking even to a city used to violence on its streets, and eventually the news of the outbreak reached the ears of the ailing Queen Anne in her palace. Her physician, David Hamilton, noted in his diary that the Queen was concerned about the events in the city streets, and how she might reform these.[23]

The Queen did not remain passive. On Saturday, 15 March 1712 she issued a royal proclamation for 'The Suppression of Riots and the Discovery of such as have been guilty of the late Barbarities within the cities of London and Westminster', which appeared in the *London Gazette.* The proclamation stated that there were 'great and unusual riots and barbarities committed in the night time upon open streets by ill disposed people, who had combined together to disturb the public peace, and in an inhuman manner, without any provocation had assaulted the queen's good subjects, and had had the boldness to insult the constables and the watch'.[24]

The proclamation continued that in order to catch and punish the offenders, who because of the 'favour of the night' had escaped, and to prevent further barbarities, the Queen's subjects were invited to inform on the offenders to the justices. It exhorted the governments of the cities of London and Westminster and adjacent areas to look 'into the statutes against barbarities',[25] and to ensure that there was sufficient watch at night. All civil and military officers were to help in this. The proclamation concluded that 'For the encouragement of persons to be diligent in apprehending the offenders Her Majesty does promise that whosoever shall discover such offenders will be rewarded with one hundred pounds and a pardon if involved with them.'[26]

Were the Queen, her privy council and the citizens of London and Westminster over-reacting to what could have been normal street violence? There is evidence which suggests that in March 1712 there was a street gang attacking passers-by in a manner that transcended normal violence. The gang became known as the Mohocks, but it is not clear whether this is what they called themselves, or whether it was a name dreamt up by the press. It was a name synonymous in the early eighteenth century with barbaric savagery, and it may have been connected with the visit to London of four Iroquois chiefs in 1710.

The Mohock gang quickly passed into literature, and this may have been one reason for the panic. John Gay's play *The Mohocks* was written while the events were taking place on the streets. Gay added to the public panic by giving the Mohocks a cannibal chief, and he devised an initiation ceremony in which a circle of drunken, kneeling Mohocks sang:

> Come fill up the Glass,
> Round, round let it pass,
> Till our reason be lost in wine
> Leave Conscience's rules
> To women and fools,
> This can only make us divine.

The chorus went:

> Then a Mohock, a Mohock I'll be.
> No Laws shall restrain

Our Libertine reign,
We'll riot, drink and be free,
We will scour the town,
Knock the constable down,
Put the watch and the beadle to flight,
We'll force all that we feel
To kneel at our feet[27]
And own the Great Prince of the Night.

In *Trivia, or The Art of Walking in the Streets*, Gay advised walkers at night to follow a watchman with a lamp because:

Rakes their revels keep;
Kindlers of riot, enemies of sleep.

Gay describes the Nickers who woke the households by throwing pennies at windows, and the Scourers who cleared the streets. He added: 'who has not trembled at the Mohocks' shame?'[28] This helped to whip up panic about the Mohocks, but what was the panic about, and was it anything but a media frenzy?

The *Spectator*, a daily journal that commented on current affairs, was apolitical but upheld morality and religion. On 12 March 1712 an article appeared about the Mohocks, which with an amazing display of misunderstood anthropology described them as a 'Nocturnal fraternity, under the title The Mohock Club, a name borrowed from a sort of cannibal from India. The president is styled the Emperor of the Mohocks and his arms are a Turkish crescent engraven upon his forehead . . .' The only qualification for joining the club, the *Spectator* claimed, was to be able to drink beyond 'reason or humanity', and then to take to the streets to attack anyone so unfortunate as to be walking abroad. 'Some are knock'd down, others stabbed, others cut and carbonaded.' The journal described 'tipping the lion', which was performed by squeezing the nose flat to the face and boring out the eyes with a finger. Or there was 'the dancing master', a ritual in which scholars were taught to cut capers by running swords through their legs, or 'The Tumblers who set women upon their heads'. The article concludes that the Mohocks were carrying out a war against Mankind.[29] The *Spectator* had a large circulation, and was read by the gentry, middle classes and professional men. What it wrote instilled fear into them. Jonathan Swift wrote in his *Journal to Stella* that there was a race of Rakes called the Mohocks 'that play the Devil about town every night, slit people's noses and beat them'. Hearing that 'young Davenant' had been set upon by them, he concluded that 'It is not safe being in the streets by night' and he was forced to go home early in a sedan chair in case he was attacked. On 16 March 1712 he reported that Lady Winchilsea's maid had been attacked when she answered the door to some Mohocks, and her face had been cut.[30] Lady Strafford, writing from her house in St James to Lady Wentworth on 11 March, repeated the rumour that Mr Davenant had been attacked. She wrote: 'Here is nothing talked about but men that goes in partys about the street and cuts people with swords and knives, and the call themselves by som hard name I can neither speak nor spell'. Lady Strafford admitted she was 'very frightened' of that gang of devils. She recounted that 'they put an old woman into a hogshead and rooled her down a hill, they cut off soms nosis, others hands and several barbarous tricks without any provocation. They are said to be young gentlemen.'[31]

The same stories were sent in a letter from Thomas Burnet, the son of Bishop Burnet, to his friend George Duckett on 15 March. Thomas Burnet, in fact, was rumoured to be a member of the Mohocks, which he hotly denied. In his letter he names 'Tim Allyn' as their emperor, and says that the Mohocks were inspired by 'potent Bacchus to run out of the Taverns at Midnight to beat the watchmen, slit noses, and cut women's arms'.[32]

It is the alleged involvement of a bishop's son that marks the Mohocks out from other street gangs. To all intents and purposes this was a relatively well-organised gang of gentlemen, and for a month in 1712 it destabilised society by disrupting the normal course of life and making people change their habits, like poor Swift who had to go home early in a chair.

The identities of some of the Mohocks were revealed on 12 March, when John Bouche, a constable of Essex Street, London, was assaulted by a gang, thought to be Mohocks. A number of young gentlemen were arrested near the scene, appeared the next morning before the justices, and were given bail. The most prominent of those arrested was Edward, Lord Hinchingbrooke (1692–1721), son of the Earl of Sandwich. His bail was set at £1,000. The next highest bail was for a baronet, Sir Mark Cole (1687–1720), whose bail was set at £500. Included amongst those arrested were a member of Lincoln's Inn, Robert Squibb, a Middle Templar Charles Dubois, Captain John Reading of a regiment of foot, and another military man, Captain Robert Beard or Bard; the group was completed by Thomas Fanshaw, Thomas Sydenham and Hugh Jones, Sir Mark Cole's servant. Jones could not afford the bail and was sent to Newgate Gaol.[33]

The *London Gazette* listed the crimes of which these putative Mohocks were accused. There were assaults on William Thomas Eldon in Covent Garden at ten at night at the beginning of February 1712, an assault on Elizabeth Fisher, the wife of Robert Fisher, a victualler, at eight o'clock at night in late February. She had drink thrown in her face, her candle was knocked to the ground and she was thrown into the street. On 23 February 1712 Mary Girdler was wounded in the arm. Ebenezer Magee, a saddler, was assaulted in the Strand and again in Russell Street. John Sells, a poulterer, was attacked on 10 March near Chancery Lane, and again in Fetter Lane as he went to Newgate market. Elizabeth Miller was assaulted on her way to the same market between four and five in the morning.

Mary Ann Kilby was set upon near the Temple Bar between seven and eight at night and wounded in the face with a penknife. Robert Ellis was attacked on his own doorstep in St Clement's Yard at eleven at night, Isaac Warner was assaulted in Ludgate Circus, and William Savage Esquire and Lady Elizabeth Savage had leaden bullets shot at them through a window by a crossbow at ten at night. Grace Joyce was assaulted in Piccadilly and wounded in the head.

Those who had been bailed appeared before the Middlesex justices in April. Hinchingbrooke, Sydenham and Fanshaw were exonerated before they had to appear. Sir Mark Cole claimed that they were simply helping the watch. This plea was rejected and all the others were fined 3s. 4d. each, hardly a punishment likely to deter them from further crime. However, two breakaway Mohocks, Captain Thomas Seaman and Mr Edward Churchill, were accused and found guilty of attacking Robert Cutmore in Charles Street and cutting off his nose. Seaman was imprisoned, and Churchill, who was wanted for a number of other crimes including murder, was hanged in June 1712.[34]

The Mohocks were tried for crimes committed against those who came forward to complain, but there may have been many more victims who did not. Those attacked were going about their lawful business, but walking alone in the streets they were vulnerable. Those targeted were women, tradesmen or figures of authority; those attacking them were exclusively male and from a different social class. Were the Mohocks asserting their masculinity through violence, committed out of doors and in a public space: exerting gentlemanly freedom in a society that was putting pressure on them to conform to a moral code?[35] This is one construction that can be put on the Mohocks' attacks. However, the attacks were centred on the Temple and the Inns of Court. Many young gentlemen were sent to the Inns of Court to learn the rudiments of law and to meet others from their own class. The Inns housed a pool of wealthy young blades often experiencing life away from parental guidance for the first time. The context of the Mohock attacks may have been nothing more than the effect of alcohol and conviviality leading impressionable young men into random violence against innocent passers-by. It is not clear, from the evidence, whether those attacked were the only people on the street at the time, or whether they were deliberately chosen as victims. As the victims had legitimate reasons for being on the streets, it would appear that they simply happened to be in the wrong place at the wrong time.[36] The Mohock attacks, were, however, a dramatic piece of street theatre, which played on the imagination of London's citizens, who could picture the dark streets, lit only by pools of light, the lone figure, and then the rush of footsteps as the Mohocks came out of the darkness.

The attackers were not necessarily members of the Mohock gang, and none of the defendants could identify any of those accused who appeared in court. Moreover, after the trial, when the Mohock scare died down, some, like Bishop William Nicolson of Carlisle, began to surmise that the whole thing had been a fabrication and the result of ill-informed rumours.[37] Others attributed a political motive to the violence. Queen Anne was nearing the end of her life. Her only son was dead, and she had no direct heir to ascend the throne after her. The Protestant heir to the throne was the Hanoverian George, but her half-brother James Stuart, the Old Pretender, was pestering her to name him as her successor. As a staunch upholder of the Church of England, she had already decided that the Crown must go to George of Hanover. But a Hanoverian succession would probably mean the end of the Tory government that had enjoyed power during her reign, and the advent of the Whigs. London in 1712 was a politically charged hotbed of faction, and an exciting if dangerous place to be. Although the attention of some of the press and the public turned to other matters, speculation about the Mohocks and whether they were politically motivated remained. One ballad, 'Plot upon Plot', suggested that the Mohocks were a Whig plot against the state, and were connected to a letter bomb sent to the Lord Treasurer, who had been saved from the explosion by Jonathan Swift, who was present when the package arrived and cut the box lid rather than untying the string, thus stopping the trigger from going off.

> Oh wicked Whigs, what can you mean,
> When will your plotting cease,
> Against our most renowned Queen,
> Her ministry and peace.
>
> . . .
>
> You sent your Mohocks next abroad,
> With razors armed and knives,
> Who on nightwalkers made inroad,
> And scoured our maids and wives,
> They scoured the Watch
> And windows broke,
> But 'twas their true intent
> (As our wise Ministry did smoke)
> To overturn the government . . .[38]

Swift was convinced that the Mohocks were Whigs with links to the parliamentary opposition, but the *Observator*, a Whig paper, claimed that the Mohocks were Jacobite Tories out to intimidate the Whigs.[39] After the events were over the *Spectator* claimed to have seen a Mohock manifesto issued from the Devil's Tavern.[40] An anonymous poem, 'The Mohocks: a Poem in Miltonic Verse', addressed specifically to the *Spectator*, claimed that the Mohocks were the reincarnation of the giants Gog and Magog, who had risen in response to a catcall from America.[41]

By April 1712, the Mohock scare had vanished. Whether the groups of young gentlemen arrested and fined were the Mohocks was not proven. A shadowy figure lurked behind the group arrested: Tim Alleyne, who may have been the son of Thomas Alleyne, a member of the Governor-General's Council for Barbados and the owner of the Black Jack estate. Tim Alleyne was educated at Queen's College, Oxford, and was a member of the Middle Temple, but his title of emperor and the tattoo on his forehead may have been inventions of Grub Street, as was the assertion, repeated by Swift, that the Mohocks numbered eighty strong.[42] The Mohocks exemplified fear of the unknown, and the attitude towards the 'savage'. It was generally agreed in London that the inspiration for the attacks had come from the four Iroquois chiefs who were in the city in 1710. The *Spectator* described the Mohocks as having the manners of 'Indian Savages', which was not becoming to English gentlemen, and suggested that there was a relationship between the Mohocks, the dominions and cannibals.[43]

The Iroquois chiefs were anything but savages. While in England, they met the Queen, dined with the nobility, attended theatrical performances and asked the Queen to send missionaries to North America, but there were basic misunderstandings about them in British society. Thomas Hearne, for example, who described the activities of the Mohocks in London, thought that the Iroquois came from the West Indies. The Native Americans were seen by the early settlers as children, unrestrained and uncivilised: the settlers felt they needed to be tamed and educated, their nudity clothed and their brutish manners changed.[44] Attitudes altered in the later eighteenth century when the Native American became romanticised as the 'noble savage', but in the early years of the century people were still coming to terms with the different peoples revealed by exploration. The differences that were observed opened up new questions about Mankind: for example, why were some black or brown, and should they have equal rights with civilised European society? The answer to this question in 1712 was no.

Since the activities of the street gang were seen as savagery, they were equated with Native Americans. They became fused in the minds of the eighteenth-century Londoner with the fear of the dark and unknown experienced when walking alone through the streets of the capital at night.

Preventive measures against the Mohocks relied on information from the public, for which as much as £100 could be paid. As far as can be ascertained, nobody ever claimed this reward. This may have been due to the conventions of the upper classes from which the Mohocks came, a class in which £100 might be spent in an evening and in which informing against a fellow gentleman was the act of a scoundrel and a duelling offence.

In the later eighteenth century the existence of such a club was doubted. For example, the *Connoisseur* suggested in 1755 that the Mohocks were a joke.[45] Nevertheless, William Hickey records in his memoirs that there had been a revival of Mohocks or Mohawks as he called them.

> In the winter of 1771, a set of wild young men made their appearance in the area of Covent Garden and drove away sedate persons. They were distinguished under the title Mohawk, and as such were severely attacked in the public newspapers, which instead of checking them, stimulated their excesses.

This gang was only four in number. Their chief was Rhoan Hamilton, an Irish rebel who, Hickey claimed, was six feet tall and well made, 'an imposing man'. The others were Mr Hayter, the son of a banker, Mr Osborne, a young American who had come to England to study law, and Mr Frederick, 'a handsome lad but without a guinea', who claimed to be the son or grandson of the King of Corsica.[46]

This quartet, Hickey claimed, was in a constant state of inebriety, and attacked anyone who fell in their way. Hickey added, self-righteously, that he had proclaimed their scandalous behaviour publicly (he was in repentant mood at the time), and he became known as an anti-Mohawk. The Mohawks persisted in their anti-social activities until 1774, when they were arrested during a riot at a playhouse. They were bailed and Hamilton fled abroad. Hayter's father who stood bail for him forfeited his recognisance and sent him to Holland to repent, Osborne went back to America, accompanied by Frederick, and they were both killed in the American War of Independence.

Thus ended the career of four young men who for a period of three years continued in one uninterrupted course of folly, intemperance and riot, to the utter disgrace of themselves, and of the police of the capital which was either so relaxed, as to permit their course of iniquity.[47]

If this quartet of thugs really existed, they present some similarities with the earlier Mohocks, and some important differences. Attacking passers-by was a feature of the earlier group, but they quickly attracted the attention of the authorities and efforts were made to curb them. If the reign of the latter group persisted as long as Hickey suggests, then perhaps their depredations were not as serious as those of their predecessors, and their victims did not complain to the constables. However, the most important difference is that the later eighteenth-century Mohawks failed to catch the imagination of the literary hacks and newspapers. The fear they spread was localised, confined to the Covent Garden area. Twentieth-century historians have also questioned the Mohocks' existence, but there does seem to have been a club of some sort operating in London in 1712, whose pleasure was to harm and humiliate others. But by April of that year they had ceased their activities and the Mohock spring was over.

CHANGES

The original Mohocks crossed the boundaries of acceptable behaviour. Public violence was common in early modern England, but in the eighteenth century a subtle change in social attitudes began to condemn violence as an outlet for male aggression and the assertion of masculine power. Although Shoemaker shows that fighting reaffirmed male superiority, and was often a form of play amongst boys,[48] the Mohocks' violence went beyond play, and took the form of the unpleasant bullying of victims going about their legitimate business. Allegedly the Mohocks came from the elite of society, and the social elite was beginning to reinterpret social behaviour. Instead of violence and exaggeration, moderation and sensibility became the acceptable norms. Politeness and civility became social virtues in the home and on the street. The drama of the street theatre as acted out by the Mohocks was no longer countenanced, and young gentlemen were encouraged to move their discourse from the public space of the street to the private space of the club or coffee-house, and to indulge their excesses within those confines. The Bridewell Boys (boys from the Blue Coat Orphans' School in Bridewell) and the urban mob might still run riot through the streets, but they were now part of legitimate protest, motivated by events and politics. Battles between Whigs and Tories took place in London and other towns on significant anniversaries such as the coronation of George I, or against specific targets such as the dissenters, but many of the riots of the second decade of the eighteenth century had a deeper constitutional meaning, and were part of the uncertainty of those years, and the growing recognition of the lower classes that they deserved a place in the government of the country.

In 1714 Queen Anne died, and was succeeded by George I, the Protestant Elector of Hanover; waiting in the wings was James Stuart, the Old Pretender, the Catholic claimant to the throne. In 1715 a rebellion broke out in his favour. Running battles between

Jacobites and Hanoverian supporters took place in the streets of towns and cities, and the Midland counties of Worcestershire, Warwickshire and Staffordshire were ablaze.[49] The rebellion was suppressed, but it added to the uncertainties of the early eighteenth century and polarised political opinion; the Whigs supported Hanover, but many Tories wavered, and some supported James Stuart. This was true of the Duke of Wharton, whose name is associated with the Hell-Fire Club.

Other changes were taking place in the early decades of the century. In 1712, at almost the same time as the Mohock scare in London, a case against an alleged witch took place in Hertfordshire. The outcome of this trial is an illustration of the demise of the belief in witchcraft. This marks how far rationalism had triumphed over superstition, adding to the dilemma faced by the hell-fire clubs, that belief in a supernatural Devil must predispose to belief in a supernatural God. It touched on one of the most important debates of the Enlightenment: Could the Devil be dethroned by reason, and Man be liberated from superstition by science? If science could show that unexpected and irrational events had a discoverable scientific explanation, fear of these events would disappear.

The publication of an English version by Balthasar Bekker of *The World Bewitched* (first published in The Netherlands in 1696) added to the debate. It claimed that scripture and reason showed that the empire of the Devil had no power over Mankind. But this was a dangerous debate. If there was no Devil, did that mean there was no God? Where did this leave the state and its government, which relied on religion to bolster its authority and was headed by a monarch anointed with holy oil?[50]

In the Commonwealth period the state had allowed Matthew Hopkins, the witch-finder general, to kill at least 128 people suspected of witchcraft. But by 1670 circuit judges were becoming less credulous, and those accused of witchcraft were likely to be acquitted. Those who followed the horrible example of the Salem witch trials of 1692 saw how panic whipped up by superstition could destroy the lives of many.[51] In 1711 Daniel Defoe revived the debate on witchcraft, and the *Spectator* took up the debate in July of that year. The writer of the *Spectator* article declared that there may have been such a thing as witchcraft in the past, but he personally had seen no evidence of it; he argued that it was the belief in witchcraft that turned old women into witches in every village and cut them off from charity and compassion.[52] At this time Defoe was working for Lord Harley, a moderate Tory. The Whigs blamed the revival of interest in witches on the Tories, and thought it was connected to the superstition of Popery and the Jacobite pretenders to the throne, thereby associating witchcraft with rebellion.

The trial in 1712 of Jane Wenham of Walkern, Hertfordshire, attracted a great deal of attention in early eighteenth-century England. The proceedings of the trial were published in full by the bookseller Edmund Curll, and pamphlets for and against beliefs in witches and witchcraft proliferated. As Curll wrote in the preface to the proceedings, these 'made a great noise in the whole country'. He appealed to rational men to consider the proceedings carefully and ask what proof there was, and whether there was any evidence for what was essentially a mere chain of absurdities.[53] The full details of the case against Jane Wenham need not concern us here. She was held to be responsible for the strange death of livestock, for bewitching John Chapman when he would not give her a penny-worth of straw, and for healing his servant's dislocated knee by witchcraft. Jane was described as old, but in the eighteenth century this probably meant middle-aged. Although there is no evidence she was educated, she knew her rights and took out a warrant against Chapman for calling her a witch. The Justice of the Peace, Sir Henry Chauncy, who heard her case, refused damages, claiming to have heard ill of her character. Chauncy brought in the local rector to oversee an agreement between Chapman and Jane. When this was not forthcoming he had Jane arrested as a witch, and once she was arrested other witnesses came forward to accuse her. After sensory deprivation and being pricked with needles and examined for supernumerary teats, she was sent to Hertfordshire Assizes, where the Grand Jury found her guilty. The only sentence the presiding judge, Mr Justice Powell, could give was death, but he was sceptical. He overturned the jury's verdict and reprieved her. She was rescued from the courtroom by the Whig peer, Lord Cowper, and taken to live out the rest of her days at Panshanger in Hertfordshire.

Jane Wenham entered Whig mythology. She was used as a figure to mock Tory superstition and to support the Whig view that the cessation of witch-hunting was evidence of the advance from the dark and superstitious past to their present enlightened thinking. A pamphlet war followed Jane Wenham's reprieve. Francis Bragge noted that the general alarm had given sceptics and free-thinkers the chance to argue about the reality of witchcraft and forget that Christ came to defeat the Devil. In another pamphlet Bragge warned that 'once men come to deny there are Spirits or witches it is a fair step to saying "There is no God"'.[54]

An anonymous pamphlet, *The Impossibility of Witchcraft*, suggested that belief in witches was irrational and impious. This idea was countered by *The Belief in Witchcraft Vindicated* and *A Full Confutation of Witchcraft, More Particularly of the Deposition against Jane Wenham*, the latter written by a Hertfordshire physician. He wrote that he would probably be accused of atheism, especially in the country, but he was glad that there was a judicious and penetrating judge on the circuit who recognised that the depositions against Jane Wenham were absurd and inconsistent.[55]

These pamphlets and others like them laid the foundations for the repeal of the Witchcraft Act in 1736. Justice Powell and other judges who acquitted those accused of witchcraft reflected the attitudes of the more humanitarian men who controlled the lawcourts. They, like the hell-fire clubs, challenged the accepted views of society.

THE DEISTS

Other elements of change added to the uncertainties of the first two decades of the eighteenth century. The abandonment of superstition by many of the educated class needed to be replaced in the intellectual's mind by something else. This led towards deism. Seen by orthodox churchmen as atheism, deism was in fact a rational ideology that rejected superstition but did not necessarily reject Christianity. Deists believed that only natural knowledge was knowable, but it also acknowledged that there was one true higher being, even if this was not a personal God. Scientific experiment, they suggested, might reveal more knowledge about the divine laws of nature and the force behind them. Or it might reveal that there was nothing behind them.

Deists held that the laws of nature were binding, and that they had inescapable ethical consequences, such as a need for philanthropy, humility, moderation, self-discipline and industriousness. These virtues were the basis of governance of the state and the family. In addition to these, the guiding principle of the ruling elite should be loyalty to the state – or patriotism, and the patriotic virtues of prudence, temperance and justice. Although as members of the ruling elite and part of the government of the country the members of the hell-fire clubs should have been adhering to these virtues, they singularly failed to do so. Natural ethics and patriotic virtues were often absent from their reasoning, and the general scepticism that was articulated after Jane Wenham's trial provided them with the opportunity to mock superstition and dare the Devil to come and carouse with them.

An important influence on the deists and probably on the hell-fire clubs as well was John Toland (1670–1722), a free-thinker and philosopher from County Donegal in Ireland, who left his native country for Scotland where he joined the Rosicrucians. The Rosucrucians were allegedly founded in 1484 by Christian Rosenkreuz, but the first documentary evidence of the group does not come until 1614. Rosicrucians claimed to have secret and magical knowledge such as how to turn base metal into gold and how to prolong life, as well as having power over the elements and elemental spirits.[56] These beliefs coincide with the general intellectual trends of the first two decades of the eighteenth century, and it is in the eighteenth century that the Rosiscrucians flourished.

From Scotland, Toland travelled to London and then on to Holland. In London he became involved with the Druids and the return to paganism. In this era Druidism was the result of antiquarian research in Britain, and desire for a past that would provide collective identity and historical consciousness for all the disparate elements of the British Isles.[57] Of course the Druids were known from Julius Caesar's *Gallic Wars*, but it was the work of English antiquarians William Stukeley and John Aubrey that led John Toland to associate megalithic monuments such as Stonehenge with the Druids and create a lasting legend, to which ritual and ceremony were added. It was Toland who took Caesar's descriptions of Druids performing sacrifices by burning humans in wicker figures and broadcast them in print. The images he created remain in the public imagination as the evil side of the Druids. Hutton argues that the atheist Toland was using the Druids as an analogy for the priests whom he hated, and this led him to create a distorted picture of them;[58] however, as a committed republican Toland stressed that there should be a civil and universal religion that would reform the old order, and that this could be based on an ancient set of rules.

In Holland, Toland founded a secret society called the Knights of Jubilation, a proto-Masonic organisation based on a business network through which seditious and erotic literature passed. The records of the chapter-general of the Knights reveal that, as in similar organisations, a great deal of wine was drunk at their meetings, and the Knights' motto was 'Good wine and a good appetite for ever.'[59] This motto summed up what many of the hell-fire clubs were about. But in the second decade of the eighteenth century the changing perception of what was acceptable behaviour, and the challenging debates on superstition and religion, meant that the clubs entered a new phase. There were still gentlemen who wanted to shock society, but now they chose to do this behind closed doors, in a concourse where they could mock religion and dare the Devil to join them. The real hell-fire clubs were born.

CHAPTER 3

The Hell-Fire Clubs

On 29 April 1721 Lord Willoughby of Brooke presented the first reading of an 'Act for the More Effectual Suppressing of Blasphemy and Profaneness', in the House of Lords. The second reading of the bill took place on 2 May 1721, then the debate was postponed for three weeks.[1] The day before the bill was introduced into the House of Lords the following Royal Proclamation had appeared in the *London Gazette*:

His Majesty have received Information, which gives great Reason to suspect that there have lately been and still are, in and about the Cities of London and Westminster, certain scandalous Clubs or Societies of young Persons who meet together, and in the most impious and blasphemous Manner, insult the most sacred Principles of Holy Religion, affront Almighty God himself, and corrupt the Minds and Morals of one another; and being resolved to make use of all the Authority committed to him by Almighty God himself, to punish such enormous Offenders and to crush such shocking impieties before they increase and draw down the Vengeance of God upon this Nation: His Majesty hath thought fit to command the Lord Chancellor to call together his Majesty's Justices of the peace of Middlesex and Westminster, and strictly to enjoin them, in the most effectual Manner, that they, and every one of them, do make most diligent and careful

Enquiry and search for the Discovery of any thing of this and the like sort tending in any wise to the Corruption of the Principles and Manner of Men . . .[2]

At the end of the proclamation was an addition: 'His Majesty hath been pleased to give Orders to the Principal Officers of his Household to make strict and diligent Enquiry whether any of his Majesty's Servants are guilty of the horrid Impieties mentioned in the Order in Council inserted above, and to make Report thereof to his Majesty.'[3] The clubs referred to were the hell-fire clubs and the proclamation and the bill were symptomatic of the deep concern of the King and the government that the country was in a deep pit of moral malaise, which would result in its destruction.

The proclamation and the bill came on the heels of the South Sea Bubble. The South Sea Company, founded in 1711, promised investors great riches through trade with Spanish America. So good was its promotional literature and public relations that investors flocked to buy shares. By June 1720 the share value had risen by 1,000 per cent, and the clamour to buy increased. But by that time Britain was at war with Spain and trade with Spanish America was at an end. The South Sea Bubble deflated and then burst with a resounding explosion. Merchants, tradesmen, gentry and aristocrats lost heavily. The company secretary fled. Landed estates had to be mortgaged to cover expenses. Britain was in economic despair.

Blasphemy, atheism and the moral climate of the country rather than greed were seen as the prime reasons for the crash. The country had been found wanting by God and had been punished. The hell-fire clubs of young sceptical and dissolute gentlemen were symptoms of Britain's moral disease. They mocked religion and had to be rooted out by the government and public opinion.

Society was becoming more materialistic and consumer-orientated. Conspicuous consumption of luxury goods and alco-holism increased and there was a general rejection of the Church.

The established Church was in crisis. It was split between tolerant clergymen who thought that conscience was a matter for God alone, and the High Churchmen who thought that only a priest had the authority to intercede between God and the individual. In 1717 the Convocation of the Church of England was suspended. This was the Church's parliament, where ideology could be discussed and policies made. Convocation would remain suspended for the next hundred years. At a local level, the power of the Church was in decline. Many churches were staffed by pluralist rectors, and had services at irregular intervals. Pastoral care was lacking for many, and there was an increase in blasphemy, swearing and Sabbath-breaking. The hell-fire clubs symbolised lack of faith, and in their mocking of religion were perceived to be part of a national moral and religious crisis. In *A System of Magic*, Daniel Defoe described being at a meeting of such a club, 'a pagan circle, near Old Charing, where God was owned, sworn by, imprecated, blasphemed, and denied, all in one breath'.[4] Defoe defined the sceptic 'as forming the notion of God in his own mind but stripping Him of his governing power, the Deist brings God down to the level with our reasoning, the atheist out-goes them all, and shuts his eyes against reason of sense and tells you there is no God at all'. He summed up the religion of his age as 'Heaven resolved with Nature, Religion with Reason, and all Gods into Philosophy'.[5] It was to prevent the descent into reason and bring the country back to the paths of righteousness that the Royal Proclamation was issued and the bill introduced in the House of Lords.

THE PROCLAMATION AND THE BILL AGAINST BLASPHEMY AND IMPIOUS CLUBS

The proclamation provoked the justices of Westminster and Middlesex into issuing an advertisement for information about the 'nefarious societies'. This was an action that appeared to be lacking in any real enthusiasm for rooting out the clubs, and on 26 May 1721 the magistrates reported that no information was forthcoming, and that in their minds the general debauchery of the town was responsible for the profanity and blasphemy.[6] Clearly, they did not believe that such clubs existed, or if they did exist it was unlikely they could be found and the members brought to trial. On the other hand, the King showed, by instituting an inquiry into the conduct of his own household, that he did believe that the clubs existed and that he was very much aware that their numbers were drawn from the upper echelons of society. He was setting an example for the justices to follow, which the justices chose to ignore.

The bill against blasphemy and profanity was not aimed directly against the hell-fire clubs, but if passed it would provide a framework by which club members could be indicted. It stated that anyone who spoke or wrote against the being of God, the divinity of Christ, the Holy Ghost and the doctrine of the Trinity as set forth in the Thirty-Nine Articles could be imprisoned for many months. Any preacher who denied the fundamental principle of the Christian religion was to be deprived of the Act of Toleration, and archbishops and bishops were to summon every person in holy orders to appear and subscribe to the bill's declaration, whilst the justices were to summon dissenting ministers to do the same.

There was considerable opposition to the bill. Lord Onslowe said he was against blasphemy, but this was a bill for persecution, and he moved that it be thrown out.[7] When his seconder stood up to speak, the House fell expectantly silent, as this was the Duke of Wharton, whose name was linked to the Hell-Fire Club as patron and founder. Wharton was reported as saying, 'He was not insensible of the common talk and opinion of the town concerning himself; and therefore he was glad of the opportunity to justify himself, by declaring himself far from being a patron of blasphemy, or an enemy of religion; but on the other hand he could not be for this bill, because he conceived it to be repugnant to holy scripture.'[8] After further debate the bill was defeated by 60 'noes' to 34 'ayes', and was put off 'to a long day'.

The bill had been ghost-drafted by Archbishop Wake of Canterbury, and was not directed at the Hell-Fire Club: it was more concerned with preserving Anglican orthodoxy. But Wake considered those who denied the Trinity to be in league with the Devil, and on the same plane as the Hell-Fire Club. The bill was to stop the anti-Trinitarians.[9] Wake's informers had been busy writing to him about the activities, real and imagined, of the Hell-Fire Club and others who mocked religion, and it is Wake's correspondence that proves the existence of such a club, and the Duke of Wharton's involvement. The Duke is the key figure of the Hell-Fire Club, and he was a man born with every possible advantage who by his own admission squandered his talents.[10]

THE HELL-FIRE DUKE OF WHARTON

Philip, Duke of Wharton, 'the Hell-Fire Duke', was born in 1698 into a Whig Parliamentarian family. His mother had estates in Ireland and the Whartons' English estates were situated in Buckinghamshire and Westmorland; they also owned Dormer House in Chelsea and a house in Dover Street, London. He had illustrious godparents: William III, Princess (later Queen) Anne and the Duke of Shrewsbury, Secretary of State. The Whartons were wealthy, and by the age of twelve Philip had his own string of racehorses. He was privately educated in the classics, but following a secluded and isolated boyhood fell short of his father's expectations when released into society. He quickly rebelled against its conventions and entered into all manner of licentiousness.

Almost immediately on entering London society in 1715, he fell in love with the beautiful but penniless daughter of Major-General Richard Holmes. His father forbade the marriage, but Philip, who was beginning to show some of the headstrong tendencies which would be his undoing in the future, eloped with Martha Holmes and married her. Six weeks later his father died, allegedly from the shock and disgrace of his son's action, having told the writer Joseph Addison that the affair with his son would break his heart.[11]

Philip inherited an estate that was worth £8,000 a year but was heavily mortgaged. Some of the London property was sold, and he was given an allowance of £1,000 a year to live on. His trustees and guardians were anxious to remove him from London society, and to continue his education on the godly lines set out by his father. In order to do this they took a disastrous decision that would have a far-reaching effect on Wharton's life: they decided to send him on a Grand Tour of Europe, chaperoned by a Huguenot/Calvinist tutor to learn more about the Protestant religion. A good Calvinist itinerary was drawn up for him with stopping-off places in Holland, Hanover and Geneva. This was a far cry from the tours of pleasure on the continent that other young gentlemen took, and in Geneva Wharton escaped from his tutor and set off for France with the aim of going to the Stuart court in exile.[12]

This was just one of the many unconsidered and rash actions that Wharton took during his lifetime. He was a restless soul, given to enthusiasm, lavish entertainment and luxury – the complete opposite of his puritan father. It is not surprising that the dourness of Calvinist Geneva did not appeal to him. He craved excitement, and perhaps the romance of a prince in exile from his throne. His father had been a Protestant through and through, true to the House of Hanover, and yet here was his son flirting with the Catholic House of Stuart, the rival to Hanover, whose supporters had been in rebellion when Wharton left England.

He met James Edward Stuart, the Old Pretender, at Avignon in 1716 and presented him with a stone horse he had acquired on his travels. James Edward bestowed the title of Duke of Northumberland on him, and awarded him the Order of the Garter. Neither the title nor the Order of Garter as awarded by James

THE HELL-FIRE CLUBS *51*

would be recognised when Wharton returned to England. From Avignon, Wharton travelled on to Paris to meet with other Jacobites and with Mary of Modena, the Old Pretender's mother.

The Jacobites had a role for him. Given that his father had been a trusted member of the Whig Junto they asked Wharton to return to England and join the Whigs in the House of Lords, where he could act as their spy and informer. He left France in December 1716, to take his seat in the House of Lords and 'smile on the Whigs, the better to cut their throats'.[13]

He bamboozled the Whigs so well that they elevated him to a dukedom for his committee work in the Irish House of Lords. On his elevation he returned to England from Ireland, and was reunited with his wife. A son was born to them in 1719, but in 1720 the baby died during a smallpox epidemic. Wharton blamed his wife for not taking the child to the country, and never spoke to her again.

It was at this time, perhaps as a reaction to his son's death, that his wild ways became well established. He became an associate of the infamous Colonel Charteris, a rake known as 'the rape-master general', an *habitué* of Mother Brett's brothel, a gambler who could not pay his debts and who indulged in massive drinking bouts. It was also during this period that Wharton became involved with the Hell-Fire Club. Was this the result of circumstances destroying a faith that was already in question? Here was a man with a Calvinist education, who had flirted with Catholicism on the continent and now was in league with Devil, mocking religion and cocking a snook at the establishment.

THE HELL-FIRE CLUB OF 1721

There is a great deal of speculation about this club, and not too many facts. Evidence suggests that it was essentially a group of young gentlemen who met together to toast the Devil and indulge in other sacrilegious actions. The young men probably included

Viscount Hillsborough and Sir Edmund O'Brien, as well as the Duke of Wharton, but it is doubtful whether their activities included meeting in rooms full of sulphur and brandy, eating Holy Ghost Pie or the Breast of Venus, calling themselves after the Trinity, martyrs and prophets, or admitting a lady with a pillow up her skirt to act as the pregnant Virgin Mary,[14] as some accounts suggest.

Once the existence of the club became common knowledge journalistic hacks quickly embellished what happened at its meetings, so that fact and fiction became merged. Since these meetings were held in secret the journalists' imagination could be given full rein. The public could be titillated with accounts of dissolute and irreligious high life, and this helped to sell papers.

The first contemporary reference to the Hell-Fire Club is in *Mist's Weekly Journal* of 20 February 1720. The article describes two clubs, the Bold Bucks and the Hell-Fires. The Bold Bucks, the journal claimed, attempted sex with all females of their own species, no matter what age, and even with their own sisters. The Hell-Fires aimed at a more 'transcendent Malignity: deriding the Forms of Religion as a Trifle. By a natural Progression they turn to Substance; with Lucifer they fly at Divinity; the Second Person of the Trinity, they leave their brethren in Iniquity, the Presbyterian teachers of Exeter, but the Third is what they peculiarly attack'. (The third member of the Trinity was the Holy Ghost.)

Mist continued that they called for Holy Ghost Pie at meetings, which took place in a tavern. The journal notes that they were university men who had completed their education in a riding academy where 'Obsceneness, Curses, Blasphemy, Exclamations are the order of the day. They play cards and dice on a Sunday. Ladies shield their faces because of the whiff of brimstone when they pass.' Mist identifies their leader as 'the unfortunate Lord Dapper, [the Duke of Wharton] whose name no longer has any reputation as it did in the days of his father'.

Mist's account was followed by a letter from 'Cato' (Joseph Addison), who wanted Mr Mist to correct the impression that there were two separate clubs. A week later Mist received a letter from 'Cordelia' whose lover 'Florio' had joined the Bold Bucks and the Hell-Fires and had told her of a plot to assassinate Mist in St Paul's Churchyard.[15]

Nathaniel Mist, the proprietor of the journal, was a Jacobite, and he may have had a political axe to grind about what he saw as Wharton's defection to the Whigs. However, Mist does emphasise that element of the Hell-Fire Club which worried the Archbishop of Canterbury, William Wake: the denial of the Trinity and especially the Holy Ghost. The exposure of this aspect of the Hell-Fires in the press eventually led to the Royal Proclamation, and the King's anxiety that members of his own household might be members of the club.

Following the proclamation *Applebee's Journal* claimed that forty persons belonged to the Hell-Fire Club, including fifteen ladies of quality. It placed their meetings at Somerset House in the Strand, a house in Westminster and another in Conduit Street. Here they met to ridicule the Holy Trinity and religion by blasphemy and profanities. They took the names of the patriarchs and prophets, and when one of their number died he or she became their ambassador to Hell. In fact, Applebee claimed, death had snatched four of them away in the midst of their foul deeds.[16] Applebee represented the Tory press. His arch-rival was the Independent Whig 'Cato' of the *London Journal*. Applebee accused Cato of being a member of the Hell-Fire Club, or at the least a friend of those who were members.

The next piece of evidence on the Hell-Fire Club comes from a satirical pamphlet, *The Hell-Fire Club: kept by a society of Blasphemers*, issued in 1721 and dedicated to the Earl of Macclesfield, who was carrying out an investigation into the clubs. The pamphlet, written in rhyme, describes in lurid and imaginative detail their blasphemy and profaneness:

> But here their curst profanity do's not offend,
> The Empire of the Devil to defend,
> They go upon diabolical theme
> Of striving who their God shall most blaspheme.[17]

At the same time as the pamphlet was published a print appeared showing *The Diabolical Maskerade* [sic] *or the Dragon's Feast as Acted by the Hell Fire Club at Somerset House in the Strand.* This showed the Hell-Fire Club members disguised as Pluto, Proserpina and various animals. Verses inscribed below the print described the blasphemous nature of the club and expressed the wish that it might soon be brought to justice.

Further speculation and embroidery of the Hell-Fire Club's activities appeared in a single-page broadsheet, *A Further and Particular Account of the Hell Fire Sulphur Club*, which is in the Wodrow Collection of the Scottish National Library. This included a list of members and their sobriquets.

> The E. . . . of W. . . . . .n The King of Hell
> The D. . . of W. . . . . . . The Door keeper of Hell
> The D. . . . of T. . . . .d Elisha the Prophet
> The M. . . . . of O . . . . The Old Dragon
> The D. . . . . . of Y. . . Lady Sodom
> M. . . . . of R. . . . .r Lady Gomorrah
> Mrs L of S. . . . The Lady Polygamy
> Mrs W. of A. . . . . .g The Lady Fornicator
> Mrs T of G. . . . .k The Lady Hell Fire

The anonymous author of the broadside blamed the club on the impieties of the late French prophets. The putative names were probably included to legitimise the account, which was in fact another journalistic effort designed to sell copies. What other evidence is there about the Hell-Fire Club of the 1720s? Much of what we know comes from memoirs of people alive in that decade but writing at a later date. However, there is one contemporary account by Thomas Smith of Shaw House near Melksham in Wiltshire, who kept a diary. In May 1721 Shaw travelled to London at the height of the Hell-Fire scandal. On Sunday, 7 May 1721 he dined with acquaintances, and the Hell-Fire Club was discussed.

> There has been of late several irreligious clubs discovered of which there is much talk, and indeed everyone that I hear speak of them with the utmost detestation as they duly deserve, such blasphemous Impieties having never been heard of and are not fit to be committed to paper. Several persons of High Rank and of both Sexes are reported to be concerned in them, and the Government has thought fit to issue a Proclamation for their Suppression, which I heartily wish may be its Effect.[18]

Decent men were shocked by the club, and the threat of the dangers posed by such organisations led a public notary, James Puckle (1667–1724), to write a conduct book, *The Club, or A Grey Cap for a Green Hand in a dialog between Father and Son*, published in 1723. This was to warn young people about the follies of the age. The son describes a club he had visited the day before 'at Noah's Ark, where in a low room that stunk like a drunkard's morning breath ... toasts were drunk'. Here a 'Rake fell a ridiculing all religion, and stated that it look'd more like a trick and contrivance of the state, than divine inspiration'.[19]

William Whiston (1667–1752), a natural philosopher of Clare College, Cambridge, and Lucasian professor, remembered the Hell-Fire Club in his memoirs published in 1753. 'At another time in King George I's reign a great noise was made about a club at court, called the Hell-Fire Club; and it was said that a maid of honour of the Princess of Wales was one of them.'[20]

In the autobiography and writings of Mrs Delany, she also remembered the hell-fire clubs of her youth. Miss Hamilton, who helped with the autobiography, wrote:

> Mrs Delany said how cautious young women should be what society they entered into and particularly whom they appeared with in public; she told me an anecdote of herself when she was young and married to Mr Pendarves; gave me an account of the Hell-Fire Club which consisted of about a dozen persons of fashion of both sexes, some of the females unmarried, and the horrid impieties they were guilty of; they used to read and ridicule the Scriptures, and their Conversation was blasphemous to the last degree; they used to act plays, some represented the Virgin Mary. The character of one of the club members, a Mr Howes was described and an account of his death, which Dr Friend (who attended him) gave Mrs Delany on the day Howes died.

Mrs Delany was in Somerset House with her aunt, Lady Stanley, when 'Dr Friend came to them quite overcome with the horrible scene he had just quitted; said he had left this miserable wretch (Howes) expiring, uttering the most horrid imprecations, and tho' denying his belief of everything sacred, said he knew he should burn in hell forever.'[21]

Mary Delany née Granville was the niece of the Tory peer Lord Lansdowne. She was born in 1700 and spent the first eight years of her life in Wiltshire, but was then sent to London to live with her aunt, Lady Stanley. In 1718 she was forced to marry an elderly MP, Alexander Pendarves, and spent eight years trapped in a loveless and miserable marriage. When he died in 1725, she returned to London under the protection of the Stanleys. In 1731 she went on a visit to London, where she met and fell in love with an Irish Anglican clergyman, Patrick Delany. Unfortunately, he was already engaged to another woman, and they had to wait until she died in 1743 to marry. Mrs Delany was noted for her botanical drawings and her garden designs. She died in 1788.[22] The identity of the Miss Hamilton who took down her memoirs cannot be traced.

These accounts should not be seen as especially reliable. Mrs Delany was making a moral point, and although she did, indeed, live with Lady Stanley, and Dr Friend is known to have existed, she did not return to London from the provinces until 1725 – four years after the Hell-Fire scare. It is possible that in her old age she was repeating something she had been told but had not witnessed herself, but in her memory it was as if she had been present at the time.[23] Whiston was writing years after the event. Most of the evidence about Wharton's Hell-Fire Club was speculative, but it would appear that such a club did exist in London in the 1720s and that it indulged in theological discussion that bordered on the blasphemous in denying the Trinity and questioning the doctrine of the established Church. There is little evidence for the Satanic and sexual rituals they were assumed to commit, though, and in the minds of later writers the Hell-Fire Club became conflated with the activities of another club that was dedicated to sex.

In 1722 the Duke of Wharton, heavily in debt and having lost £100,000 on the South Sea Bubble, retired to a villa at Twickenham. Here he became friends with the traveller and writer Lady Mary Wortley Montagu, which led to accusations that she was a member of the Hell-Fire Club. It is Lady Mary who gives us information about the club that has become confused with the Hell-Fire Club. In March 1724 she wrote to Lady Mar about Viscount Hillsborough, 'who has turn'd his house, one of the handsomest in Hanover Square into an Edifice . . . He open'd it on Ash Wednesday by the best Contriv'd Entertainment in the World, and the only remedy against Spleen and vapours occasion'd by the Formality of that Day which still subsists amongst the rags of Popery.' In opening at the start of Lent Viscount Hillsborough's club was committing blasphemy by mocking one of the central tenets of the Christian religion: self-denial in Lent.

The club was called the Schemers, 'and they are sworn to several articles absolutely necessary for the promotion of public good and the conservation of peace in private families. 1st that every member shall come at the hour of 6 mask'd in a Dominie leading in their predominant Lady of his affection mask'd also.'

The lady was to remain anonymous and masked, and no one was to reveal her name. The partners chose what they wanted for supper, and then departed to eat and make love in luxuriously appointed private apartments. These gallantries continued throughout Lent, and Lady Mary suggested that the 'whole generation of fathers, mothers and husbands raise a great clamour against this institute 'tis true they have the envy and curses of the old and ugly of both sexes and a general persecution from all old women . . .'[24]

Hillsborough was running a high-class brothel for his friends. Lady Elizabeth Hastings named the Duke of Wharton and Sir George Oxenden as members of the Schemers, and claimed that members of the club wore purple favours to identify themselves.[25]

Wharton's involvement with the Hell-Fire Club probably came to an end in 1722, as he had found a new interest, the Freemasons. He was elected Grand Master in June of that year. He showed his true colours to the Whigs in 1723 when he supported the Jacobite Bishop Atterbury when he was on trial for treason, and in the publication of a twice-weekly paper the *True Briton*, which he published in 1723–24. The *True Briton* promoted a Jacobite Tory view, which was anathema to the Whig government. In 1724 he resigned from the Masons and founded a new club, the Gormogons, which met at the Castle Tavern in Fleet Street with the aim of ridiculing the Masons.[26] Nothing was sacred to the Duke and everything was open to ridicule. Perhaps in order to save him from himself and to prevent further scandal touching his family name he was sent on a diplomatic mission to Vienna. Now over £70,000 in debt, he decided not to return to England after the mission, and went to Madrid instead. Here he met and fell in love with a maid of honour at the Spanish court, the daughter of an Irish colonel. When his wife in England died, he converted to Catholicism and married the maid.[27]

The couple were penniless. By 1728 they had moved to Rouen, where Wharton tried to borrow money from English gentlemen passing through the city on the Grand Tour. From Rouen he sent a series of letters to *Mist's Weekly Journal* accusing English courtiers of being pantomime figures of vanity and folly, and the government of being corrupt. The publication of these letters resulted in Mist's printing presses being smashed. Undeterred, Wharton published a mock will of George I and a lewd poem about Sir Robert Walpole. He also wrote to England justifying his exile abroad, giving the maintenance of a standing army, the repeal of the Triennial Act that meant Parliament no longer had to be re-elected every three years, and the suspension of the Convocation of the Church of England as his reasons. He conveniently forgot about his debts and his creditors.

They did not forget about him, though, and to escape them he fled to Paris, sending his wife to live with her uncle while he lodged with a surgeon from Birmingham who had taken pity on him. Wharton, who had claimed that he had fully espoused the Jacobite cause, saw a way of making money and threatened to sell Jacobite secrets to Walpole's agents, forcing the Stuarts in exile to give him a small allowance to prevent this.

On his first visit to Madrid he had joined the Spanish army, and had appeared in arms against Britain at the siege of Gibraltar. He was described by a British observer as 'going to a battery to show his Garter Ribbon, crying out a thousand times "Long live the Pretender", and using a quantity of bad language'.[28] As if in retribution, a musket ball shattered his foot.

Bearing arms against His British Majesty's forces was treason on a large scale. A Bill of Indictment for high treason was brought against him in England, and in his absence he was stripped of his title and outlawed. His dignity was further damaged by his subsequent activities in France, where by his own admission he was involved in a series of foolish and sometimes dangerous episodes, such as kidnapping a band of musicians or challenging Lord Cranston to a duel that neither of them intended to fight.[29]

In 1729 he was recalled to his Spanish regiment. On the ensuing campaign he was taken sick and died at the monastery of Poblet on 31 May 1731.

Wharton had converted from Whig to Tory to Jacobite and back to Whig when it suited him. He was variously a Calvinist, an upholder of the Church of England and a Catholic. He was a rake in many senses, a libertine, drunkard and gambler, and he was also a poet. His restless spirit flitted from craze to craze, but for us he was the Hell-Fire Duke.

The gentle conservative Catholic Alexander Pope used him as an example of Folly in 'The First Moral Essay' (in *The Epistle to Cobham*).

> Wharton, the scorn and wonder of our days,
> Whose ruling passion was the Lust of Praise;
> Born with what'ere could win it from the Wise,
> Women and Fools must like him or he dies;
> The wond'ring Senates hung on all he spoke,
> The Club must hail him master of the joke.
>
> . . .
>
> An angel Tongue, which no man can persuade;
> A Fool, with more of Wit than half Mankind,
> Too rash for Thought, for Action too refin'd:
> A Tyrant to the wife his heart approves;
> A rebel to the king he loves:
> He dies, sad out-cast of each church and state;

And (harder still) flagitious, yet not great!
Ask you why Wharton broke thro' ev'ry rule?
'Twas all for fear the Knaves should call him Fool.
Nature well known, no prodigies remain,
Comets are regular, and Wharton plain.[30]

The Duke of Wharton was a rake bent on self-destruction. He was always seeking new experience, and his actions were rash and ill considered. It is doubtful whether, apart from a desire to shock, he really believed in anything, be it Whig or Tory, Hanover or Stuart, God or the Devil. The Hell-Fire Club, like the Masons and his performance in the House of Lords, was part of his self-dramatisation and foolish enthusiasms.

HELL-FIRE IN IRELAND

Many of the rakes that haunted London society were also to be found in Dublin, as English peerages often included an Irish title and estates: the Duke of Wharton, for example, or Viscount Hillsborough of the Schemers, who was an Irish peer. They were part of a centuries-old occupation by a colonising power, and, removed from the constraints of the mainland, in a country where the established Church had less control over the bulk of the population and where revolutionary and secret movements flourished, they were able to indulge themselves. The hell-fire clubs in Ireland were not the anti-Trinitarian debating shops of London in the 1720s, but more the full-blooded expression of contempt for religion and society that the sobriquet 'Hell-Fire Club' might suggest.

In the early eighteenth century, Ireland was governed by a Protestant minority, and the idle young gentlemen of the clubs came from the Protestant landowner ascendancy. The Catholic landowners were dispossessed and their lives ruled by penal legislation. There were few signs of improvement in towns or countryside, except in Dublin where the era of great Palladian houses commenced in 1722, and there was a burgeoning professional middle class. The gentry occupied themselves in drinking, hunting, horse racing and gaming, and the highlight of the Irish aristocracy and the gentry's social year was when the Lord-Lieutenant was in residence and held court in Dublin Castle. The country was garrisoned with soldiers to deter rebellion, and poverty was endemic. With no poor law legislation to alleviate it, the poor had to rely on collections at the church door. The chief manufacturing area was Ulster, where the linen industry prospered and went hand in hand with Presbyterianism and a Protestant work ethic.[31]

Evidence of the Irish Hell-Fire Club, like that of the English, is sparse and based on rumour, but there are some more facts that emerge and these point to its existence in the 1730s. It was supposedly founded in 1735 by Richard Parsons, Earl of Rosse, who was already infamous in polite society for his blasphemy and obscene wit, and his eccentric habit of receiving visitors in the nude. The club met at first in the Eagle Tavern in Cork Street, Dublin, but later moved to an isolated hunting lodge at the top of Mont Pelier, seven miles south-west of the city. Ironically, it was situated on land that the Duke of Wharton had once owned but that had been purchased by the speaker of the Irish House of Commons in 1721.

'Set upon a prominent rounded hill in the centre of a walled deer park, by the 1770s the lodge was in ruins; some said blasted by the Devil at his evil work.'[32] Information about the club's members comes from a little-known painting in the Irish National Gallery entitled *The Hell Fire Club*. This shows five members seated round a table on which are a punchbowl and glasses. It was painted by James Worsdale, a member of the club, and probably dates from after 1741 as the Earl of Rosse is absent from the picture, having died by then. The five men at the table are Harry Barry, Lord Santry; Simon Luttrell, Lord Irnham; Colonel Henry Bessborough; Colonel Richard St George; and Colonel Clements.

James Worsdale was a patron of Mrs Laetitia Pilkington, who had slid downwards through society after she had been divorced when found *in flagrante delicto* with a young surgeon. She turned to making a living as an author and ghost-writer of plays.[33] She was acquainted with the Delanys, and Worsdale was an acquaintance of Jonathan Swift, who complained of a 'brace of monsters', blasphemers and bacchanalians, of whom Worsdale was the leader.[34] This network of disparate people indicates the narrowness of eighteenth-century Dublin society, in which everyone who counted was acquainted with each other. Mrs Delany must have been aware of the rumours attached to the Irish Hell-Fire Club, but used the English club to make her moral statement.

It was the Irish Hell-Fire Club that was alleged to have indulged in Satanic rituals and to have made pacts with the Devil. These accusations have come down to us through oral tradition and have probably been embellished on the way. Eventually they were committed to print in the nineteenth century in books such as Chambers's *Book of Days* and in the *Gentleman's Magazine*.

According to the stories, the club members met at the lodge to drink 'saltheen', hot whiskey and melted butter, standing in front of a great roaring fire which melted the marrow in their bones so that they dropped to the floor. One chair at their meetings was always left vacant for the Devil, and their mascot was a fierce black cat. A clergyman who bravely came to confront them at one of their meetings saw the cat served first at dinner and asked why. He was told that it was because the cat was the oldest person in the room, whereupon he suggested that it was no cat but the Devil incarnate. Hearing this, the club members were up in arms, and declared the cleric should die. He begged for a few minutes' grace in which to say his prayers, and in doing this exorcised the Devil from the cat, which changed to its real Satanic shape and shot through the roof.

This tale is obviously apocryphal but it was also a way of rationalising what locals thought went on in the lodge. By the 1770s the lodge did have a hole in the roof. What could be more logical than for the Devil to have made it? It was known that a group of gentlemen met there, and before they met quantities of firewood and whiskey were delivered. It was common knowledge that these same gentlemen were members of a club in Dublin known as the Hell-Fire Club.

Two of the club's leading characters, Lord Santry and Lord Irnham, added to its reputation for evil. Harry Barry, Lord Santry, was known throughout southern Ireland for his drinking and his quick temper. In 1739 he was tried for the murder of Loughlin Murphy and found guilty. He had been drinking with his cronies in Palmerstown when Murphy appeared. The drinking went on into the evening, and an argument ensued between Santry and Murphy. Santry tried to draw his sword but at first was too drunk to do so; however, he told Murphy if he uttered another word he would run him through. Murphy replied that he did not wish to offend his lordship, whereupon Santry at last managed to drag his sword from its scabbard and stabbed Murphy, who collapsed and died six weeks later.

There is evidence that Santry tried to cover up the deed. He removed the dying Murphy to Dublin and sent his own physician to treat him, and when Murphy died he was quickly sewn up by Santry's doctor, who gave the cause of death as inflammation of the lungs. At his trial Santry called various witnesses who claimed they had seen Murphy going about his normal business in the weeks before his death; and others who claimed that Santry had acted in self-defence. Despite this he was found guilty. But a peer, even an Irish peer, could not be allowed to die on the common gallows. His friends made efforts to secure a pardon for him, which was granted in June 1739. By 1740 he was so heavily in debt that his estate was placed in the hands of trustees, and he moved to England, where he died in Nottingham in 1751.[35]

There was definitely a smell of brimstone about Harry Barry, and the same smell came from his friend Simon Luttrell, Lord Irnham. Simon Luttrell was a bastard in all senses of the word, as his parents did not bother to get married until he was four years old. Nevertheless, he was given an education befitting a peer's son at Eton, before returning to take control of his Irish estates, where he achieved lifelong unpopularity: 'The name Luttrell has come to mean in Ireland, traitor, villain, bastard, coward and profligate, and everything that can be conceived odious and horrible'.[36]

He was rumoured to have settled his debts by making a bargain with the Devil in return for giving him his soul seven years hence. The Devil came to collect his soul while he was at a meeting of the Hell-Fire Club at Mont Pelier Lodge, and claimed that he would have the soul of the last man out of the room. This was indeed Luttrell – but he distracted the Devil and escaped.[37]

In 1744 Luttrell married an English heiress and moved to England where he became involved with another protagonist of the Hell-Fire story, John Wilkes. In 1769 Luttrell's son, Henry Lawes Luttrell, who was his father's bitterest enemy, stood against Wilkes in the election for Knight of the Shire for Middlesex. Wilkes won the poll, but Parliament awarded the seat to Luttrell. A pamphlet war followed, and Simon Luttrell, to spite his son, became Wilkes's firm friend.[38]

Simon Luttrell is thought to be the anti-hero of the anonymous poem *The Diaboliad* dedicated to 'the worst man in England' and published in 1777. In this poem the Devil grown old leaves Hell for earth with his imps to seek a suitable successor. They collect statesmen, courtiers and 'lordlings from the arms of whores', and take them to Hell, where Satan says that the person who should have his throne 'must be false to God, defy every law, thief, traitor, hypocrite [and] patricide'; he then asks for a volunteer. Luttrell is assumed to be the volunteer. The poem ends with the onset of the American Revolution.

The legends surrounding the Irish Hell-Fire Club are more colourful than those surrounding the 1720s English version, and more in keeping with ideas of how such a club acted: an empty chair kept at feasts for the Devil, Satanic visitations, pacts with the Devil, and a familiar in the shape of a cat. Yet these legends have been grafted on to what was probably no more than a drinking club. The accretion of tales about the Irish Hell-Fire Club may be due to the more rural nature of Irish society, and the gulf between the occupying aristocracy and the indigenous people with their superstitions that were far removed from the sophisticated theological debates of London society. Did the Irish Hell-Fire Club really exist? Undoubtedly there was a club of that name in the Dublin area in the 1730s and 1740s, and it had a rival called the Blasters. They caused the authorities enough anxiety for them to investigate its activities in 1738, but although an artist, Peter Lens, admitted drinking the Devil's health in public and using obscene language, no other proof of its existence was found. An attempt to revive the Irish Hell-Fire Club was made in 1771 when a letter in the *Freeman's Journal* referred to idle young gentlemen who drink to the Devil.[39] The revival will be discussed later in this book.

REFORM OF MANNERS IN IRELAND

Ireland was not immune to attempts to reform society and to stop blasphemy and Sabbath-breaking. Local societies for the reform of manners were founded using English models. They relied on informers to tell the magistrates about backsliders, and the informers were encouraged to do this by the promise of material and spiritual rewards. Gangs of vigilantes hunted prostitutes and grabbed them out of brothels, and reported those who profaned Sunday. However, the Irish societies were never as numerous or effective as the English ones. Irish magistrates often refused to convict those brought before them, and much of the information came from religious rivals and informers eager for reward. Informers became despised and the societies for the reformation of manners in Ireland quickly faded from view.

One of the problems that such societies faced was that relying on informers went against the social code of neighbourliness. It destroyed trust in the local community, and could even split families, and therefore was viewed with distaste by most sections of society.

HELL-FIRE IN THE PROVINCES

There is one provincial hell-fire club for which good evidence exists, the Hell-Fire Club of Norwich. This was active in the 1750s, involved in inciting riots against a charismatic breakaway Methodist preacher.[40] Norwich in the 1750s was a large prosperous city, with an upper class of resident gentry and wealthy capitalists. The city was governed by a mayor and corporation, and it had a vibrant social life, with many taverns, coffee-houses, clubs and places of entertainment. It also had a hard core of Jacobite Tories who were supported by the Jacobite gentry of the surrounding county, such as the Le Stranges of Hunstanton or Sir Armine Woodhouse of Kimberley.[41]

The ultra-conservative, upper-class Jacobite, papist and neo-Catholic Protestants came into direct conflict with the labouring-class Nonconformists when James Wheatley, a Methodist preacher, probably of Welsh origin, arrived in the city in 1751 and started to attract large crowds to his open air meetings. The climax of the meetings came when sinners publicly repented and promised to give up swearing, blasphemy, Sabbath-breaking and lives of idleness, and be saved. Between September and November 1751 thousands of Norwich's citizens were 'saved'.[42]

Wheatley was a lay preacher, in fact a renegade lay preacher, who had been banned from preaching on the Methodist circuit by John

Wesley in 1751 because of his Calvinist belief that Man was answerable for his own actions through free will.[43] To the oppressed labouring population of Norwich this was an attractive proposition: it meant that morals and respectability were their responsibility rather than being dictated by Church and state. Oddly enough this was a doctrine that should also have been attractive to the Hell-Fire Club members, who were also on the fringes of the law and acting of their own free will. But they viewed Wheatley in political terms. The Norwich Press saw much in Wheatley which was commendable, and described his meetings favourably, while deploring the action of the Hell-Fire Club which behaved 'audaciously, acting in defiance of all laws'.[44] The so-called gentlemen of the Hell-Fire Club, the press claimed, were 'Papists, Jacobites and Non-Jurors', who were against the government and wanted to create havoc. They met at the Blue Bell on Orford Hill, where they sang treasonable songs and distributed money to the mob to encourage them to attack those going to Wheatley's meetings. The club was comprised of 'indolent, rich young men'.[45]

The anti-government Jacobite element of this club adds a further dimension to the character of hell-fire clubs, and the way in which they drummed up support has distinct similarities to the Oxford Riot fomented in 1715 by Jacobites who plied a mob with drink and encouraged them to riot.[46] The Norwich club members had the resources to remain anonymous and behind the scenes. On 21 November 1751 they plied the mob with alcohol and sent them off with blackened faces to disrupt Wheatley's meeting with violence. From then until May 1752 the nights in Norwich were rent by riot and violence. The Riot Act was read in February, and in March Wheatley was attacked and nearly killed by the Hell-Fire Club's mob; men, women and children in the crowd were beaten up. The dragoons were called in, but before they could restore order the Methodist tabernacle had been destroyed. Sixteen ringleaders were captured and imprisoned. However, they were not club members, but were merely used by the Hell-Fire Club to create havoc. A pamphlet, *A True and Particular Narrative of the Disturbances and Outrages that have been committed in the City of Norwich since November to the Present*, gave details of the arrested rioters, and what little was known about the Hell-Fire Club members.

Wheatley stayed in Norwich, and the Hell-Fire Club members became responsible adults and moved on to become model citizens. By 1752 the Jacobite cause in England had had its day and it was felt that political protest could be better achieved through legitimate channels and a parliamentary opposition.

HELL-FIRE IN THE UNIVERSITIES

Youthful high spirits amongst the wealthy were to be seen in abundance in the universities of Oxford and Cambridge. Two previous writers on the hell-fire clubs, L.C. Jones and Geoffrey Ashe, claim that both Oxford and Cambridge had their own versions of the clubs. On closer examination, however, it seems that they have, to some extent, been led astray by works of literary fiction on the subject. Jones claims that the Oxford Hell-Fire Club was centred on Brasenose College. His clue for this comes from the *St James Chronicle* of 1 December 1763 that mentions a hell-fire club at Oxford in connection with Reverend John Kidgell, who had been involved with the prosecution of John Wilkes's *Essay on Woman*.[47]

In the nineteenth century the stories became embroidered and part of local tradition, and Jones is rightly suspicious of these. The tale went that in 1827 the Reverend T. Churton, a fellow and tutor at Brasenose, witnessed, through a window, a meeting of the Hell-Fire Club in the rooms of a wealthy undergraduate, at which one of its members burst a blood vessel in the course of a blasphemous speech. Churton claimed to have witnessed the Devil carrying off the dead member's soul. Jones points out that there are similar tales current from the medieval period onwards, but he also suggests that the Phoenix Club at Brasenose was a revival of the Hell-Fire Club of 1721.[48]

The Phoenix Club was founded in the late eighteenth century as an exclusive undergraduate dining club. In 1781 it had four members, rising to twelve in 1786. It was a genuine club with officials, rules and subscriptions. Each member had to host a dinner in his own rooms, and the club was wealthy enough to have its own cellar. Excessive drinking was common but no member was allowed to take more than two dozen bottles of sherry or port from the cellar per week. There were many complaints about the club, its drunkenness and the noise made by its members.[49] It was probably a meeting of the Phoenix Club that the Reverend Churton observed and, given the amount of alcohol available if each member had drawn his allocation from the cellar, it is not surprising that someone died during the evening.

In Cambridge the alleged variant of a Hell-Fire Club was located at Jesus College and was known either as the Appalling or the Everlasting Club. Geoffrey Ashe claims that the club was founded in 1738, and that the Master of Jesus had 'an alleged minute book' containing its records.

The club met in a lumber room on the Cow Lane staircase, known in the college as 'the Ghost Room'. The rules of the club were that no member could resign, whether dead or alive, and the club was to meet on All Souls Night every year to sign the book, no matter where they had to come from, Heaven or Hell. On 2 November 1743 the club assembled but one member, Henry Davenport, had been killed overseas. As the decanter went round the table it is claimed that his ghost appeared to sign the book. The next year allegedly another ghost appeared, that of Alan Dermot, who had been killed in Paris. More club members died until only one survived, Charles Bellasis. Eventually he became a fellow of the college, and had rooms on the same staircase as the Ghost Room. On 2 November 1766 he locked himself in his room, and dreadful moans and screams were heard coming from it. When the doors were knocked down the next morning Bellasis was found dead, sitting at the table, round which six chairs, one for each of the dead members, were drawn up. The minute book was open and had been signed by the dead members. Ashe adds plaintively that there is no record of the alleged members in the university records.[50]

It is not surprising that Ashe could find no record of the club members in the university or college records as Arthur Gray, Master of Jesus College from 1912 to 1940, made up the whole story and published it in a collection of ghost stories, *Tedious Brief Tales of Granta and Gramarye*, in 1919 under the pseudonym Ingulphus.[51] Gray restored the Ghost Room to student use, but there is no record of why it was called that. Nevertheless, he may have taken the name of at least one of the protagonists of the story from college records, as the Bellasis family of Newburgh in Yorkshire was associated with the college, and a Charles Bellasis entered the college in 1572. Names of the other actors do not appear in the college records.[52]

MORAL REFORM IN ENGLAND

The hell-fire clubs were symptomatic of an increasingly sceptical and ungodly society, which blasphemed and ignored the Sabbath practices in a way that the Church and reformers were determined to stop. Laws were passed to prosecute those who worked on a Sunday, and prosecutions for this reached a peak in 1720–24 at the height of the Hell-Fire scare.[53] The authorities appeared to believe that if they could not name and shame hell-fire club members, they could at least take those who were publicly flouting the Sabbath to task. By 1757 a Sunday Observance society had been founded, and Sabbath-breaking was debated in Parliament.

The Societies for the Reformation of Manners continued to flourish in the 1720s and 1730s, and as information about the

Hell-Fire and Atheistical clubs became public the societies stepped up their prosecutions, reaching an average of 2,000 successful prosecutions a year for blasphemy between 1715 and 1720.[54]

The societies were not formed specifically in opposition to the hell-fire clubs, which after all comprised a small percentage of the population, and a wealthy elite at that. Instead they represented the growing gulf between the burgeoning respectable middle-class professionals and capitalists, and those who did not have to labour to earn a living but had the time and luxury to experiment and indulge themselves in new and radical ideas while they were still young enough to do so.

What Were the Hell-Fire Clubs?

The hell-fire clubs of the eighteenth century were not the Devil-worshippers of popular belief. The earliest, that patronised by the Duke of Wharton, probably had, beneath the feasting and drinking, the serious intent of discussing the existence of the Trinity, and it was because this went against the teaching of the established Church that they came to the notice of the authorities. Later clubs such as the Irish versions were wilder, but dedicated to drinking.

The members of the clubs specifically known as hell-fire clubs were invariably young and wealthy, and it seems that it was something that young men grew out of in time. They called them hell-fire clubs in order to shock their elders, and perhaps to draw attention to their rebellion.

Many of their contemporaries believed that they had strong links with earlier clubs such as the Ballers and the Mohocks. John Oldmixon in his *History of England* (1735) wrote that 'these lewd young rakes were branch'd out of the Scourers or the Mohocks'. In 1755 *The Connoisseur* made the same connection: 'The Mohocks and the members of the Hell-Fire Club, the heroes of the last generation struck out mighty good jokes from all kinds of violence and blasphemy.' Anti-Whig historians were also at pains to point out that present day society had not progressed beyond that which had come before, and that the fires of Hell were still being enthusiastically raked.

CHAPTER 4

Interlude Abroad:
the Grand Tour, Dilettanti
and Divans

One element that many of the members of these infamous clubs had in common was that they had been on the Grand Tour of Europe. Usually a young man set off on the tour accompanied by a tutor, or 'bear leader' as these functionaries became known. The itinerary would have been decided in advance with the family, and religious allegiance may have had some bearing on this. Thus, the Duke of Wharton who came from a Calvinist background was sent to the Low Countries and Geneva, although, as we have seen, he escaped his 'bear leader' and made for the fleshpots of France and Roman Catholicism.

The job of the tutor was supposed to be to enhance his charge's moral and spiritual welfare, help him learn a foreign language, introduce him into polite society, and return him home in one piece, with a broadened mind and cultivated taste. Depending on the quality of the student, this was not always possible. It was often the first opportunity the lad had of getting away from the rules and strictures of parents and school, and excessive drinking, gambling and whoring were usually more attractive than polite society.

For some, however, what they saw on the Grand Tour, and their experience abroad, had a lasting impression, and they brought back ideas, art and artefacts which were to change their lives and add to

the national treasure-house of fine art. They also brought back journals and diaries written during the course of their travels. As many
of them had these published,[1] there is a great variety of sources on
the Grand Tour for the historian to work on,[2] and it has become a
popular topic for research.

It is clear from the evidence that the Grand Tour influenced
tourists in different ways. For some, exposure to other cultures
merely reinforced their own identity, but there were those who were
open to new ideas, embraced them and translated them into
action when they returned home. Clubs were formed where travellers could meet to relive their adventures, houses were remodelled
using architecture seen on the Grand Tour, and art galleries were
plundered to bring home original works and copies of the great
masterpieces seen on their travels. It is this element that makes the
Grand Tour part of the discourse on the hell-fire clubs.

GENESIS OF THE GRAND TOUR

The Grand Tour is usually seen as an eighteenth-century phenomenon, but in fact it had earlier origins. In his essay *Of Travel*
published in 1597, Francis Bacon wrote: 'Travel, in the younger sort,
is a part of education; in the elder, a part of experience'; and he
describes the situation as it was to become in the eighteenth
century, with young men travelling 'under some tutor, or grave
servant' and keeping an account of their impressions of what they
observed. The aim was to see as much as possible of the royal courts
of Europe, the cabinets and rarities, the weddings, feasts and
funerals. When the traveller returned home, Bacon suggested, he
should 'let his travel appear rather in his discourse than in his
apparel'.[3]

The sixteenth-century tourists were in the ancient tradition of
pre-Reformation pilgrims to Rome, Santiago de Compostela or
Jerusalem. They followed in the footsteps of the many priests and

cardinals who travelled to Rome to consult the Pope, or students from all over Europe going to the Italian universities of Padua or Verona. Some seventeenth-century tourists from Britain went to escape the Civil War or religious persecution. But others, like John Milton or Rochester's nemesis, Bishop Gilbert Burnet, went because they were curious and wanted to see continental Europe for themselves.[4]

It was at the start of the eighteenth century – once Britain was a more settled and Protestant country under William III and Queen Anne and the Catholic Church was seen less as a threat and more as a curiosity – that the Grand Tourists set off in numbers. Of course, their travels were interrupted by spasmodic European wars that meant they had to avoid some countries. For example during the Seven Years War (1756–63) France had to be avoided, and it was also out of bounds during the Franco-British war in the North American colonies and the American War of Independence. The War of Spanish Succession (1701–14) meant that travelling in Habsburg/Austrian possessions was difficult, and during the War of Austrian Succession (1740–48) parts of Italy became 'no-go' areas. Treaties that ended wars were followed by a flood of tourists, and after the Battle of Waterloo in 1815 that flood became a torrent.

Another feature of Grand Tourism that we must not forget is that tourism is a two-way process. Foreign visitors made their Grand Tours to Britain, and they were just as likely to record their impressions as the British abroad. Tourists writing about Britain provide a valuable comparison with British tourists writing about the continent. British writers on the continent show that they were likely to seek out their countrymen wherever they went, whereas Continental visitors to Britain interacted freely with the native population and joined in social events, soaking up the culture of the coffee-house and the tavern. Joseph Spence, Professor of Poetry at Oxford who accompanied a number of young men on the

Grand Tour, noted down the number of Englishmen they met on their journey. There were 112 in France in 1731–33, and 175 in Italy in 1739, including Sir Francis Dashwood in Bologna.[5] But as Laurence Sterne waspishly remarked, 'An Englishman doe not travel to see Englishmen'.[6] Another tendency of British tourists was to compare everything they saw with similar features at home (usually unfavourably to the Continent). Continental visitors to Britain were entranced and sometimes bemused by the novelty of Britain, which they saw as totally different from where they came from. The difference in attitude may have been part of the natural insularity of the upper-class British, which the Grand Tour was supposed to change.

The Grand Tour was an expensive undertaking for a family to fund. Why were so many noble and gentry families sending their young men on these tours, and what outcome did they hope for? The young man was certainly not meant to indulge in excessive drinking and sexual licence, to make unfortunate liaisons, catch a dose of clap, or convert to Roman Catholicism. Most families saw it as a way to complete his education and to enable him to acquire polish and experience. Some saw it as an alternative to sending him to Oxford or Cambridge, institutions seen either as nests of Jacobites or schools of scandal. Lord Shaftesbury, who went abroad for his health in 1720 and died in Naples in 1721, saw the Grand Tour as a way of 'making the virtuoso to become virtuous' and 'increasing knowledge and industry amongst its participants'[7] (a vain hope in many cases).

In *A Sentimental Journey* (1766), Laurence Sterne asked the question: Why do people travel? He came up with the following list. People travel for their health, bodily and mental; through necessity; delinquents are sent on the tour with a tutor recommended by a university; and it is a way of saving money, as life on the Continent is cheaper than in Britain. He also listed the types of traveller who were likely to be on the Grand Tour: the idle, the inquisitive, the liar, the proud, the vain, the spendthrift, the innocent, the simpleton, the sentimental and those in search of knowledge and improvement.[8]

The young men who were later to become members of hell-fire clubs and other institutions of a similar genre fit many of these descriptions. The Duke of Wharton was sent on the tour, being a delinquent who was likely to bankrupt his estate. Sir Francis Dashwood was inquisitive and, like the other members of his club who accompanied him, an inveterate and curious traveller. But whether the travellers went in search of knowledge and improvement is doubtful. Horace Walpole, who met up with Dashwood and some of his colleagues in Italy in 1743, suggested on their return when they founded the Society of Dilettanti for travellers who had been to Italy, that the real qualification for joining was to have been continually drunk in Italy, as he had rarely seen Sir Francis Dashwood sober in that country. The actor David Garrick, himself a Grand Tourist, suggested that the fine gentlemen skimmed the cream of every nation, but never got beyond the surface.[9]

In 1764 Richard Hurd published *A Dialogue on the Uses of Foreign Travel*, which was an imaginary conversation between Lord Shaftesbury defending the Grand Tour and John Locke opposing it. The words put into Shaftesbury's mouth help to sum up why young men were sent on the Grand Tour. Foreign travel, says Shaftesbury, is part of modern breeding and education. 'It polishes the life and manners of our liberal youth, and fits them for the business and conversation of the world, which they will observe.' Travel broadened the mind, supplied good manners and civility, bestowed a liberal education on participants and an insight into the customs, policies and government of other countries.[10]

The imaginary Locke countered this by asserting that he sees only mischief coming from travel, which has brought back 'what we have dearly paid for. Irreligion and even atheism; whilst degeneracy is the usual acquisition of our travelled youth'. In sending raw,

ignorant, ungovernable boys out into the world with shallow, saun-
tering tutors, foreign travel, Locke concluded, was a disaster. 'Travel
will not help the future ruler to understand his own country; for that
he needs understanding and a moral framework.' Locke declared
that foreign travel was a waste of time and that 'polishing' did not
mean the acquisition of good sense or morals.[11]

In this dialogue Hurd skilfully identified the advantages of the
Grand Tour, and its disadvantages. The disadvantages gave way to
scandal when the young man returned home and these follies were
publicised by the increasingly important media, while the quieter,
more restful experience of the 'Shaftesburys' who sought virtue went
unnoticed. These were young men who had had a classical education and wanted to see the places they had read about; often they
received a shock of recognition when they identified these places.

Some confined their activities to ritual visits to museums and art
galleries, but others had a more serious interest, and took the
opportunity to buy originals or copies of art and artefacts to add to
the family collection. Their eyes were opened to the different
architectural styles they saw, and these styles were to be translated
into remodelling of their country houses and landscaped parks.

But as Locke, Hurd's mouthpiece, pointed out, what was brought
back could have unfortunate results, for on the continent they were
exposed to dangers they had not encountered at home; and this did
not only include the charms of the ladies they met and the cheap-
ness of the wine. They were travelling in the main in Roman
Catholic countries. Although it was part of the tutor's duties to
protect his charges from Rome and its influence, by the third decade
of the eighteenth century it had become normal for the Grand
Tourist to visit the Pope, where he was allowed to bow to him,
rather than kiss his slipper as Catholic visitors did.[12]

Many British tourists derided the Catholics because of their
rituals, the worldliness of their clergy, their belief in miracles and
the gulf perceptible in Italy between the affluence of the Church

and the poverty of some of the people. Itineraries often brought Grand Tourists to Italy during Holy Week, where they either marvelled at the ceremonies or mocked them unmercifully as derived from paganism.[13] The holy house at Loreto amazed many British travellers. William Bromley noted that the inhabitants of the town were 'miserably poor', but in the holy house he saw images wearing silk vestments covered with pearls and diamonds. His Protestant sensibility was shocked here and at Rome. 'Protestants want to expose the grossest superstitions of the Catholics', he wrote.[14] However, judging by the subsequent behaviour of some of the Grand Tourists on their return, such as Sir Francis Dashwood, it is obvious that Catholicism had a lasting effect on their imagination.

Another danger for the Grand Tourists was that they might fall under the spell of the Stuarts in exile and become Jacobites. The Duke of Wharton is an example of this, and Sir Francis Dashwood was accused of having Jacobite leanings. Some tourists, like Sir John Hynde Cotton IV of Madingley Hall, Cambridgeshire, sought out Prince Charles Edward to satisfy his curiosity, and was shocked by what he saw: an elderly drunken failure of a man.[15]

Even if a young man was sent on the tour mainly to gain education and polish, what he actually brought back with him was something else. It could include an enhanced knowledge of the world beyond the British Isles, but also incipient alcoholism, venereal disease, or even a wife. He had also been exposed to sights and sounds different from those at home. Classical temples and Palladian architecture inspired Grand Tourists. They collected antiques, copies of famous statues, and paintings. A rather modest gentry traveller from Cheshire, George John Legh of High Legh, returned from his Grand Tour of Italy and Switzerland with a large number of prints, paintings, books and cork models of antiquities, and he continued to add to his collection through agents long after he had returned home.[16] Although the young gentleman tourist viewed the world as an exhibition put on for his delight, and travel as a commodity that was his by right, it is clear that most of the tourists were not immune to what they saw. The influence of buildings, statues and ideas can still be seen in the parks and houses of rural England, where classicism was transformed into an idiom acceptable to the English gentry. Stourhead, Stowe, West Wycombe and other great houses are evidence of this.

Can the influence of the Grand Tour and the hell-fire clubs be related in any way? In order to look at this question it is necessary to go to the opposite end of the Grand Tour and ask: What did the Grand Tourist find when he got to his destination? Were there political, social, cultural and moral situations that were likely to change his views, and influence him in years to come? Might they give him ideas at odds with British polite society and its social values?

Eighteenth-century Italy and the Grand Tourist

The ultimate destination of many of the Grand Tourists was Italy. This was partly because most young gentlemen had had some modicum of a classical education. They knew the Roman authors and they knew about the Roman sites in Italy.[17] In 1732 Joseph Spence wrote with amazed delight that 'one of the pleasures of being at Rome, is that you are continually seeing the very place and spot of ground where some great thing was done ... *This* is the place where Julius Caesar was stabbed by Brutus.'[18]

Earlier in the century Joseph Addison had written that 'There is certainly no Place in the World where a Man may travel with greater pleasure and Advantage than in Italy.' He described astonishing works of nature, great schools of music, paintings, architecture and sculpture; and an abundance of cabinets of curiosities, antiquities and varieties of government. But Addison also saw Italy as a mausoleum, enshrining the past as a place still alive.[19] The past itself was one reason why Grand Tourists flocked to Italy. This was related to the Antiquarian movement in England, where ancient structures such as Stonehenge were being rediscovered and theories as to why they existed being put forward. The past helped to give an identity to the present. The other reason for the Grand Tour to Italy was more mundane: it was cheap, the wine was good, and the women were said to be beautiful and willing. These made the dangers of travel, Catholicism and the bandits worth risking.[20] When British tourists got to Italy a period of adjustment was often necessary. First they found a heavily urbanised country, with large, densely populated cities with populations often over 100,000. In Britain only London could rival this, and the Italian cities possessed larger conurbations than the travellers would ever have experienced before. Italian cities teemed with life. They were centres of manufacturing, and they had their own structures of government and authority. The cities were in complete contrast to the countryside where serfdom still existed up to 1781, and tenancies were on a sharecropping basis unknown in England. They found not a coherent nation state but a patchwork of kingdoms (Sicily, Naples and Sardinia), dukedoms (Tuscany, Milan, Modena) and republics (Lucca, Genoa, Venice and San Marino), and of course the Vatican State and Rome.[21] This network of absolutist states had their own civil and criminal law codes and were governed by a patrician urban elite, or aristocracy, which spread its culture into the public sphere. They dispensed patronage to artists and craftsmen, and organised the dissemination of knowledge. Over this lay the Roman Catholic Church. It was a different system to that which the Grand Tourists were accustomed to at home. Britain was a nation state, governed by a constitutional monarchy. The patrician urban elite and the aristocracy participated in this government, but their culture inhabited a private space rather than the public sphere. In the first half of the eighteenth century the elite patronised artists, but usually for their own consumption. Public art had still to make an appearance in

Britain, and the landscaped parks and rebuilt houses were for private use. And yet the dissemination of knowledge and access to works of art was beginning. By 1759 the British Museum had opened, followed by other public institutions and galleries. The democratisation of art and leisure in England had the effect of sending clubs into the country, where their activities and artefacts could be kept in secret. The Medmenham Friars and Crazy Castle, a gentlemen's club based at Skelton Castle in Yorkshire, are examples of this.

Grand Tourists were both fascinated and appalled by the hold the Roman Catholic Church and its Inquisition had over the country. Tourists observed the Church's ceremonies and marvelled, and they made a point of visiting monasteries and nunneries to see something that had been absent from Britain for 200 years. In fact these institutions seemed to have a fascination for tourists such as Joseph Spence.[22] Others who were there at the start of Lent enjoyed the carnival, when the world was turned upside down and the master became the servant. But many were worried that this was a country where witchcraft still inhabited the same sphere as religion, and heretics could still be burned at the stake.[23] Atheists were put on trial in Italy, and intellectuals looking for a dialogue between ancient and modern philosophies and trying to reconcile this with religion were looked at with suspicion by the Church and civil authorities. However, Carparetto suggests that the intellectual debates did not penetrate through to the Grand Tourists. They could not read Italian for a start, and came with inbuilt prejudices against intellectuals.[24] The Italian institutions that the Grand Tourist did applaud were the social institutions such as hospitals, almshouses and orphanages, and the programme of prison reform taking place.[25]

The difference between the Italian temperament and the British often perplexed the Grand Tourist. Especially difficult to understand was the role of women in some Italian states. In Sicilian society for example women dominated the household, but had no role outside it – an idea alien to many British tourists. However, they were sometimes amazed at the licence that married couples had in some Italian states, where it was accepted by the elite that both husband and wife would take lovers but dress this up as a platonic relationship.[26]

The Italian 'Enlightenment' was still in its infancy in the 1740s,[27] but Italian art and architecture dazzled the tourists and it was the visual images of classical temples and Palladian villas that remained with them when they returned home. The architecture, sculpture and paintings they saw 'influenced the mind and manners of them, filling them with great ideas'.[28]

Whig travellers identified with the heroes of the Roman republic, and had busts and statues made of themselves draped in togas. On their return home they continued republican themes in their houses and gardens. Stowe in Buckinghamshire is an example of a Whig republican park and garden, while Stourhead in Wiltshire is a Tory construction based on peace, patriotism and virtue.[29] The visual influence of the Grand Tour can be seen in Sir Francis Dashwood's remodelling of the house and park at West Wycombe. Sir Francis was the founder member of the Medmenham Friars, a species of hell-fire club, and the influence of the Grand Tour can be seen in his ideas and activities. The physical landscape he created at West Wycombe and Medmenham Abbey is full of classical allusions and copies of statues and buildings he saw on the Grand Tour. The rituals of the clubs in which he was involved can be seen as imitations of Roman Catholic rituals. He even had a portrait of himself painted in the guise of a Catholic friar worshipping a classical figure of Venus.

Conyers Middleton, chief librarian of the University of Cambridge, who travelled to Italy for his health, fell to musing about the relationship of Catholicism to paganism; his musings were eventually published in 1729 as *A Letter from Rome Shewing Conformity between Popery and Paganism.* By 1742 this book had been through five editions. In it Middleton drew parallels between religious practices he had seen in Rome and what he knew about the ancient world from classical texts. For example, the sprinkling of holy water in the church had a parallel with Virgil's description of sprinkling the pagan shrine with water; and there was a similarity between votive offerings in saints' chapels and votive offerings to pagan gods. Middleton noted how antique statues had been converted into Christian saints, and the Pantheon, 'that noblest Heathen Temple, dedicated to Jove and all the gods is now reconsecrated to the Blessed Virgin and all the Saints'.[30]

Middleton showed how the heady combination of the Roman Church and classical remains in Italy had a lasting influence on those who saw them, and for the educated young Grand Tourist paganism/heathenism meant Greek and pre-Christian Rome.[31] The classical idiom of the Graeco-Roman temples was taken back to England and similar temples began to adorn the landscape, while the harmonious architecture of Palladio would soon transform the country seats of the nobility and gentry as well as townscapes such as that at Bath, whose Circus is a tribute to the Roman Colosseum.[32]

The architecture was not only visually stunning, but it had a deeper meaning. For example, the classical temples at Stowe as illustrated by the Temples of Ancient and Modern Virtue were political and moral statements: symbols of liberty against despots and in favour of the civic virtues of an unblemished public life dedicated to the common good.[33] The temples that Sir Francis Dashwood erected at West Wycombe were, as we shall see, symbols of something much more earthy, and could be said to be an inversion of the gardens at Stowe, showing how the classical elements could be redefined into something that represented sex and pleasure.[34]

Perhaps the most important effect of the Grand Tour was visual. The tourists brought back ideas about art and architecture, and to remind them of what they saw they purchased books of prints and copies of statues; and, depending on their nature, their incorporation of classical elements into their estates could represent the victory of virtue, or it could pay homage to the female form and to sexual licence, as it did at West Wycombe and Medmenham in Buckinghamshire.

TRAVELLERS AND CLUBMEN

Two men who link the hell-fire clubs and the Grand Tour are Sir Francis Dashwood and the Earl of Sandwich. Sir Francis was a keen traveller and encouraged others to follow him, and to publish their observations. The Earl of Sandwich came from a naval family, and was himself the First Lord of the Admiralty at various times. He was an enthusiastic explorer, venturing to Egypt and beyond.

Sir Francis (1708–81) set off on his first tour in 1726, at the age of eighteen, two years after he had inherited his baronetcy. On this trip he visited France, but three years later he was in Italy, crossing the Alps in the company of Thomas Nugent, spending Christmas in Venice and, in the spring of 1731, signing the visitors' book at Padua University.[35] It was probably on this visit that the story originated about Dashwood's exploits in the Sistine Chapel on Good Friday. At the Good Friday service in the Sistine Chapel the congregation received small scourges in order to inflict physical punishment on themselves as a penance. All the lights were extinguished and the penitents howled with pretend pain. Dashwood who had secreted a horsewhip under his coat, leapt up and began whipping the penitents in earnest, leading to cries of real pain and 'Il Diavolo! Il Diavolo!' (the Devil, the Devil).

This story has been attributed to Horace Walpole, but it first appeared in print in 1764, in a fictional account of Sir Francis, *Chrysal* by Charles Johnstone. This episode, if it existed, has been seen as evidence of Dashwood's anti-Catholicism, but it could also be interpreted as anger at the pretence of the penitents. As it only came to light thirty years after the event, when Dashwood's private life had become public, it is doubtful that it ever happened. However, Horace Walpole did write that in Rome Sir Francis had been openly profane and mocked the Catholic Church.[36] Even Dashwood's dislike of Roman Catholicism and his profanity can be disputed, as he became a firm friend of the abbé Niccolini, a Catholic antiquarian who helped to inspire Dashwood's love of the classical world and its art.

Dashwood's next tour abroad was more exotic: in 1733 he accompanied Lord Forbes, envoy extraordinary to the Russian court in St Petersburg. This tour was sufficiently unusual for him to keep a diary during his journey through Denmark and Sweden and his sojourn in Russia. The diary shows his keen interest in everything he saw, and while what we know about him in Italy comes from other people, the diary provides an insight into him personally as a traveller. However, there is much in the diary that could be construed as information that would be useful for the government at home. He describes fortifications, armaments, sea power and regiments, and discusses the different forms of civil and military government he saw. But his real interest was in the architecture and the art collections he visited, the people he observed, their clothes and their customs. Some of what he saw obviously had an influence on his later life. In Vasiliostoff, an island on the Baltic side of St Petersburg, he saw 'a Vast Globe of nine feet in diameter, and on the inner side, a seat around a table where several of us got in'.[37] This was presumably the inspiration for the great golden globe placed on the top of his remodelled West Wycombe parish church, which was hollow and in which revellers could be seated round a table. At a later date, Horace Walpole suggested that Dashwood had 'in early life made a voyage to Russia dressed like Charles the Twelfth [of Sweden] in the hopes of making the Czarina Anna fall in love with him – an improper hero to copy, when a woman was to be captivated'.[38] Later writers have taken this as fact, but like so much of Walpole's comments it comes from a fertile imagination and a predilection for gossip. There was no hint of impropriety in Dashwood's visit to Russia.

He took what was for the eighteenth century another exotic tour in 1738, visiting Greece and Turkey. Again what he saw, especially the colourful life in Turkey, was to have a lasting effect on him. He was back in Italy in 1739–41, and for this visit there is some evidence about the life he led. On 11 November 1740, Lady Mary Wortley Montagu wrote to the Countess of Mar that 'an English lady called Mrs D'Arcie (what D'Arcie I cannot imagine) lodged in the house where I now am, and Sir Francis Dashwood was with her everyday . . .'

Seven years later, on 17 December 1747, Lady Mary wrote to the Countess of Bute asking for information about whom Sir Francis Dashwood had married: as in Italy he seemed 'so nice [pernickety] in the choice of a wife, I have some curiosity to know who it is that had charms enough to make him enter into an engagement that he would speak of with fear and trembling.'[39]

The Oxford don Joseph Spence met Dashwood in Italy in 1741 and made no comment about his morals, but trusted him enough to give him letters from the young nobleman he was accompanying to take back to England. Spence also met another inveterate traveller, clubman and libertine in Italy, the Earl of Sandwich. John Montagu, fourth Earl of Sandwich, born in 1718, was the grandson of the Earl of Rochester, and lived up to his grandfather's reputation. He was educated at Eton and Trinity College, Cambridge, where he was the exact contemporary of Horace Walpole who was at King's College, and Thomas Gray, the poet, who was at Peterhouse. Walpole heartily disliked Sandwich, and lumped him together with Dashwood as moral reprobates, but, as we have seen, Walpole's waspish comments must be read with care.

After leaving Cambridge, Walpole and Gray embarked on a conventional and leisurely tour of the continent, but Sandwich, who was a keen athlete and cricketer, never did anything conventional. He wanted to go further into the world, and because he came from a naval family and the sea was in his blood he was not content to take the slow overland routes: instead he chartered a ship at Naples and set off round the Mediterranean. Joseph Spence, who was given the chance to accompany him as a tutor, wrote later that he was glad he had refused the offer; in his place the Reverend John Cooke became Sandwich's 'bear leader'. Sandwich left an account of their travels, *A Voyage Performed by the Late Earl of Sandwich Around the Mediterranean*.[40] As well as Cooke, Sandwich was accompanied by Mr Ponsonby, the Earl of Bessborough and a painter to record the journey. Amongst Sandwich's purchases were two Egyptian mummies, eight embalmed ibises, papyrus scrolls, intaglios and medals.[41] Spence wrote in his diary that Sandwich was expected back in Italy in January 1740, but did not appear until February as he had been put in quarantine owing to an outbreak of plague in the Middle East. In February 1740 Spence wrote to his mother that Sandwich had developed a passionate love of art on his travels, and was proposing to visit Malta and the Greek island of Chios. Sandwich spent many hours describing his voyage to Spence, perhaps to show him what he had missed.[42]

Sandwich was fascinated by the different cultures he encountered, and especially by the Ottoman Empire with its despotic Sultan and subjugation of women.[43] When he returned to England he sought out Sir Francis Dashwood, who had also been to Turkey, and together they founded two societies for those who had experienced the joys of travel to the East and to Italy: the Divan Club for those who had been to Turkey, and the Dilettanti Society for those who had visited Italy.

THE DIVAN CLUB

The Divan Club was the result of Dashwood's and Sandwich's visits to Constantinople where they had been fascinated by the customs and society to the extent they were keen to imitate them. This gave them a chance to dress up. Sir Francis Dashwood in particular seems to have been an enthusiastic fancy dresser and had his portrait painted in a number of costumes and roles. For example, he appears in a jewelled turban and gold-encrusted shirt in a portrait entitled *Il Faquier Dashwood Pasha* by Adrien Carpentier.[44]

The club held its first meeting on 8 January 1744 at the Thatched Tavern in St James Street, London. As well as Dashwood and Sandwich, its first members included Lord Duncannon. The qualification for membership was that 'none but such as can prove that they have been in the Sultan's Dominions be qualified to be chosen of this club'.[45] Officers of the club took oriental names: the secretary became the Hasnadar, the person who took the chair at each dinner was the Vizier, and the president was the Reis Effendi. Sandwich was the first Vizier.[46] The club minute book was the Al Koran, and allegedly this still exists in the hands of Sandwich's descendants.[47] The club's toast was 'The Harem'.

In view of this toast and the treatment of women in the Ottoman Empire it seems odd that women were allowed to join the Divan Club. However, Sir Francis Dashwood's half-sister Mary Walcot appears in Turkish costume in a portrait called *Sultana Walcotiana*. Lady Mary Wortley Montagu, who lived in Constantinople while her husband was ambassador there, Fanny Murray, a courtesan and one of Sandwich's mistresses, and Lady Dashwood also appear in similar costumes. Was this club anything more than an escape from reality into a fantasy world of rich clothes and convivial companionship? The fact that Sir Francis Dashwood's wife and sister were members seems to belie the accusation that the club was a private brothel; or that it was an opportunity for married men to get away from their wives. Was it mocking Islam or applauding it? Probably neither, as it took elements of the culture that its members had seen in Constantinople and adapted these to form a pleasant drinking club for like-minded people.

Nine founder members were joined by twelve more, including Lady Mary Wortley Montagu's husband. But by 1746 enthusiasm for the club was on the wane and there was a great deal of absenteeism from meetings. The last meeting was held on 25 May 1746.

This short-lived club was significant because it was a forerunner of the much better-known Medmenham Friars, Dashwood's inter-pretation of a hell-fire club. It is likely that meeting in the relatively public environment of a London tavern curtailed activities, which were easier to arrange in the country retreat of Medmenham Abbey. The Divan Club demonstrated how impressions of a foreign society and its culture influenced British observers and were translated into British club life. The second public club that Dashwood and Sandwich were involved with survived into the twentieth century, and has had a long-lasting effect on art and culture.

THE SOCIETY OF DILETTANTI

The Society of Dilettanti was formed in 1732 as a small private society for gentlemen who had been to Italy, had developed a taste for fine art and classical ruins and wanted to encourage this appre-ciation of art and classical sites in England.[48] Horace Walpole, of course, attributed a different motive for the formation of the Dilettanti – a predilection for alcohol.[49] The society first met in Bedford Head Tavern and it was here that they decided to keep minutes of their meetings. The first minute book records the names of forty-six members, of which Sir Francis Dashwood is the second. It includes Simon Luttrell of the Irish Hell-Fire Club, the Earl of Sandwich and Bubb Dodington, another of Dashwood's cronies.[50] The members were mostly young and wealthy.

As in the Divan Club, dressing up in unusual costumes was a feature of the Dilettanti. The society's president wore a scarlet toga and sat in a specially commissioned armchair of mahogany covered with crimson velvet. The secretary dressed as Machiavelli, and the Master of Ceremonies wore a crimson taffeta pleated gown and a Hungarian cap and carried a Toledo sword.[51] Sir Francis Dashwood was responsible for designing and procuring the costumes, and the first Master of Ceremonies was the Earl of Sandwich, although he was suspended from that office in 1748 due to a 'misdemeanour'.[52] There was much drunkenness in the early days of the society, and in 1749 it was resolved that health-drinking should be discontinued.[53]

In 1736 the society decided it must have its own regalia and furniture. A box called the Bacchus Tomb intended for use as a ballot box was commissioned. This was made of mahogany with a classical pediment supporting a bull's head and Justice with a book sitting astride a hole in which the black or white balls would be placed. A figure of Bacchus was added at a later date.[54] Some modern authors have suggested that the society's regalia contained covert sexual messages, but it should be pointed out that the ballot box and another society box where papers were kept necessarily had to include openings or holes. This did not stop a twentieth-century writer suggesting that the Society of Dilettanti had a 'sexual orientation' which was symbolised by the regalia and in the portraits that every member of the society was obliged to have painted by its official artists, George Knapton and Sir Joshua Reynolds.[55] Portraits of club members were a familiar feature of clubs of this era. For example, there are portraits of the members of the Kit-Kat Club in the National Portrait Gallery. But the Kit-Kat Club members were in the ordinary dress of eighteenth-century gentlemen, whereas the Dilettanti wear costume and are dressed as Romans, Elizabethans, cardinals, Venetians and orientals. Costumes added to the feeling of escapism from the humdrum world that such a club could bring, and served to remind the members when meeting on a grey English November evening of the blue skies and sun of Italy.

Horace Walpole's comments on the portraits provide a link between the Dilettanti and the Friars of Medmenham, a species of hell-fire club: 'Their pictures were drawn ornamented with symbols and devices and the founder [Dashwood] in the habit of St Francis, and with a chalice in his hand, was represented at his devotions before a statue of the Venus de Medici. These pictures were exhibited in their club room in a tavern in Palace Yard.'[56] A twentieth-century author, S. West, also links the Dilettanti and the Medmenham Friars. He suggests that Dashwood's Dilettanti portrait is openly blasphemous as it refers to him as a saint paying homage to a pagan goddess of love by means of a glass of wine. This symbolises, West suggests, a hidden agenda of atheism amongst the Dilettanti.[57] The reason for painting Dashwood as a friar will never be known, but there is no evidence that he was an atheist, or that he subscribed to the deism of earlier hell-fire clubs. He was, at least in public, a conventional English gentleman, a pillar of the Anglican Church, and the fact that Robert Hay, the future Archbishop of York, belonged to the Dilettanti suggests that any agenda of atheism remained well hidden.

West also accuses the Dilettanti of being a front behind which homosexuals and republicans could hide. There is no evidence of any homosexuality or republicanism in the society. The Dilettanti were drawn from the ranks of Whigs, Tories, Independents and Jacobite Tories. It was a club more concerned with friendship, drinking in good company, role-play and a lust for travel than with playing with the Devil. The society even had its educational side. It promoted Italian opera, and in 1755 proposed that an academy of painters should be formed, an idea which was to materialise as the Royal Academy in 1768. The Dilettanti wanted to create a gallery of casts of Greek and Roman statues in London for artists to study: an early forerunner of the cast court at the Victoria and Albert

Museum. They financed expeditions of artists to make sketches of antiquities in Greece and Asia Minor, the instructions for which were drawn up by Sir Francis Dashwood. The sum of £2,000 was made available for archaeological work in Turkey, at Troy, Attica and Morea. In 1767 the society financed the publication of *Ionian Antiquities*, and this sponsorship of artists and publications continued throughout the eighteenth century. They also purchased Greek and Ionian marbles and presented them to the British Museum in 1785.[58]

In its early days the Society of Dilettanti had several roles. It was a drinking club that offered the opportunity for male bonding and talk about travels and adventures in Italy. It provided its members with a place where they could escape from their heavy responsibilities in England, it had an element of masquerade about it, which might have been the result of visits to the Venetian carnival, and it was ultimately responsible for the study and acquisition of Greek and Roman artefacts that form part of the national collection of antiquities. It was not, as has been suggested, a private brothel, and although its membership was exclusively male it was not a covert organisation for homosexual activity. It would have been difficult for it to have been particularly secretive because it met in taverns, and its activities seem to have been common knowledge to non-members such as Horace Walpole. However, it seems that meetings were too public for some members, especially Sir Francis Dashwood. We do not know what conversations he had with fellow members, but at some point he decided that a club which met in seclusion might better fit his needs. To this end he took out a lease on Medmenham Abbey, and here the Medmenham Friars, or the Knights of St Francis, erroneously known as the 'Hell-Fire Club', met.

This move represents another phase of the hell-fire clubs: a withdrawal from the public sphere of the street and the tavern to the private sphere of the country house, away from the prying eyes of journalists and gossips.

CHAPTER 5

The Medmenham Friars

Although in the eighteenth century the Medmenham Friars, or the Knights of St Francis as they were also known, were never called the Hell-Fire Club, this is the title by which they are known today, and their activities have become the model of how a hell-fire club should proceed. Ironically, we would not know of their existence if some of the members had not fallen out with each other, and one of them, John Wilkes, had not decided to publicise their meetings, and bring the club into disrepute. His revelations opened the floodgates of speculation and fiction. However, there was some fact embedded in the fiction. There was indeed a group of men who met at Medmenham Abbey in Buckinghamshire, for conversation and convivial dinners. Letters and cellar books owned by the Dashwood family of West Wycombe show that they met at regular intervals through the year, and that each member could draw a number of bottles from the club's cellar. What happened at these meetings has to be untangled from the fictional accounts that followed Wilkes's revelations. *Chrysal, or The Adventures of a Guinea*, a novel by Charles Johnstone, is a prime source of fiction about the Friars, and one that some authors have taken as fact.

The first edition of *Chrysal* was published in 1760 before Wilkes brought the Friars to public notice, but its author was quick to capitalise on Wilkes's account, and a new enlarged edition was soon published. Book III of the enlarged edition was about Medmenham and based loosely on Wilkes's revelations. Other imaginative accounts followed, each adding to the story of the Friars, until they were accused of being members of a Satanic cult, practising black magic and other lewd rites. The reality was less sensational, but it had an overtone of sexual indulgence.

Medmenham Abbey

Sir Francis Dashwood leased Medmenham Abbey from Sir Francis Duffield in 1751. The abbey had been a Cistercian monastery. After the dissolution of the monasteries, a small Elizabethan courtyard house was built on the site, but by the eighteenth century the abbey was in ruins and the Elizabethan house in disrepair. Dashwood and his friends set about reviving the conventual buildings and the grounds to their own design. The abbey chapel was rebuilt, and a refectory and cells added. John Wilkes described it in a letter to John Almon, who reprinted the letter in his collection *The New Foundling Hospital for Wit*, Book III. Wilkes described a large house on the banks of the Thames, in 'a remarkably fine situation, with woods, meadows and a chrystal stream running through, venerable elms gather round the house'. Over the great entrance was carved a motto taken from Rabelais's Abbey of Thélème: '*Fay ce que vouldras*', or 'Do what you will.'

Wilkes continued his description. 'At one end of the refectory is a statue of Harpocrates, the Egyptian goddess of silence, and at the other end a blind goddess, to remind members that this is a secret organisation.'

'The garden, the grove, the orchard and the neighbouring woods, all spoke of the loves and frailties of the younger monks, who seemed at least to have sinned naturally.' Inscriptions and statues in the gardens all pointed to this being a garden dedicated to sexual pleasure. A statue of Venus taking a thorn out of her foot stood at the entrance to a cave. 'The statue turned from the viewer so that

1 Philip, Duke of Wharton, 1698–1731. Portrait by John Simon, after Charles Jervas. The Duke of Wharton was known as the Hell-Fire Duke because of his involvement with the club of that name, which met in London from 1720 to 1721. He denied his involvement in the House of Lords, but the accusation stuck to him through life and after death. He was an enthusiast who took up projects on a whim and dropped them when a new one came along. After leaving the Hell-Fire Club he joined the Freemasons, and finally went into exile, becoming a Jacobite and a Roman Catholic.

2 John Wilmot, 2nd Earl of Rochester, 1647–1680. Portrait by an unknown artist. This handsome fellow, in a full-bottomed wig, was one of the original rakes of the Restoration. His main interests were wine, women and the theatre. The first exposed him to bouts of excessive drinking that led to riot and disorder; the second resulted in him taking many mistresses; and the third meant that he patronised playwrights. In one piece of personal theatre he dressed as a quack doctor and advertised himself as a specialist in women's ailments.

3 *He and His Drunken Companions Raise a Riot in Covent Garden* depicts the result of alcohol, high spirits and the lack of organised law enforcement which allowed young men, such as the Mohocks to terrorise passers-by. The Piazza in Covent Garden was a favourite gathering place for shady characters including prostitutes and young men out for mischief and committing atrocities after dark.

4 *The Diabolical Maskquerade.* The print is subtitled *The Dragon's-feast as acted by the Hell-Fire Club, at Somerset House in the Strand*, and it was produced at the time when the Duke of Wharton's club was meeting, Somerset House being one of their alleged venues. Members of the Hell-Fire Club are dressed as the classical figures Pluto, the God of the Underworld, Proserpina, and various animals. Verses below the print describe the club as blasphemous and express a wish that it will soon be banned.

5 Sir Francis Dashwood, 1708–1781, in a work attributed to Nathaniel Dance. This is a subdued portrait of Sir Francis Dashwood; other portraits show him in fancy dress as a friar worshipping Venus, but here he is in the sober guise of a country squire. This was his public face as MP, JP and solid member of the community. It masks his private and secret life as the founder of the Medmenham Friars and the colourful Divan club, and the owner of a garden landscaped in the shape of the female pudenda.

6 Paul Whitehead, 1716–1774, in a portrait by John Downman. Paul Whitehead was the secretary of the Medmenham Friars, and Sir Francis Dashwood's closest friend. He was known as 'Ancient Paul' because of his cadaverous appearance. He started from relatively humble beginnings, but gained Dashwood's friendship and patronage through his satirical writings. It was Whitehead who kept the Friars' records, and it was he who destroyed them shortly before his death. His heart was buried with great ceremony in Dashwood's mausoleum at West Wycombe.

7 Charles Churchill, in a portrait by J.S.C. Schaak. Charles Churchill was a Medmenham Friar and close friend of John Wilkes with whom he sometimes shared mistresses. His nickname 'Bruiser' described his appearance, which was large and frightening. He seduced and eloped with a fifteen-year-old girl, taking refuge in Wilkes's house in Aylesbury. A libertine and a poet, his verse 'The Candidate' describes the events and personalities of the Medmenham Friars.

8 John Wilkes, 1726–1797.
John Wilkes had the doubtful
distinction of being expelled
from the Medmenham Friars
when his politics diverged from
those of Dashwood and the other
Friars, and it was Wilkes who
drew the public's attention to
Medmenham. He was a radical,
defender of civil liberties, and a
libertine, whose treatment of his
wife was reprehensible, but he
was a loving and supportive father
to his children, legitimate and
illegitimate.

9 West Wycombe Park, Temple of Venus. English Heritage work on West Wycombe
Park started in 1735 and took nearly fifty years to complete. The Temple of Venus, one of
the glories of the park, was finished in 1752. It stands on a conical mound, which has an
oval opening into an underground room. This is allegedly a portrayal of the vagina, and
original planting of shrubs around were said to represent pubic hair. John Wilkes referred
to the Temple as 'the entrance by which we all come into the world…'

10 West Wycombe Mausoleum. This unusual hexagon structure is open to the sky. It was built by Sir Francis Dashwood with money left to him by Dubb Dodington, a fellow MP and Friar. It is situated so that it catches the eye of travellers on the London Road. It was to this mausoleum that Paul Whitehead's heart was brought to be interred in a marble urn.

11 West Wycombe Church. Sir Francis Dashwood remodelled West Wycombe Church in classical style, based on the Temple of Palmyra. The interior resembles a drawing room rather than a church, with armchairs, benches covered in green felt, and wine bins. The church is crowned with a golden globe.

12 West Wycombe House was originally a plain rectangular building until Sir Francis Dashwood started to remodel it in 1740. The front and east portico were modelled on the Temple of Bacchus at Smyrna, while the façade of the south front is a two-storey colonnade of Corinthian columns at the top, and Doric at the bottom, reminiscent of the façade of the church of St Sulpice in Paris. Inside, the classical theme is continued as the interior is based round an atrium as seen in Roman villas and heating is supplied by a system similar to a Roman hypocaust.

13 John Montague, 4th Earl of Sandwich 1718–1792 in a portrait by Joseph Highmore. The Earl of Sandwich, alias Jemmy Twitcher, was a politician, admiral, libertine, musician and sportsman. A close friend of Sir Francis Dashwood and a member of the Medmenham Friars, he prosecuted John Wilkes for the obscene publication *Essay on Woman*, partly as revenge for Wilkes's politics, and partly because Wilkes exposed the Friars to ridicule. His reforms at the Admiralty were unpopular at the time, but stood the country in good stead during the French Wars.

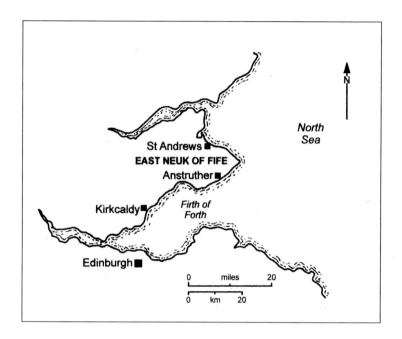

North
Sea

St Andrews ■
EAST NEUK OF FIFE
Anstruther ■

Kirkcaldy ■

Edinburgh ■

Firth of
Forth

0   miles   20

0   km   20

14 The Firth of Forth, Scotland. This shows the relationship of the location of the original Beggar's Benison meeting with its surrounding area.

The East Neuk of Fife. Members of the original Beggar's Benison were drawn from the five royal burghs of Crail, Kilrenny, Anstruther Easter, Anstruther Wester, Pittenweem and their hinterland. Although now an area of pretty villages and tourist attractions, in the eighteenth century salt pans, coal pits, fishing and a large merchant fleet meant that the East Neuk was a hub of industry and trade.

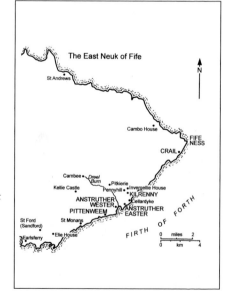

The East Neuk of Fife

St Andrews

Cambo House

FIFE
NESS

CRAIL

Carnbee • Dreel
Burn
Kellie Castle   • Pitkierie
Pennyhill • • Invergellie House
• KILRENNY
ANSTRUTHER • Cellardyke
WESTER ANSTRUTHER
PITTENWEEM EASTER
St Ford
(Sandford)   St Monans
• Elie House
Earlsferry

FIRTH   OF   FORTH

0   miles   2

0   km   4

15 Beggar's Benison Medal. The Beggar's Benison had a number of different designs for their medals and diplomas, but all on the same theme. The obverse of this medal shows Adam and Eve and has the legend 'Go forth and multiply'. The reverse has the legend 'May Prick and Purse never fail you', and the image of a female with legs akimbo pointing to a man's penis. The mixture of the sacred and the profane is typical of the Beggar's Benison.

THE BEGGARS BENISON. ANSTRUTHER 1732

THE WAY OF A MAN WITH A MAID
TE ST
PLATTER

16 Beggar's Benison Testing Platter. This is the trial platter on which the initiate seeking membership of the Beggar's Benison had to masturbate and fill a spoonful.

17 Wig Club Wig Stand. The Wig Club was founded in 1775. The wig it was named after was allegedly made of pubic hair taken from royal mistresses. Although the club had sexual overtones, one of its functions was as a gambling den.

18 Beggar's Benison Wine Glass. The glass shows an anchor symbolising the maritime nature of the place where the Benison was found, a penis that should never fail, and a representation of Castle Dreel where the Beggars met.

19 Wig Club Phallic Glass. This drinking glass in the shape of an erect penis was made for the Wig Club. It is assumed that each member had to empty it in one go.

20 Beggar's Benison Bible. This is the annotated bible from which the initiate had to read verses from the Song of Solomon after masturbating on the test platter. The design on the keyhole allegedly represents the vagina, and the Latin inscription translates as 'The Tree of Knowledge of Good and Evil'.

21 Castle Dreel, Anstruther Easter, Fife. These are the remains of Castle Dreel where the original members of the Beggar's Benison met, performed their initiation rites, and paid for local girls to expose themselves in the interest of 'science'. It overlooks the Dreel Burn, which divides Anstruther Easter and Anstruther Wester.

22 The author at Anstruther Easter.

the observer could see the two hills of snow [her buttocks] over which a Latin inscription read:

> This is the place, show where we go to cleave behind
> This is our Elysium, and soft gladness.

Inside the cave was a mossy couch with an invitation to use it. Wilkes added that

> The favourite doctrine was not penitence, for in the centre of the orchard was a grotesque figure, and in his hand he had a reed stood with flaming tips of fire. To use Milton's expression,

> > Pene Tente (Penitence)
> > Or
> > Peni Tenti (Erect Penis)[1]

Sex therefore was one of the main preoccupations of the Friars. Blasphemy was also suspected. The original number of Friars was twelve, including Sir Francis, representing, it is thought, the twelve apostles. These were the inner circle. As membership increased, a novitiate was added, in which new members had to serve before joining the inner circle. Some later writers have suggested that Wilkes never succeeded in becoming one of the twelve, and that his is only a hearsay account of what went on when they were in closed session.

Most of what we know about the twelve comes from Johnstone's fictional account, but it is possible that he got his information from Wilkes. Johnstone's *Chrysal* is about the spirit of gold, appearing in the form of a guinea, which travels from pocket to pocket. In one incarnation it ends up in the pocket of a Friar where it observes an initiation test that took place in the chapel at Medmenham between John Wilkes and the Earl of Sandwich, rival candidates for the inner circle.

They are taken to the chapel to put their case to a solemn assembly, and a vote is taken to decide who should become an apostle. Sandwich wins this, causing Wilkes much anguish. Sandwich and Wilkes were known political enemies, so this section of the book is playing on their political rivalry. But it was not until Wilkes had dramatically different political opinions to Dashwood and the other Friars that he expressed any dissatisfaction with them. Prior to that he seems to have enjoyed himself greatly at Medmenham, and made full use of its facilities.

It is in *Chrysal* that blasphemy and Satanic rites are mentioned: 'Every sacred rite of religion was profaned, hymns and prayers were dedicated to the Devil.' Banquets were held in the chapel, and brothers vied with each other in 'gross lewdness and impiety'.[2]

Horace Walpole visited Medmenham in 1763, after Wilkes's revelations but while the Friars were still using the abbey. He adds to the description of how the Friars operated. Each 'monk had his own cell, in which there was little more than a bed, and into which they could take any woman they wanted'. Walpole noted the Rabelaisian inscription over the door and the statues mentioned by Wilkes. He added that in the common or chapter room there were prints of the kings and queens of England, but that of Henry VIII, who had dissolved the monasteries, was papered over. Walpole also described portraits of the Friars with their pseudonyms. 'John of Aylesbury', wrote Walpole, 'was John Wilkes, who had been expelled for abusing the Prior, Sir Francis Dashwood.'

The Friars' garments were still hanging on pegs when Walpole visited, and he scotched the rumour that they dressed in hooded habits. 'The habit is more like a water man's than a monk's, and consists of a white hat, a white jacket and white trousers. The Prior has a red hat like a cardinal's, and a red bonnet turned up with coney skin.' Walpole was not allowed into the chapel, but added all the same, 'It is said to be furnished with bawdy pictures.'[3]

Thomas Langley, who visited the abbey in 1796, described it:

The abbey-house, with its ivy-mantled roof and falls forms a very picturesque object. The late addition of a ruined tower, cloister and other corresponding parts, is made with much taste and propriety . . . Within the cloister is a room fitted up with good taste . . . Some few years since the house was tenanted by a society of men of wit and fashion under the title the monks of St Francis, whose habit they assumed. During the season of their conventual residence they are supposed not to have adhered very rigidly to the rules of life which St Francis had enjoined.

The only witness to the activities of the Friars that Langley could find was a female domestic who claimed to know nothing.[4] Walpole suggested that all servants were dismissed before the Friars met.[5]

The Friars of Medmenham would appear to have been a private club for gentlemen, where they could indulge in alcohol and sex. It also allowed them to pursue that peculiar eighteenth-century fascination with fancy dress: a shucking off of the everyday for a fantasy world, a trend we have already seen in the Divan Club and the Society of Dilettanti.

MEETINGS AT MEDMENHAM

Sir Francis Dashwood arranged the meetings and sent out invitations to members. The cellar books show that meetings took place on Wednesdays and Saturdays between June and October.[6] Summer activities, therefore, took place when Parliament was in recess, as many of the Friars were MPs. Summer also allowed the Friars to enjoy the garden and the nearby river. A gondola was provided for river trips, and it is likely that fishing trips to a nearby island took place.

At least one letter, from John Wilkes to his friend Charles Churchill, the poet, shows that the Friars met at the summer solstice.

> June 15th 1762
> Pray remember the ghost for me tonight, and next Monday (June 21st 1762) we meet at Medmenham.[7]

Other letters hint at sexual activity. On 3 September 1758 John King of Ashby, Lincolnshire, wrote to Sir Francis Dashwood to apologise for missing one of the Medmenham meetings because of family commitments, but presents his mirth to the sisterhood, 'who are determined to exert their spiritual entreaties there, as far as their spirits are willing . . .'[8] On 5 September 1761 William Stapleton wrote to Sir Francis Dashwood accepting an invitation to a meeting of the Friars: 'I shall be extremely glad: hoping there be now and then an extraordinary ejaculation to be sent up to heaven.'[9] And from Sir William Stanhope to Sir Francis: 'my compliments to all your Brethren and assure them that they have my prayers, particularly in that part of the litany, when I pray the Lord to strengthen them to stand.'[10]

Sex was clearly part of the Friars' activities, but who were the 'nuns' who partnered them? Various suggestions have been made as to their identities. Perhaps they were local girls, enticed into the abbey for payment, or local gentlewomen seeking to escape from their husbands and experience some sexual variety, or prostitutes brought down from London? In his book, *The Hell-Fire Club*, D. McCormick names one of the latter as Fanny Murray, a courtesan and one-time mistress of Beau Nash and the Earl of Sandwich. Another lady of easy virtue who may have visited Medmenham was Agnes Perrault, who may have been the author of *Nocturnal Revels*, which described activities at Medmenham. Another potential female member at Medmenham may have been Mary Walcot, Dashwood's half-sister.[11]

There is no real evidence as to who the sisterhood were. It is likely that, like an earlier club called the Schemers, they were the mistresses and concubines of the Friars, who for one reason or another wanted to remain anonymous. Secrecy and silence were the watchwords at Medmenham, for which some ladies may have been grateful. The culture of secrecy, to which Wilkes must have subscribed, makes it all the more reprehensible of him to expose the Friars, but it should be noted that apart from Dashwood he named no names.

MEMBERS OF THE MEDMENHAM FRIARS

The cellar books and other evidence help us to compile a list of possible members, and there are others that we know were Friars. There is no doubt that Sir Francis Dashwood was involved as founder and organiser, and his friend, the one-time poet Paul Whitehead – known at Medmenham as 'ancient Paul' on account of his aged and cadaverous appearance – was a member, acting as steward and secretary.

Whitehead (1710–74) was born in Holborn, London. He was the son of a tailor, who had him educated at Hitchin in Hertfordshire, and then apprenticed him to a London mercer. This did not suit him, as he had ambitions to become a writer. He started by writing satires, and he organised a mock Freemason march through London; it was as a result of this march that he met Sir Francis Dashwood. Whitehead needed a rich patron, and Sir Francis fitted that role exactly. They became firm friends and allies, and Whitehead was determined to protect the reputation of Dashwood and his fellow Friars. Shortly before he died he burned all his papers, which probably included more information on the Friars. In his will he left £50 to Dashwood and asked to have his heart buried in the mausoleum at West Wycombe, which had been funded by Bubb Dodington.

In August 1775 Whitehead's heart was brought to West Wycombe with a great procession of choirboys, musicians and the Bucks Militia. In 'The Candidate' John Wilkes's friend Charles Churchill describes Whitehead at Medmenham:

> Whilst Womanhood in the habit of a nun
> At Medmenham lies, by backward monks undone,
> At nation's reckoning, like an ale house score
> Whilst Paul the aged chalks behind the door,
> Compell'd to hire a foe to cast it up,
> D[ashwood] shall pour, from a communion cup
> Libations to the Goddess without eyes,
> And hob or nob in cyder or excise.[12]

Mention of cider and excise referred to Sir Francis Dashwood's term as Chancellor of the Exchequer when he imposed an extremely unpopular cider tax and caused riots in the cider counties of the West Country. A satire, *Secrets of the Convent*, published in 1763, after Wilkes had exposed the Friars, suggested that Sir Francis obtained the office of Chancellor through his friendship and possible blackmail of Lord Bute, the chief minister.

Whitehead was an opportunist, born into the lower middle class but with aspirations beyond it. He wanted to live a life in which he did not earn his living by hard graft, but could consort with and imitate the life of his 'betters'. He was, in fact, a member of a new breed that flourished in the eighteenth century, symbolised by figures such as Whitehead and, of course, John Wilkes. It was through men like Dashwood and the Earl of Sandwich that they could enter a society unknown to their fathers.

Medmenham was a place for exhilaration and pleasant enjoyment, and the inclusion in the Friars of men such as Whitehead and Wilkes shows that those with similar interests but from different backgrounds could mix socially with those who might be considered their superiors.

Another member of the Friars was, like Dashwood, a founder member of the Divan Club and Dilettanti Society: the Earl of Sandwich. It was Sandwich who was to become Wilkes's chief prosecutor when he abused his parliamentary privileges. In *Chrysal*, Johnstone suggests that this was due to a practical joke that Wilkes played on Sandwich at Medmenham. Wilkes obtained a baboon from another Friar, allegedly Sir Henry Vansittart who had been Governor of Bengal. Wilkes hid the creature in his cell, dressed it up as a devil and then placed it in a chest with a spring lock that would open the lid through the attachment of an invisible piece of string, tied to Wilkes's finger. When Sandwich was kneeling in the chapel at Medmenham with hands and eyes pointed towards Heaven in one phase of the perverted holy ritual, Wilkes released the baboon amongst the terrified Friars. It jumped on to Sandwich's shoulder as he lay prostrate on the floor: turning his head, he saw its grinning face and thought the Devil had come to carry him away. As the baboon put its paws around Sandwich's neck and gibbered at him, Sandwich cried, 'Spare me, gracious Devil, spare a wretch who was never sincerely your servant. I have sinned only from the vanity of being in fashion, never have I been able to commit the thousandth part of the vices which I have boasted of.' While Sandwich was uttering these words, one of the Friars who had recovered his senses opened a window and the baboon leapt through it, never to be seen again.[13]

The tale is pure fiction. It does not appear in the account of the Friars given by John Wilkes to John Almon, and this was surely an episode he would have boasted about, as it showed Sandwich in an unfortunate light. It sounds like a variation of the equally fictional account by Horace Walpole of Sir Francis Dashwood whipping communicants in the Sistine Chapel. Simply owing to the logistics of hiding, dressing and putting a baboon in a chest, this story is impossible. And how convenient that the wretched animal disappeared.

However, there is another version of this story in the *Dictionary of National Biography* under the entry for Robert Vansittart, who allegedly presented the Friars with a baboon, to which Sir Francis Dashwood habitually delivered the Eucharist. If this did happen, it was sacrilege in two senses. Sir Francis, who was not an ordained minister, could not dispense the Eucharist; and if he did so, then administering it to an animal that had no soul was equally sacrilegious. Unfortunately there is no direct reference to the origin of this story.

Sandwich was a known libertine, but he was also a politician, and First Lord of the Admiralty. Another politician who was probably a member of the Friars was Bubb Dodington, later Lord Melcombe. Dodington started life as plain George Bubb, but inherited a fortune. In his case, social mobility came through wealth as well as connections. Dodington was a long-time friend of Sir Francis Dashwood and visited West Wycombe many times. It is assumed that he was a member of the Friars as the pages in his diary that coincide with meetings at Medmenham are left blank, and he was an assiduous diary-keeper.[14]

Other MPs who were Friars were Sir William Stanhope, Sir John Dashwood-King (Sir Francis's half-brother), John Tucker, Arthur and Robert Vansittart, Sir John Aubrey, John Martin, Richard Hopkis and John Wilkes.

Sir John Aubrey (1739–1826) was from Boarstall in Buckinghamshire and was educated at Westminster School and Christ Church, Oxford. He was MP for Wallingford from 1768 to 1774, and again in 1780, after representing a number of constituencies between 1774 and 1780. In 1782 he became Lord of the Admiralty under the Rockingham administration, and then served in the Treasury in 1783–89. He was a liberal who supported

Wilkes, and this would have made him unpopular with his fellow Friars. He attacked the proceedings against Wilkes in the House of Commons, and this probably ended his association with the Earl of Sandwich, Dashwood and the other Friars.[15] John Dashwood-King (1716–93) represented the constituency of Bishop's Castle, a seat in the pocket of his brother-in-law John Walcot, and so was returned unopposed at each election. He had the doubtful distinction of never speaking once in the House of Commons. (This was not unusual in the eighteenth century.) Like his half-brother, he was a member of the Tory opposition.[16] Richard Hopkis (*c.* 1728–99) represented a number of constituencies, including Dartmouth, Thetford, Queenborough and Harwich. He held the offices of Clerk of the Board of Green Cloth from 1767 to 1777, Lord of the Admiralty 1782–91, and was Lord of the Treasury 1791–97.[17] As this shows, the Friars had a significant presence at the Admiralty.

How John Martin became a Friar is a mystery. His estate was Overbury Court in Gloucestershire and he was MP for Tewkesbury. But he was a Whig, while most of the Friars were opposition Tories. As membership seems to have been by the recommendation of an existing member, he must have been on good terms with another Friar. How Sir William Stanhope MP (1702–72) became a Friar is less of a mystery. Although he represented Lostwithiel in Cornwall, his estate was in Buckinghamshire. He was the second son of the Earl of Chesterfield, and his second wife was Elizabeth Crawley, the daughter of Sir Ambrose Crawley an ironmaster and Jacobite.[18] Along with Dodington and Dashwood, Stanhope was a member of the Prince of Wales's set.

Another member with Jacobite antecedents was Sir William Stapleton of Rotherfield Greys in Oxfordshire. His grandfather fought for the Royalists in the Civil War and went into exile with Charles II, and his father had invited the Hell-Fire Duke of Wharton and other Jacobite sympathisers to a dinner where the

Pretender's health was drunk in public.[19] The other MP in the Friars, apart from John Wilkes, was John Tucker, who died in 1779. He was probably introduced to Medmenham by Bubb Dodington, whose seat of Melcombe Regis he took over when Dodington was elevated to the peerage. He joined with Dodington and Dashwood in opposing Sir Robert Walpole, and in his will he left all his property to Dodington.[20]

The Vansittart brothers came from a family that originated in the Netherlands and came to England via Danzig in the 1670s. They were involved in trade with Russia, India and the South Seas, and their father became a director of the East India Company. One of the brothers, Henry, was sent to Madras from 1745 until 1752, where he gained a reputation as a rake-hell. He was back in India as Governor of Bengal in 1753, but resigned and returned to England in 1764, becoming MP for Reading in 1768. The dates when he is known to have been in India show that he can have had little overlap with the heyday of the Friars.

The eldest Vansittart brother, Robert, was a lawyer who eventually became Regius Professor of Law at the University of Oxford in 1767. By that time he had amassed well-paid sinecure posts as recorder for a number of towns, including Maidenhead, Newbury and Windsor. He was a friend of William Hogarth, who painted him wearing a turban embroidered with the words 'Love and Friendship'. He was an early patron of George Knapton, who became the Dilettanti's official artist, and was also a friend of Dr Johnson.

Other Friars came from local Buckinghamshire gentry: Francis Duffield, the actual owner of Medmenham Abbey, Mr Clarke and Dr Benjamin Bates of Henley. Dr Bates was the last surviving member of the Friars, and he strenuously denied any scandalous goings on to his dying day. The Friars' membership also included Wilkes's friends Thomas Potter and Charles Churchill, Dr Thomas Thompson, John Norris of Magdalen College, Oxford, Robert Lloyd, a poet, and perhaps William Hogarth, the painter. John

Hall-Stevenson was a visitor to Medmenham, as were Edward Lovibond and Henry Collins.[21]

A second generation of Friars *may* have included Sir Francis Delaval, William Douglas, Earl of March, the Duke of Queensberry, the Earl of Westmorland who was related to Dashwood, the politician Henry Fox, the Prince of Wales, Simon Luttrell of the Irish Hell-Fire Club, the Marquess of Granby, the Duke of Kingston, the Earl of Bute and the third Earl of Orford.[22] If this exotic bunch were indeed Friars, then it shows a change in the character of the membership, from a locally based society to one that attracted the most prestigious nobility of the country. But the evidence that Lewis Jones gives for this line-up is based on works written after the event, and on secondary sources. For example, the claim that Frederick, Prince of Wales, was a member is taken from the old *DNB* and the *Victoria County History* for Buckinghamshire. Although the Prince lived close to Medmenham at Cliveden, and was a friend of Bubb Dodington there is no hard evidence that he was a Friar. In fact the only surviving accurate list of Friars comes from the cellar books.

Was Benjamin Franklin a Friar? Probably not, although there is no doubt that Franklin and Dashwood were firm friends. Franklin visited Dashwood at West Wycombe and collaborated with him on a revision of the Book of Common Prayer, with Franklin working on the catechism and the Psalms. He reduced the catechism to 'What is your duty to God?' and 'What is your duty to your neighbour?' and Jones suggests that this is evidence of Dashwood's and Franklin's deism.[23] The Prayer Book was privately printed, but never adopted by the Church of England.

Franklin was first brought to Dashwood's notice in 1762, when Dashwood as the newly appointed Chancellor of the Exchequer was trying to get to grips with higher economics. He asked for advice from William Denny, a fellow member of the Royal Society and former Governor of Pennsylvania, who suggested that he contact

Franklin who was in London as the Agent for Pennsylvania. At this time they seem only to have corresponded, not actually meeting in person until 1772, after the Friars were disbanded. From that date onwards Franklin was a regular visitor to West Wycombe. He described the gardens there as a paradise, and praised the wit and humour of his host.

It is clear from the cellar books and letters amongst the Dashwood family papers that not all members attended every meeting. Wilkes, who was present at twenty meetings, was one of the most regular Medmenham attenders. But Friars could use their cells and draw wine from the cellar between meetings. An inventory of the cellar showed that it contained sherry, port, rum, hock and claret. There were twenty-nine cups, twenty-seven knives, twenty-nine forks and twenty-four glasses.[24] If each of the twenty-six members listed in the cellar book brought along a female companion then there would not have been enough glasses and cutlery to go round, although there were a number of teacups and saucers that may have been for the ladies.

The idea that women were admitted to Medmenham appears in *Nocturnal Revels*, published in 1774 and allegedly written by Agnes Perrault, one of the courtesans who visited the abbey, and in *The Confessions of Sir Francis of Medmenham and the Lady Mary his wife* (1795).

Nocturnal Revels claims that every member was allowed to introduce a lady of 'a cheerful, lively disposition'. The ladies were not compelled to take a vow of celibacy when they joined the Order, but could consider themselves the lawful wives of their sponsors when they entered Medmenham. They subscribed to the secrecy of the rites and were admitted in masks so that their identity was hidden. Should they fall pregnant, there was a doctor on hand to perform the obstetric art.[25]

The Confessions of Sir Francis . . . and the Lady Mary his wife was written by John Hall-Stevenson, a wealthy eccentric who supported

Wilkes and thus became an enemy of Dashwood. It is obscene in the extreme. In it Sir Francis confesses to a Friar that

> Like a Hotspur Young cock, he began with his mother
> Cheer'd three of his sisters, one after another
> And oft tried little Jen, but gained so little ground
> Little Jen lost her patience and made him compound.

It continues in this vein. Sir Francis confesses eight sins, and challenges the Friar to confess his; the Friar can find only five sins, but thanks God that Sir Francis had no brother or he would have had a dozen to confess. Lady Mary then confesses her sins, claiming that she was taught at sixteen by a 'masculine nun'. She ends up copulating with the Friar in the garden.[26] However, all of this is fiction, and John Hall-Stevenson's main concern was to titillate his friends and blacken Sir Francis Dashwood's name.

Do What You Will

'*Fay ce que vouldras*' presumably meant that inside the abbey anything was permitted, including excessive drinking, sacrilege and unlimited sexual licence. This has led more imaginative writers to conjure up a picture of orgies, the Black Mass and Satanic rituals around Sir Francis and the abbey. But Sir Francis Dashwood did not mean unlimited freedom of expression. In *An Address to the Gentlemen, Clergy and Freeholders of Great Britain* published in 1747 he wrote that freedom does not mean that the individual should act as he wants, but that he should do what he wants only within the law. What went on at Medmenham was almost certainly within civil and criminal law. The Medmenham Friars were not alone in using the motto *Fay ce que vouldras*. In his *London Journal*, James Boswell mentions that he had joined the 'Soaping Club' – 'A club that let every man soap his own beard and *fay ce que vouldras*'.

Soaping your own beard could be a euphemism for masturbation.[27] Boswell as a friend of Charles Churchill would have known about the Medmenham Friars, but was not asked to join.

There was no rape of virgins or human sacrifice at Medmenham Abbey, but neither was it the country club suggested by Betty Kemp. She puts forward the idea that the Rabelaisian motto was an 'exhortation' to be honourable and considerate, and that Medmenham was a pleasure park by the Thames, where a group of gentlemen met to eat and drink together and take part in fishing expeditions and picnics. She admits that probably some rituals did take place, but this was the age of the Freemasons, and other clubs had their formalised rituals and dress.[28]

We only know about these rituals from fictional accounts, and there is no evidence that they parodied the Roman Catholic Mass. If indeed rituals were performed at Medmenham, then any resemblance to the Mass was probably the result of the influence of the site on the Friars' imagination. It was a Cistercian ruin, with Gothic structures grafted on to it; and as well as being the age of the Freemasons this was the age of the Gothic, and the Gothic horror novel as satirised in *Northanger Abbey* by Jane Austen. Is there any evidence that Sir Francis Dashwood was anti-Catholic? His behaviour in Italy, discounting the alleged incident in the Sistine Chapel, suggests that he may have been shocked by the elaborate religious rituals he saw. Stripping the Prayer Book of its additions and paring it down to the essential Anglican belief structure might be further evidence of this. But if the evidence shows that he was anti-Catholic, this suggests that he was not, as some of his contemporaries and later historians claimed, a Jacobite, since the Stuarts in exile were Catholic and would have restored Britain to Rome had they been returned to the throne.

However, there is also evidence which suggests that Dashwood was not anti-Catholic. To start with, he loved dressing up and performing formalised rituals. This can be seen in his activities with the Divan Club and the Dilettanti. Furthermore, Wilkes tells us that in the chapter room at Medmenham Abbey, the print of Henry VIII, who dissolved the monasteries and abandoned the Roman Catholic Church, was covered up. Was this the statement of a hidden agenda?

There is no evidence of any witchcraft or magic, black or otherwise, at Medmenham. In fact when Wilkes wrote of 'English Eleusinian mysteries' in connection with the abbey he is at pains to point out that he is referring to a classical past that inspired the rituals of pouring libations to the gods or paying homage to the mother goddess. He also indicated that, like the Eleusinian mysteries, those at Medmenham were secret. It was the secret and enclosed nature of the Friars that fascinated the eighteenth century and led to fiction and speculation. Here was a mysterious scandal that hack writers could use to boost the sale of their books, a scandal that touched public men. Ironically, the Friars could have remained a secret organisation, had not these public men fallen out over politics.

Had the Friars been a club similar to the Divan club or other eighteenth-century men's clubs it would not have received so much attention. Had its members been seen in a brothel this would have been accepted as normal for the time. Had they entertained their mistresses at Medmenham, that too would have been accepted, and little made of it. It was the fact that the evidence of what went on was so slim that attracted attention and led to wildly inaccurate accounts, which have persisted into the twenty-first century.

What we can say is that there was a secret club at Medmenham which indulged in role-playing. The garden ornaments and inscriptions around the abbey, described by John Wilkes who had seen them with his own eyes, suggest that sex played a part in abbey life, and the cellar books show that drink played another part; there were probably also some formalised rituals and initiation ceremonies. However, secrecy was the byword at Medmenham Abbey, and when the code of secrecy was broken by one of the Friars, chaos followed.

CHAPTER 6

Essay on Woman:
the Friars Exposed

The Medmenham Friars came to public notice through the political differences of its members. John Wilkes (1725–97) was elected to Parliament in 1757. A poor speaker, his talent lay in his pen, and the aggressive way in which he carried his argument to his opponents. When a new journal called the *Briton* appeared, arguing against the continuation of the Seven Years War and promoting peace, Wilkes countered this with the *North Briton*, which was in favour of continuing the war. Although Wilkes wrote anonymously, it was common knowledge that it was he who penned the articles that satirised ministers and their policies.[1]

The Seven Years War was a contest for overseas domination by European powers seeking to extend and consolidate their empires. In 1756, tension between Britain and France in North America spilt over into war, and in Europe a war between Austria and Prussia managed to involve all European states, including Britain but with the exception of Spain. Britain was drawn in as a result of diplomatic blunders by the then Prime Minister, the Duke of Newcastle. Concerned to ensure the safety of Hanover, the King of England's personal possession, he approached Austria for a guarantee that it would not attack. When he was rebuffed by Austria, he turned to Russia for help. This panicked Austria into offering to defend Hanover for a payment of £500,000. However, it was a bluff: at the same time as negotiating with Britain, Austria activated the anti-British Franco-Austrian alliance and attacked Hanover after all. Britain was now committed to the war.

At first the war went badly for Britain. The Duke of Cumberland, the hero of Culloden, was defeated on land, and the naval base of Minorca was lost at sea, this loss resulting in the court-martial and execution of Admiral Byng for cowardice. In Canada the French under General Montcalm had considerable success, and the French also triumphed in India.

The turnaround of Britain's fortunes of war was due, in part, to the leadership of a new Prime Minister, the Whig William Pitt the Elder, whose direction of the war and provision of supplies was efficient and encouraged his generals to more effort. In 1757 Robert Clive re-took Calcutta from the French, and in 1758 General Wolfe began to push back the French in Canada, while in Europe the French were defeated at the Battles of Rheinberg and Krefeld. In 1759 Britain defeated the Franco-Austrian alliance at Minden, the French fleet was routed off the coast of Lagos, and Quebec fell to the British. By 1761 Britain had taken the West Indian island of Dominica, and in 1762 Martinique, St Lucia, St Vincent and Grenada. The war was going well for Britain, but at this point the Earl of Bute, now Prime Minister, started peace negotiations, at the King's instigation. The pro-war Pitt faction of which Wilkes was a member saw this as a dreadful waste of effort and lobbied for the war to continue, fearing that the gains made would be lost. Despite this opposition, the Peace of Paris was signed in February 1763. As soon as the treaty was signed Wilkes departed for Paris with his daughter.[2]

The Earl of Bute may have been one of Wilkes's fellow Friars, and one of Bute's supporters, the Earl of Sandwich, definitely was a Friar. Whereas once they had dined peaceably at Medmenham, now Sandwich and Wilkes were on different sides, and Wilkes was not prepared to back down. When he heard that Bute had resigned, Wilkes wasted no time in returning from France to join in the ensuing fray.

THE *NORTH BRITON* NUMBER 45

After Bute's resignation, Parliament reconvened on 19 April 1763, with the King's Speech and the creation of new peers, including Sir Francis Dashwood, who became Baron Le Despencer and was given the office of Chancellor of the Exchequer. Issue number 45 of the *North Briton* was published on 23 April 1763. It contained an article criticising the King's Speech and his government ministers in language that could be accounted treasonable. Wilkes was known to be the author of this article, and a warrant for his arrest was drawn up, but parliamentary privilege gave him immunity. After some debate the warrant was held to be legal and on 26 April 1763 three of the King's messengers arrested Wilkes, and took him to the Tower of London.

By this time Wilkes's account of the Medmenham Friars had been sent to John Almon, who published it. This was followed, in May, by a poem written by Wilkes's friend Charles Churchill, called 'The Conference', which mentioned the Friars, and in June 1763 an article about them appeared in the *Public Advertiser*. Scandal and speculation about the identity of the Friars and what they did was rife. Tales began to circulate, and within the closed circle of MPs and peers Wilkes was seen as a traitor not only to his country but also to his friends and colleagues.

Wilkes was released from the Tower of London, but worse was to come that would affect him and the Friars still further. Among the papers impounded in Wilkes's house by the King's messengers was the manuscript of a lewd poem called *Essay on Woman*.

ESSAY ON WOMAN

Essay on Woman was written some time between 1754 and 1759.[3] The poem was mainly the work of Thomas Potter, with interpolations by Wilkes. Potter was the disreputable son of the Archbishop of Canterbury, and MP for St Germans in Cornwall. He and Wilkes were boon companions in immorality of all descriptions, Potter having once allegedly sodomised a cow on Wingrave Common, Buckinghamshire.[4] It may have been Potter who introduced Wilkes to the Medmenham Friars in the first place.

The *Essay on Woman* was a parody of Alexander Pope's *Essay on Man*. It also ridiculed Bishop Warburton of Gloucester, who had edited Pope's essay. Potter had personal reasons for ridiculing Warburton, as he was allegedly Warburton's wife's lover, and the father of her son.[5]

The poem was not only lewd, it was blasphemous as well, referring to the Holy Trinity as 'cock and balls' and mocking the Church of England. But the overall theme of its ninety-four lines was that a woman's body is a world of wonder to be explored.[6]

Only twelve copies of the *Essay* had been printed, probably one for each of the apostles or inner circle of the Medmenham Friars, although, with what must have been consummate hypocrisy, they claimed to be shocked by the book. The title-page stated it was written by Pego Borewell Esq.[7] (Pego was the eighteenth-century slang word for penis.) The essay claimed that it contained notes written by Rogerus Cunaeus and the colophon on the title-page was an erect penis. The book was dedicated to Fanny Murray, a well-known courtesan, the mistress of, amongst others, Beau Nash and of Colonel Joseph Yorke, the son of Lord Hardwicke, the Chancellor and a member of the Duke of Cumberland's victorious army at the Battle of Culloden.[8]

The structure of the poem mirrored Pope's *Essay on Man*. Where Pope had started his poem, 'Awake, my St. John! leave all meaner things', Potter and Wilkes began:

> Awake my Fanny, leave all meaner things
> This morn shall prove what rapture swiving brings
> Let us since life can little more supply

> Than just a few good Fucks and then we die
> Expatiate free o'er that lov'd scene of Man
> In mighty Maze! For mighty Pricks to scan.[9]

In verse 3 of *Essay on Man* Pope writes that 'Philosophers agree that the two great duties Nature has explained to all her children, are to preserve the individual and propagate the species'. In Wilkes and Potter's version this becomes

> The latent Traits, the pleasing Depths explore
> And my Prick clapp'd where thousands were before
> Observe how Nature works, and if it rise,
> Too quick and rapid, check it ere it flies.[10]

Pope's 'The Dying Christian to his Soul' becomes 'The Dying Lover to his Prick'.[11]

The King's messengers had found the manuscript copy of the poem, and the twelve printed copies came into the hands of Wilkes's enemies through the efforts of the Reverend Kidgell, rector of Godstone and Horne in Surrey and chaplain to the Earl of March. He bribed the printer to give him the printed copies, and passed a copy to the Earl of Sandwich, who saw this as a chance to punish Wilkes for *North Briton* 45, for exposing the Friars to public gaze, and for libelling the Bishop of Gloucester. Wilkes was summarily expelled from the Friars and Dashwood and Sandwich set about finding hostile witnesses against him. Their aim was to break Wilkes's parliamentary privilege, and charge him in the House of Lords with libel of the Right Reverend Dr Warburton, Bishop of Gloucester.

At the new session of Parliament in November 1763 Wilkes was charged with having produced 'a most scandalous obscene and impious libel. A great profanation of many parts of the Holy Scripture; and a most wicked and blasphemous attempt to ridicule and vilify the Person of Our Blessed Saviour.'[12]

The Order of the Day for the House of Lords on 17 November was consideration of the essay. Witnesses against Wilkes were Lord Stanhope, James Watson and seven others. Stanhope produced a letter taken from Mr Keasley, a printer of Ludgate Street, which was attested under oath to have been written by Wilkes, and in which were instructions to the printer to produce twelve copies of the *Essay on Woman*. Bishop Warburton started proceedings by claiming that he had been libelled by the poem, but the Earl of Sandwich was the star of the show. He had a copy of the poem, and he proceeded to read it out loud to the assembled peers. The *Journal of the House of Lords* states drily, 'And some passages of the paper being read', which does not convey the chaos and hilarity gleefully described by Horace Walpole. He wrote that the pious Lord Lyttleton 'groaned in spirit and begged they might hear no more, but his fellow peers cried "Go on, go on" and urged Sandwich to continue.'[13]

Bishop Warburton declared that he had not written one word of what was being read out, and when the peers laughed at him, he began to rage at them that the fiends of Hell would not keep company with Wilkes, and then apologised to Satan for the comparison.[14] Sandwich produced his witnesses to show that Wilkes was the author of the essay, but Lord Mansfield intervened, pointing out that any criminal had the right to be heard. Wilkes was sent for, and the session adjourned until he could be present.[15]

Wilkes was thunderstruck at the proceedings in the House of Lords, and surprised that it was Sandwich who accused him. He said that Sandwich's conduct was not considered sufficiently moral to make him a champion in such cases.[16] Sandwich was unpopular with the London crowd, and Wilkes was a hero. At a performance of *The Beggar's Opera* when the hero Macheath declared 'That Jemmy Twitcher should peach me, I own surprised me', the whole audience burst into applause, identifying Macheath with Wilkes, and Jemmy Twitcher with Sandwich. The nickname Jemmy Twitcher was to stick to Sandwich for the rest of his life.[17]

There was a problem in Sandwich's charges against Wilkes, as the *Essay on Woman* had been printed for private circulation and therefore did not fall foul of libel or obscenity laws. It could only be prosecuted if it had been published for general sale. Unfortunately, Wilkes had advertised it as a joke in the *Public Advertiser* of 10 May 1763.[18]

The furore over the *Essay on Woman* was really a by-product of the political enmity between Sandwich and Wilkes. The real reason that Sandwich personally and Parliament as a whole wanted to break Wilkes's parliamentary privilege was the publication of the anti-government and anti-monarch *North Briton* 45. On 25 November 1763 the House of Commons discussed the journal, and resolved that it should be burned by the public hangman. The House of Lords agreed with this on the 29th, but debated whether or not parliamentary privilege extended to the written word. The Lords affirmed the decision of the Commons that it did not, but there were many who spoke up for the extension of parliamentary privilege to the written word, including Lords Temple, Grafton and Cornwallis, the Dukes of Portland and Devonshire, and the Bishop of Lichfield and Coventry. They claimed that if MPs could not write what they wanted for fear of prosecution this would be 'a parliament under perpetual terror of imprisonment, it would never be free, nor bold, nor honest . . .'[19]

North Briton 45 was burned by the public hangman on 3 December 1763. Parliamentary privilege had been removed from the written word. Wilkes now faced prosecution and possibly a charge of treason. He fought a duel in which he was injured and then fled to France, arriving in Paris on 28 December.[20]

The publicity surrounding the *Essay on Woman* and Wilkes's exposure of the Medmenham Friars resulted in tourists visiting the abbey. Dashwood stripped the chapel and the chapter house, and the Friars seem to have disbanded. But Dashwood had not given up his predilection for dressing up and secret societies.

Sex was obviously one of the preoccupations of the Friars of Medmenham. But this was a symptom of the age. During the eighteenth century sexual discourse became public discourse, at least for the wealthy literate men who could afford to buy books, pictures and prints, or had access to them. Painters began to show women's nipples, and there were literary descriptions of 'ideal breasts' (from the man's point of view).[21] Hogarth's series of prints *The Harlot's Progress* was issued in 1732. These not only showed woman as the victim, but also illustrated the dangers of promiscuity. Prints such as these were reasonably priced, but even cheaper and with a wider circulation were books, and it can be argued that the Friars and other clubs like them were feeding off a culture of obscenity current in the eighteenth century.

HELL-FIRE CLUBS AND DIRTY BOOKS

In the eighteenth century sex became a popular subject for writers and journalists attempting to make a living by their pen, and a growing number of sexually explicit books were published. Sex would sell, and authors knew there was a demand for it. Although much of what they wrote was clearly physically impossible, it fed on the imagination of the readers who wanted to experience and experiment for themselves – exactly as the hell-fire clubs did. Wagner notes that much of the sexual literature was also anti-religious, and was part of the trend towards atheism that characterised the Enlightenment. He points out that many works were in the form of 'confessions', and the clergy were often ridiculed in these books.[22] This is also true of the non-sexually explicit but enjoyable sexual romps of Henry Fielding's *Tom Jones* and Daniel Defoe's *Moll Flanders*. But these two books were the socially acceptable end of the novel; a gentleman could have them on open shelves in his library. Hidden away would be an underworld of books, a cabinet of sexual curiosities available only to his closest friends; a literary parallel of the closed membership of the Medmenham Friars. Gentlemen were often troubled by guilt about owning such collections. Pepys demonstrates this in his diary entry for 13 January 1668. When he came across a French novel *The School of Venus* at a bookseller's shop, his wife, who was French, translated some of it for him and he found it a 'bawdy, lewd book' and put it back on the shelf. However, he was unable to resist it, and eventually went back and purchased it in a plain binding, took it home, read it and then burned it.[23]

The School of Venus was translated into English in the early eighteenth century and remained in publication up to 1744, but by this time there were a number of home-grown sexually explicit books on the market. Some were in verse, such as *The Fifteen Plagues of a Maidenhood* published in 1707 and followed by fifteen other plagues, such as *The Plagues of a Wanton Wife* and *The Plagues of a Whore*. The earliest surviving English pornographic prose novel is *A Dialogue between a Married Lady and a Maid*, published in 1688, and taking as its model the Earl of Rochester's poems.[24]

Popular themes for pornographic books were girls' schools, nuns and flagellation. A link with Sir Francis Dashwood and the Friars comes in the anonymous *Secrets of the Convent*, which includes a woodcut of a Friar with a goblet, Sir Francis, toasting a naked goddess with another Friar (Paul Whitehead), looking on. Beneath the woodcut are the lines:

> Once on a Time, as Fame Reported,
> When Friar Paul St Francis Courted
> This Francis answered, your no Novice
> You well deserve the jewel office

> A place of trust your faith will suit
> You shall demand it of Lord Boot [Bute]
> Your Manner, Morals, Virtue, Grace
> Call loudly for a goodly place
> Success attend you, I'll be blunt
> My dearest brother here is c..t.[25]

It was not only Roman Catholics and Church of England clergymen who appeared in pornographic novels. The Quakers came in for sexual ridicule as well. Edmund Curll's *Post Office Intelligencer* of 1736 included 'letters' from a Quaker to his friend describing his copulation with his lover in biblical rhetoric. In 1739 the same publication described a conversation between a Quaker and his maid that ends in the comforts of copulation.[26]

In 1760 'Jolly Quaker' Obadiah Broadbum appeared in an anonymous novel *The Rule of Taste*. Obadiah sets out by coach for Bath accompanied by a 'lascivious old dog', a widow Honoria bent on satisfying her passions at Bath, and Miss Polly Witts, the virginal daughter of a rich London merchant. The Quaker bets the others a hundred guineas that Polly will lose her maidenhead by the end of the journey. But of course Polly is no virgin, already having been seduced by the author, who found out for himself that he was not her first lover:

> Well – the short and long of the story was this
> For mutual and deep was the dart
> I beg'd and she yielded to love's seducing kiss
> And Hymen made everything smart.[27]

Eventually the author and Polly marry, and become Quakers themselves.

There was much discussion of the female anatomy and female libido in novels and treatises, and 'girl on girl' sex was an extremely popular subject; that the textbooks on female anatomy were snapped up by the buying public may have been due to the fact that gentlemen rarely saw their wives naked and wanted to see the female form in more detail. But these books could stimulate the male and lead to masturbation, and there were many books published about this 'sin'. There were also handbooks on sexual techniques, and medical reference books on venereal disease. Perhaps the two most influential erotic books of the eighteenth century were *A Complete Set of Charts of the Coasts of Merryland*, which was a chart of female anatomy couched in nautical terms, and John Cleland's *Memoirs of a Woman of Pleasure*, known in its expurgated editions as *Fanny Hill*. This was published in 1749, but it appears to have been in circulation in manuscript before that date, as a club on the Fife coast of Scotland had access to it before publication. The same club also had a copy of *Merryland*, and the link between *Merryland*, *Fanny Hill* and Anstruther in Fife will be discussed later in this book. *Merryland* had been through ten editions by 1742.

The Memoirs of a Woman of Pleasure was to be denied the chance to go into multiple editions. When it was first published, Cleland, its printer and publisher were charged with producing an obscene book, and the novel was banned and remained banned until the twentieth century. This was a bitter blow for Cleland, who had written it in order to pay off his debts, so he went on to publish the expurgated edition, *Fanny Hill*. The *Memoirs* were full of explicit scenes of a sexual nature, narrated by the heroine, Fanny Hill, and it was one of a growing genre of fictional histories and biographies that were used as vehicles for descriptions of sex.

John Cleland (1709–89), its author, was born in Kingston upon Thames in Surrey, to a Scottish family. He was educated at Westminster School, and in 1728 was sent to Bombay to work for the East India Company. He returned to Britain in 1740, bringing the manuscript of the *Memoirs* with him. Cleland's father was a customs officer, and the language of the sea and customs and excise invades the text of Cleland's book. There is no doubt that Cleland makes Fanny Hill enjoy and participate in sex, receiving as much as she gives. But she was 'a woman of pleasure', a courtesan or harlot, who, like Hogarth's harlot, had come to London to make her fortune and had fallen in with the madam of a brothel. She experiences every conceivable sexual adventure, relating them all with gusto and in unblushing and forthright language.

Cleland and Wilkes were prosecuted after publication because, although censorship had been reinstated at the Restoration, in 1695 the Licensing Act that controlled censorship was allowed to lapse, and pre-publication censorship came to an end. Printing became a free market, with copyright confined to the publishers for twenty-one years after the death of the author. More publishers and book-sellers set up in business and the demand for books increased. However, pre-publication literary censorship was re-established partly as a result of the *Essay on Woman* in the late 1760s.

The sexually explicit books were written mainly for men, by men. In them women become objects to be bought and sold, playthings of the rich, or observed through curtains, as in *The School of Venus*. In these novels women are equated with sex rather than valued as individuals. It was a view of women manufactured and manipulated by men, and by the law. The law made married women their husbands' property, meaning they had no rights except through him. Spinsters and widows had independence, but were ridiculed. Respectable women were encouraged to marry, and to respect the body more than the mind. Too much education, it was felt, would spoil a woman for her future husband. Whether the wives of the men who read about Fanny Hill and women like her had the same sexual appetites as their husbands became a matter for debate, especially after the publication in 1716 of *The Ladies' Physical Directory*, which suggested that a woman's libido was slower to arouse than a man's.[28]

Women were prevented from breaking this mould by patriarchal authority that made rules to keep them in their place. At the same time men had no compunction about taking a mistress or pleasuring themselves in a brothel. Representatives of this patriarchy included members of the order of St Francis, the Medmenham Friars. They read pornographic novels for titillation and delight, and it is doubtful that they ever stopped to think about the role of women in these books. Perhaps they should not be blamed for this. They were the products of their age, living in a male-dominated society where the wealthy could buy what they wanted, and where women were turned into a commodity.

It was, perhaps, the obvious licentiousness of public men – the MPs, landowners, gentry and aristocrats – that made Methodism attractive to the middle classes and well-to-do tradesmen. It provided an antidote to the immorality and libertinism of those who might be described as their betters, and an avenue to respectability and meeting with other God-fearing and respectable people who believed in hard work and the sanctity of marriage. These people provided the backbone for the Societies for the Suppression of Vice, which in 1787 widened their remit to include the prosecution and banning of obscene literature. Their petitions to Parliament led to a Royal Proclamation to magistrates urging them to suppress all loose and licentious prints, books and publications that dispensed poison to the minds of the young and unwary. This was followed by the foundation of Proclamation Societies, which had the sole aim of searching out and prosecuting indecent books.

The growth in the eighteenth century of the middle section of society – professionals, industrialists or Nonconformist ministers, for example – meant a change in public attitudes to indecency; clearly, books such as *Merryland* or *The School of Venus* could no longer be tolerated, at least not in public. But who would have read these volumes anyway?

In the eighteenth century the reading public expanded, although, as Altick points out, some who could read chose not to do so.[29] The increase in those who could read was the result of wider access to education. Charity schools were set up for the lower orders, but the government was worried that educating the labouring class might lead to revolution, so the curriculum for these schools was usually restricted to learning to read the Bible, and learning the catechism by heart. However, these schools did at least give their pupils the ability to read other publications if they wanted. The middle class could send its sons to endowed grammar schools or Nonconformist academies, and the gentry either employed private tutors for their children or sent their sons away to public school and then to university.[30]

The middle class and the Wesleyan Methodists were the largest group of readers,[31] but they were the group least likely to buy 'dirty books', although they did buy novels such as Samuel Richardson's *Pamela* or Henry Fielding's *Joseph Andrews*. Moreover, the cost of books meant that they were not universally available. Quartos and folios cost 10–12s., octavos 5–6s., and small octavos 2s. 6d. The four-volume set of *Tristram Shandy* by Laurence Sterne cost 2s. 6d. per volume in paper wrappers. Bound novels cost 3s., or 2s. for unbound sheets.[32]

The average wage of a literate clerk was one pound a week, so buying books was a luxury most could not afford. The labouring class earned 4–6s. a week, so books were beyond their budget, but they may have been able to buy pamphlets, which cost between 6d. and 1s. 6d. depending on the number of pages, or chapbooks brought to the door by pedlars. It is important to remember that one book or pamphlet purchased could be read by many people, and read out loud to whole congregations.

On the whole, the purchase of sexually explicit novels was possible only for the very wealthy who could hide them in their libraries and clubs. The Medmenham Friars, for example, were alleged to have a library of occult and pornographic material.[33]

'Dirty books', like membership of a hell-fire club, were the prerogative of the upper classes, those in authority who sat in Parliament and made and administered the country's laws. As Wilkes remarked of the Earl of Sandwich, there was a certain hypocrisy about this, and especially about Sandwich's attitudes, as his morals were suspect. But Sandwich's actions may have been caused by personal spite and political anger at Wilkes, rather than shock at the contents of the poem. Ultimately, however, the prosecution and subsequent publicity destroyed the secrecy of the Medmenham Friars, and eventually caused them to disband.

CHAPTER 7

Public Men and Private Vices

Most of the Friars of Medmenham held public offices as peers of the realm or Members of Parliament. This was usual for the members of hell-fire clubs, and the other secret clubs of the eighteenth century. The Earl of Rochester and the Duke of Wharton and their cronies were courtiers, military or naval officers. The members of the Irish Hell-Fire Club were members of the Irish Parliament and when scandal hit in the eighteenth century politicians were not forced to resign. They might have been held up to ridicule for a time, but provided that they were on the same side as the government they kept their posts.

As well as taking part in national politics, they were also in the local public domain as magistrates, militia officers, church patrons, lords of the manor, landlords, and employers of estate workers and domestic servants by the dozen. These multi-faceted roles were expected of the eighteenth-century gentleman and landowner, and were part of their personal context in national and local life.

A closer examination of the lives of four Friars might help us to understand them better as men and as figureheads of society, and explain their involvement with clubs that met in secret. The four men to be discussed are Sir Francis Dashwood, founder of the Friars, magistrate, militia officer and MP; George Bubb Dodington, an eccentric, MP, patron of the arts, one of Dashwood's closest friends, and almost certainly a Medmenham Friar; the Earl of Sandwich, peer of the realm, first Lord of the Admiralty, owner of Hinchingbrooke House in Huntingdonshire, Friar and libertine; and lastly John Wilkes, MP, journalist, Friar and libertine.

SIR FRANCIS DASHWOOD (1708–81) AND WEST WYCOMBE PARK

So far we have seen Sir Francis on the Grand Tour, and as founder member of the Divan and Dilettanti clubs and the Friars of Medmenham. His own estate at West Wycombe in Buckinghamshire was not far from Medmenham, and his remodelling of the house, garden and park there reveal more of his personality and the influence the Grand Tour had over him. West Wycombe, although now in the hands of the National Trust, is still the home of the Dashwood family.

The Dashwood family did not start out as landed gentry, but as City of London merchants, members of the East India Company importing silk from Turkey and India and porcelain from China. Sir Francis's father, another Francis, was made a baronet and purchased the country estate at West Wycombe in 1698.[1]

This part of Dashwood's background is well known, but it is less well known that some of his money came from slavery, as he was a member of the Royal African Company. The Royal African Company had two branches of trade: the purchase of gold and ivory for England, and the purchase of slaves in Africa for the West Indian plantations. The company's original shareholders included the Earl of Sandwich, the philosopher John Locke, Sir Francis Dashwood senior, and Sir Samuel Dashwood, his brother. All were on the Court of Assistants that provided goods for export to Africa. Robert Vansittart, the father of three Medmenham Friars, was also a member of the Court of Assistants.[2] The involvement of the Dashwoods and the Vansittarts in the Royal African Company was common knowledge in eighteenth-century London; guidebooks to the capital listed Royal Africa House as a place to see, and often listed the company's directors.[3]

Dashwood's father married four times. Sir Francis was the son of the second marriage, to Lady Mary Fane, while his half-brother, another Friar, was the son of the third wife, Mary King. John Dashwood-King was eventually to inherit West Wycombe. Sir Francis Junior was educated at Eton, and on leaving set off on the Grand Tour.[4]

As the second generation of a landed family whose background was in the City, he was one of a growing breed of gentry who had come from the ranks of finance and trade. They were a newly rich group, eager to rise up the social ladder and join the ranks of the squires and gentry with the aim of acquiring a peerage.

Land rather than the money they had earned through trade gave them status, but the difference between them and the old county elite was that they had purchased their land rather than inheriting it. However, once the estate was purchased they set up an inheritance system through entails that passed it through a sequence of male heirs. If the surname of the next male heir was different to that of the founding family, a condition of inheritance was to take the family name. This accounts for the many hyphenations to be found in the surnames of aristocratic and gentry families today.

Once the country estate had been purchased, the *nouveaux riches* had to become accepted into county society. But, as in the case of the Dashwoods, a fortune helped to facilitate this: Sir Francis junior's mother was a daughter of an earl (Westmorland). The upper echelons of eighteenth-century English society were probably more fluid than its middle and lower ranks. The membership of the Friars illustrates this, as it included dukes, earls, new wealth and johnny-come-latelies such as John Wilkes.[5] The families of Wilkes and Whitehead were tradesmen, and although Wilkes was to marry into money, they had to define their social status for themselves; becoming part of the network around the Friars helped them in this. With land came responsibility. The gentry provided the back-bone of the justices of the peace, and were the patrons of the parish church, its appointing incumbents. Benign gentry provided almshouses for the poor, and their estates gave work to labourers and land for tenant farmers. Their consumer demands stimulated manufacturing industry and overseas trade. It could be argued that without them society could not have flourished. They put the country's laws into action, provided manpower to defend it, and represented constituents in Parliament. However, these roles were part of their public face.

On his return from his Grand Tour, Sir Francis entered Parliament in 1741 as MP for New Romney, where he succeeded his brother-in-law, Sir Robert Austin.[6] In opposition he taunted Sir Robert Walpole and the Whigs at every opportunity, and through this earned the reputation of supporting the Jacobite court in exile. This assumption was reinforced by a speech he made in 1744 against sending a loyal address to the King when a French invasion threatened. Sir William Young who replied to the speech claimed, 'It had the most pronounced Jacobite tendency of any speech that was ever pronounced in Parliament.'[7] Dashwood was forced to jokingly deny any connection to the Jacobites when a resolution on the army was passed from the Lords to the House of Commons by the Duke of Marlborough, and Dashwood opened the debate on it by 'much disclaiming of Jacobitism'.[8]

On 13 May 1751 Dashwood spoke against a bill to create a Regency while George II was out of the country. Walpole described him at this time as 'a man of sense, without eloquence; and of honour without good humour; naturally inclined to adventures'.[9] Later, he saw him as cultivating 'a roughness of speech, affecting to know no more than he learnt from unadorned understanding'.[10]

Walpole's comments show that Dashwood, unlike some of his contemporary MPs, was an active attender at the House of Commons; and a regular speaker, who was not afraid to champion unpopular causes. In February 1757 he stood up to defend Admiral Byng who was under court-martial for cowardice after the loss of Minorca. When sentence of death was passed on Byng, Dashwood moved that mercy should be extended to him, a man, he added, to whom he felt personal animosity but in whom he could see no wilful error.[11] Dashwood worked hard to save Byng, to no avail, but his spirited defence of the unfortunate admiral brought him firmly into the public eye.

Although he was in opposition for most of his political career he did have his moment in government in 1761 when he was returned as Member for Weymouth and Melcombe Regis, and entered the house for the government. In 1762 the Earl of Bute, the first minister, appointed him Chancellor of the Exchequer, a post for which he was totally unfitted. John Wilkes suggested that the new Chancellor, now Lord Le Despencer, could not settle a tavern bill without trouble.[12] Horace Walpole, who heard Dashwood's budget speech, described it as coarse and blunt with 'neither knowledge nor dignity, his style is naked, vulgar and irreverent to an assembly that expects to be informed . . . Men were puzzled to guess why he was chosen . . .'[13] What Dashwood proposed in his speech caused an uproar as he placed a tax on cider, the staple drink of the labouring classes and a staple product of much of rural England. Riots followed in the cider counties, and Dashwood lasted only a year as Chancellor. In 1763 he left to become the Keeper of the Great Wardrobe, a sinecure, and in 1766 he became one of the Postmasters-Generals, an office that he served conscientiously until his death in 1781.

He was an active politician. He proposed a bill for triennial parliaments instead of septennial, and a bill for the reduction of the peacetime army, and he presented the militia bill. He was on committees to repair and build roads and bridges and to establish turnpikes, draining and navigation, and he presented a bill that would set up public works for the relief of the poor. He does not seem to have gone out of his way to collect offices and preferment, but he was a long time in opposition. In 1747 he became part of Frederick, Prince of Wales's Cliveden set. The Prince was at odds with his Whiggish father and supported the Tories instead, especially 'right-wing Tories'.

Sir Francis Dashwood's public face at a national level was prominent. He was also a visible influence in his native county of Buckinghamshire where he was on the bench of justices and served as Lord-Lieutenant of the County from 1763 to his death in 1781; and he was a colonel in the Bucks Militia raised in 1759 during the Seven Years War. As a prominent member of the parish of West Wycombe he put the poor to work constructing a road from West Wycombe to Oxford. The chalk for this was dug from his estate, and the resulting caves gave him access to another secret place (the caves are now known as the Hell-Fire Caves).

He remodelled West Wycombe church. The architecture of the new church shows the influence of the Grand Tour, as it was built as a copy of a classical temple that Dashwood had seen at Palmyra. It has red porphyry columns, a black and white marble floor, a magnificent mahogany pulpit and lectern and armchairs that could be turned into steps. Instead of pews there were benches covered with green felt. One side of the church was for men and the other for women. Beneath the windows stood wine bins, and in the chancel a *Last Supper* probably painted by Giovanni Borgnis. The wooden font had four doves drinking from the basin, and a serpent on the pedestal reminiscent of the Dilettanti Society's seal. Was this representative of Dashwood's taste, honed by his travels, or was it, as Ronald Fuller asked in his book on Dashwood, a joke? He points out that the old church was in need of rebuilding, but the new church was more like a ballroom, and more to the glory of Dashwood than God.[14] It is a mixture of sacred and profane that sums up Sir Francis's character.

The crowning glory of the church was the large golden ball on top of the spire which may have been modelled on a globe seen by

Dashwood in Russia.[15] An amazed John Wilkes wrote to the Duke of Grafton that 'it is the best Globe Tavern I have ever seen'. When Wilkes published an account of West Wycombe church he described the globe as a convenient place for secrecy or a jolly singsong. What the parishioners thought of their new church is not recorded, but the village was at the bottom of the hill, and the church at the top, suggesting that Dashwood was more interested in display than in serving the villagers.

To the east of the church was an unusual hexagonal mausoleum open to the sky, built with money left to Dashwood by Bubb Dodington. The whole was designed to catch the traveller's eye on the road from London.[16] It was to this mausoleum that a great procession brought the heart of Paul Whitehead, 'ancient Paul' of the Medmenham Friars, to be interred in a marble urn. Was this intended to be the resting place of all the Friars? Although Medmenham was closed down after Wilkes's revelations, Sir Francis still had West Wycombe and his remodelling of the house, garden and park are further reminders, if all the theories about the gardens are correct, of Sir Francis's love of secrecy, intrigue and sexual metaphors.

SIR FRANCIS DASHWOOD AND WEST WYCOMBE HOUSE AND GARDEN

The original house at West Wycombe was a long rectangular building completed in 1707. Sir Francis started to remodel West Wycombe in 1740, but the work took over thirty years to complete. A number of architects were employed and various members of the Dilettanti Society submitted their ideas. The professionals involved with the building included Louis Jolivet who completed a survey of the house and garden in 1751, John Donowell who claimed he had planned the north and south fronts, and Nicholas Revett who worked on the structures in the gardens and the west portico.[17]

Perhaps none of the architects could realise what Sir Francis really wanted; but between them they managed to create a masterpiece based on classical temples and Palladian architecture. The first parts of the house to be completed were the north front and the east portico. The entrance portico completed in 1753 was modelled on the Temple of Bacchus at Smyrna, and was one of the first Greek revival buildings in England.[18]

The most stunning façade is the south side of the house, which is a two-storey colonnade of Corinthian columns at the top and Doric at the bottom, inspired by the façade of Saint-Sulpice in Paris.[19] The whole colonnade is a synthesis of classical and Palladian architecture and it transformed a relatively modest and oddly shaped house. Inside the colonnade were busts of Roman heads and copies of classical statues. This led into the Great Hall, which recalled the atrium of a Roman villa. The ceiling of the hall was copied from the Temple of Bal at Palmyra and its under-floor heating was based on the Roman hypocaust. Further busts stood on pedestals in the hall, some representing Medmenham Friars, while portraits of the Divan Club members hung in the Palmyra Room. Other rooms were opulently decorated with paintings based on classical mythology. Giuseppe Borgnis painted *The Power of Love* and *The Triumph of Bacchus and Ariadne* that hang in the Blue Drawing Room. He also painted a copy of Raphael's *Banquet of the Gods* and *Cupid and Psyche* for the Music Room.[20] The classical theme was continued in the park and gardens. West Wycombe park was created in 1735 but not completed until 1781. This was, therefore, undertaken by Sir Francis with the aim of leaving something to posterity, as he would never see the trees he planted grow to maturity. English gentlemen landscaping their grounds were doing this for the future as much as for their generation, creating something that would tell succeeding generations about their taste and beliefs.

Eighteenth-century parks and garden landscaping and architecture have been the subject of much speculation by architectural, garden and social historians. Will Pearson, using work by Richard Wheeler, the National Trust's historian, suggests that Dashwood set out to ridicule the garden at nearby Stowe. Stowe's Whig owner, Viscount Cobham, had a number of temples named for ancient and modern virtues in his grounds, thereby using his gardens to reinforce his view of morality. But where Cobham's garden had serious overtones, Pearson claims, Dashwood's garden was one of jokes of a 'carnal kind', imbuing Stowe's temples with a more earthy symbolism.[21] Stowe has been seen as a masculine garden, and West Wycombe as a feminine garden in a masculine world.[22]

The central lake at West Wycombe, artificially created by Sir Francis, is allegedly in the shape of a swan, 'to recall Leda and her fate'.[23] The lake was dotted with islands that could be reached by gondolas, protected by a full-scale model of a gunboat. The gardens and park have also been described as a 'ribald quest' based on the female form that reaches a centrepiece with the Temple of Venus completed in 1752. This was set on a conical mound with an opening beneath, allegedly representing the vagina.[24] The temple itself was a circular arrangement of Ionic columns. Maps of 1752 and 1767 show it at the southern edge of an enclosure containing statues, vases and figurines, flanked by a symmetrical triangular parterre and mirrored by a semicircular horseshoe-shaped clearing.[25] This has also been interpreted as representing female pudenda. John Wilkes obviously thought that the Temple of Venus represented the female form, as he described the oval entrance to the room constructed underneath it, sometimes known as Venus's Parlour, 'as the entrance by which we all come into the world, and the door is what some idle wits have called the Door of Life'.

In 2000–1 the National Monuments Record surveyed the park and garden. Their survey revealed that the Cascade was built at the same time as the Temple of Flora. The Cascade was on the eastern side of the lake, and included piles of rocks, basins and the reclining figure of Neptune. It was rebuilt in 1770 as a tiered waterfall with nymphs. The Temple of Apollo housed a statue of the Apollo Belvedere and an entablature inscribed in Latin 'Sacred to Liberty and Friendship'. Other temples included the Temple of Diana, the Temple of Winds and the Temple of Flora.[26] The Temple of Flora was completed while the Friars were still operative, so it is possible that they had some influence on its design, and that some of them used it. The rest of the temples were later constructions.

Sir Francis added one more feature to his park that illustrated his own peculiar tastes. The chalk dug out for road-building had left him with a considerable complex of caves. These now became the entrance to the Underworld, which was crossed by the River Styx, a stream running through the caves. It was here, allegedly, that Sir Francis and the remaining Friars met to complete their rituals, orgies and Black Masses.[27]

Sir Francis also had an estate in Lincolnshire. Here he erected the Durston Pillar to guide travellers across a trackless heath. This was an inland lighthouse with a lamp, standing at the junction of Ermine Street and the track to Lincoln from Sleaford.[28] However, Sir Francis's private life was not totally concerned with secret societies and extra-marital activities. His relationship with his wife remained cordial. He seems to have been a devoted husband and nursed his wife tenderly through her last illness.[29]

George Bubb Dodington 1691/2–1762

Another public man with private vices was George Bubb Dodington. As an intimate friend of Sir Francis Dashwood, he was an obvious candidate to be a member of the Medmenham Friars. Bubb Dodington left Dashwood £500 in his will so that he could construct the hexagonal mausoleum at West Wycombe.

Bubb Dodington had a relatively humble beginning: he was born plain George Bubb, the son of an apothecary of Herefordshire.[30] The name Dodington and the fortune he was to inherit came from his maternal uncle who died in 1720. Dodington was a distinctive and well-known figure in eighteenth-century society. Short and over-weight, his stamina and the amount of food and drink he could consume were legendary. He deliberately dressed in an old-fashioned style to enhance his eccentricity and impress his country voters.[31]

He was educated, probably at the expense of his maternal rela-tions, at Winchester School and Exeter College, Oxford, moving from there in 1711 to enter Lincoln's Inn, but leaving almost imme-diately to go on the Grand Tour. At this time he had not come into his fortune, and a common avenue of advancement for an impover-ished social climber such as Bubb Dodington was to enter Parliament. He was lucky in having influential relatives who had the borough of Winchelsea in their pocket. He served as MP for Winchelsea from 1714 to 1722, when he transferred to Bridgwater in Somerset, and in 1754 took over his own pocket borough of Weymouth and Melcombe Regis in Dorset.

Another source of income for the ambitious young man was to seek government employment overseas. Dodington was Britain's envoy to Spain from 1715 to 1717, but three years later his uncle died and Dodington inherited his fortune. This allowed him to devote his full attention to politics, indulge his rather capricious tastes, and buy land.

In 1725 he married Katherine Beaghan from Ireland. He always referred to her as Mrs D. and supported a train of her impoverished relatives, as well as providing for numerous kin of his own. His fortune enabled him to become a generous patron of the arts, for example of James Thomson, the poet of *The Seasons*, and Henry Fielding, who dedicated *Jonathan Wild* to him.[32] He purchased land by the River Thames at Hammersmith and built a fantastic house that he called La Trappe, perhaps after the French monastery. No expense was spared on this house and its furnishings, which abounded with gilts, tapestries, peacocks' feathers, a fireplace with a false stone idol, and ceilings painted by Servandoni.[33]

Sir Francis Dashwood was a frequent diner at La Trappe. Dodington's diary shows that from 1749 to 1762 they dined together almost very week, either at La Trappe or at Sir Francis's town house. Sometimes this was in exalted company and sometimes with other men associated with the Friars. For example, '21st January 1751 Monday the King's Birthday. Dined with us Marques de Mirepoix, General Wall, Monsieur d'Abrieu, Comte de Perron, Abbe de Grossa Testa, Monsieur de Lausandine, Marquess de Arge, Baron de St. Fiorent, Comte de Haslane, Duke of Queensberry, Lord Talbot, Sir Francis Dashwood and Mr Breton.'[34]

Dodington's diary suggests that he was a member of the Medmenham Friars, or at least a visitor to the abbey. According to the editors of the diary, the evidence for this can be found in the fact that days when other sources such as Wilkes's letters show that the Friars met are not mentioned in Dodington's diary, although he was otherwise punctilious about his daily entries.[35] He was definitely a visitor to West Wycombe. 'September 11th 1750 At Wycombe, Sir Francis told me what he had learned from Mr Boone.' From West Wycombe Dodington went on to Cliveden, and then 13 September is blank: to the diary editors, this 'strongly suggests a meeting of the Medmenham brotherhood', especially as the next entry for 14 September reads: 'Sir Francis and I returned to Wycombe by ten this morning.' On 3 June 1762, in a letter to the Mayor and Corporation recommending Sir Francis as their MP, he describes him as 'my best friend'.[36]

La Trappe was a place for political negotiations and Dodington's diary reveals what might be described as the underbelly of mid-eighteenth-century politics. In 1750 political power was in the hands of elderly men. George II was 67, Lord Hardwicke, the Chancellor, 60, and the Duke of Argyll, the king's adviser, 72. Frederick, Prince of Wales, was 43 and there was a new breed of politicians in their forties who formed an opposition party around him. He was in disagreement with his father about his policies and with the government over his allowance and the Civil List.[37]

Dodington wanted to include Dashwood in the Prince's party and succeeded in enticing him to Cliveden and introducing him to the Prince's set. Dodington's diary is the source of suspicions that Sir Francis may have flirted with the Jacobites. On 28 March 1751 Dodington records that Sir Francis had been in contact with the Earl of Westmorland (a suspected Jacobite) about forming a party to reduce the land tax the following year, and to vote to reduce the army. In May of that year Dodington, Sir Francis, Lord Trentham and General Oglethorpe, the last two known Jacobites, resolved to put forward a bill to pave Pall Mall. Dodington prepared a bill that went to the House on 13 May 1751. Dodington was not present at the time, and Sir Francis went out to La Trappe to tell him that Pitt had spoken against the bill.[38] Like Sir Francis, Dodington was involved in local politics as well, and in 1762 he became Lord-Lieutenant of Somerset.

Was Bubb Dodington just a chubby eccentric with a taste for the exotic, or a serious politician and public figure? His public life shows him to have been eminent in the 1740s and 1750s, a manipulator consulted by other politicians. About his private life he was more secretive than his companions. There is no record of sexual orgies at La Trappe, but he almost certainly belonged to the Medmenham Friars, and probably introduced members to the second generation of Friars, such as the Marquess of Queensberry.

JEMMY TWITCHER: THE FOURTH EARL OF SANDWICH (1718–92)

The third member of this quartet of public men with doubtful private lives is John Montagu, fourth Earl of Sandwich. As we have seen, after his education at Eton and Cambridge his Grand Tour took an unusual turn as he chartered a ship and sailed round the Mediterranean, visiting European classical sites as well as Turkey, Egypt and Palestine. This trip had a profound influence on him and led him to found the Divan Club and the Society of Dilettanti, along with Sir Francis Dashwood.

Sandwich's great-grandfather was the Earl of Rochester, and Sandwich seems to have inherited his disposition. He inherited the earldom of Sandwich at the age of ten from his grandfather, as his father was already dead. The family seat was Hinchingbrooke House in Huntingdonshire, but the family was impoverished, and after his Grand Tour it was imperative that Sandwich find some gainful employment, especially as there was a rift between him and his grandmother, who had a personal fortune and threatened to leave it to a friend rather than to her grandson. Sandwich's relationship with his relatives was generally strained, as he was also estranged from his mother, who eloped with Francis Seymour in 1730.[39]

Sandwich took his seat in the House of Lords in 1740, and his friendship with Sir Francis Dashwood and other members of the Divan and Dilettanti clubs naturally put him in opposition to Sir Robert Walpole. He was part of a group in the House of Lords headed by the Duke of Bedford. It was probably through Bedford that he met Charles Fane, the MP for Bedford's pocket borough of Tavistock in Devon, and his daughter Dorothy, whom Sandwich married in 1740. At this time, Britain was engaged in the War of Jenkins's Ear against Spain and France. Walpole fell in 1740 but no government post was available for Sandwich in the Pelham/ Newcastle administration, although he was gaining a reputation as an orator. In 1744 Newcastle was dismissed and the 'Broadbottom' administration took over – so called because it was a coalition of many different opposition groups. Unfortunately the name could also be applied to many of its supporters. This gave caricatures and cartoonists ample scope for ridicule.

The Broadbottoms appointed the Duke of Bedford as First Lord of the Admiralty, and Sandwich joined him as Second Lord. Sandwich's family had long associations with the Admiralty, so the post was one to which he was ideally suited and he set about his work with gusto, investigating the workings of the department. What he found was a service in need of reform, but reform had to wait until after 1745 and the Jacobite rebellion. Sandwich was no Jacobite. In 1745 he was commissioned as a captain in the regiment that Bedford had raised to protect the Hanoverians, later transferring as a colonel to the Duke of Manchester's Regiment.[40]

He replanned the dockyards and reorganised the supply system for the Royal Navy. He had previously been the British representative at the Conference of Breda where the government had told him to spin the proceedings out for as long as possible, which he did for two years. He had shown himself to be a competent administrator and a good diplomat, but politics is a fickle game. His investigations into the corruption surrounding supplies to the naval dockyards made him unpopular in certain quarters, and he was dismissed from the Admiralty. He remained out of public office until 1763: these years coincide with his membership of the Medmenham Friars.

He spent some of this time with his family in Huntingdonshire, but his wife was suffering from depression, and in 1755 the couple separated. Lady Sandwich was given a grace and favour apartment in Windsor Castle, where she lived with her sister, but her condition deteriorated and in 1767 she was declared insane and made a ward of court. She died in 1768.[41] How far her depression was due to her natural condition and how far it was brought about by Sandwich's neglect and libertine behaviour can no longer be ascertained. At least in public, Sandwich was a devoted family man.

Sandwich's finances were improving. In 1757 his grandmother died, and despite her threats she left her fortune to him.[42] But inactivity did not suit Sandwich: in order to get a post he was prepared to talk to the opposition, and in 1762 he was made Ambassador to Madrid. Before he left to take up his post the political scene changed, and to his great joy he got his old job at the Admiralty back. Here was a chance to continue with his reform, and to make sure that the demobilisation following the Treaty of Breda could proceed smoothly. It was at this time that he and Wilkes parted company. Wilkes was against the treaty, and in the House of

Commons he spoke against everything that Sandwich wanted to do at the Admiralty. The division culminated in Wilkes's arrest, and the affair of the *Essay on Woman*. The incident had no effect on Sandwich's public life, but a change of ministry did. In 1765 he was out of office again.

In 1770 Britain was once more at war with Spain, this time over the Falkland Islands. Sandwich was back at the Admiralty, and set about further reforms and ensuring that there was a constant stock-pile of timber to build more ships.[43] He was very much a 'hands on' First Lord who visited the dockyards frequently, and kept a close eye on appointments of ships' officers. It was Sandwich who had to see the navy through the American War of Independence. Not only did it have to fight its way across an Atlantic patrolled by French warships; it also had to keep the British troops supplied. Although the American colonies were lost, Sandwich's part in the war was honourable.

The opposition tried to place part of the blame for the loss on him but he could not be held responsible. The government, however, could, and when it fell on 15 March 1783, Sandwich was out of office again. In his term as First Lord he had set up a system of supplies and victualling which was to hold Britain in good stead during the Napoleonic wars.

He was, by 1783, in eighteenth-century terms, an elderly man, but he remained a politician. In his own county of Huntingdonshire he had great political influence, as he controlled the elections of MPs to the borough of Huntingdon. He was frequently at his country house, and it was there that some of the diverse elements of his private life emerged. Sandwich was not only a rake and a liber-tine but also a patron of the arts, of music and the theatre. He hired actors to put on performances at Hinchingbrooke and assembled choirs to perform oratorios. His own preferred instrument was the drums, but he also had a good voice and founded The Noblemen and Gentlemen's Catch Club, which met to sing rounds, and he was patron of the Concert of Ancient Music. Other private passions included yachting, fishing and cricket. (Cricket in the eighteenth century was a popular pursuit to gamble on, and punters would travel for miles to bet on all aspects of the matches.)

Gambling was one of Sandwich's private vices, and although he may not have played for high stakes, his was a class caught up in a culture of gambling. Cards, dice, and betting on billiard games were common at dinner parties, balls and country house visits, and Huntingdon boasted its own racecourse for further betting jaunts.

Women were Sandwich's other vice. As we have seen, he was a member of the Friars of Medmenham. He was also a founder member of the Divan Club and the Society of Dilettanti, which were, according to some commentators, private brothels, although there is no evidence for this. Like many other noblemen of his day, Sandwich kept mistresses. One of these was allegedly Fanny Murray.[44] But the love of his life was Martha Ray, a milliner's apprentice whom he met through his love of music. Sandwich had her voice professionally trained, and sent her to France to learn social graces so that she could accompany him into society. When she returned they lived openly as man and wife, which may have contributed to his wife's nervous breakdown. They had five children, and Sandwich's relationship with them was better than that with his legitimate family. However, despite his love for Martha, Sandwich, whether through lack of funds or stinginess, failed to make any financial provision for her. Seventeen years Sandwich's junior, she was likely to be left penniless after his death, so proposed to him that she should go on the stage and earn herself a nest egg. Sandwich was horrified, and his friends told him to give her an allowance. Lord Loudon pointed out that Sandwich had debauched her 'very young'. Nicholas Rodger, Sandwich's biographer, suggests that Sandwich was not faithful to Martha, and another biographer G. Martinelli suggests that Sandwich was having a liaison with Lady Mary Fitzgerald at the same time as living with Martha.[45]

Martha herself attracted the attention of an unbalanced young army officer, James Hackman, who fell hopelessly and obsessively in love with her and wanted to marry her. Whether she reciprocated is debatable and the letters that allegedly passed between them are probably fakes. But Hackman abandoned his army career and took holy orders in order to impress Martha with his good intentions. He stalked her for seven years, but in 1779 could stand it no longer. On 7 April of that year, as Martha stepped into a coach after a performance at Covent Garden, he shot her, and then tried to shoot himself. He was convicted of murder and condemned to death.

Sandwich was described by Fanny Burney as being tall, stout and weather-beaten, and not at all popular with his peers or the people.[46] Yet in his public life he had been a conscientious First Lord of the Admiralty, who understood the problems facing the navy. It was his treatment of John Wilkes that lost him public popularity and confidence and gave him the nickname 'Jemmy Twitcher'.

John Wilkes

John Wilkes was born in the City of London, where his father Israel was a distiller.[47] In this his origins mirror those of Dodington, but unlike Dodington he had no wealthy uncle to leave him a fortune. However, his maternal grandfather, a tanner, was relatively wealthy and may have paid for the Wilkes brothers' education at a private Nonconformist school in Hertford, and later with a private tutor, Matthew Leeson. The first, John Wilkes found stimulating; the second, he did not. In 1742 Wilkes was enrolled in Lincoln's Inn but, it seems, he may never have studied there as shortly afterwards he is recorded at the University of Leiden in the Netherlands.[48] (His family's Presbyterian background barred him from attending Oxford or Cambridge.)

Later he claimed that it was at Leiden that he acquired a taste for women. In effect this stay at Leiden had a liberating and lasting effect on Wilkes, much as the Grand Tour had on wealthier young men. But unlike them, on his return to England he had no income or country estate to go to: he had to find himself either an heiress or a job. Through his acquaintance with Matthew Leeson, Israel Wilkes, John's father, found him the former, and a marriage was arranged between him and Mary Mead, a wealthy woman with an estate in Buckinghamshire. A Presbyterian like the Wilkeses, she was ten years older than her husband.

Mary Mead has been badly treated by historians. She has been described as ugly by some, an imbecile or simple by others, or 'pitifully neurotic'.[49] Yet her portrait by Joshua Reynolds shows her to be a pleasant-looking modest woman, who was probably painfully shy rather than simple, as we know she was given to panic attacks if separated from her mother. At thirty she would have been a failure in the marriage stakes, an old maid and the subject of the pity of her peers. Wilkes had known Mary since his time with Matthew Leeson yet later he was to claim he had been dragged to the altar as a schoolboy to please his father, and that this was a 'sacrifice to Pluto' (the god of the underworld) rather than to Venus (the goddess of love).[50] In fact Wilkes was twenty-one years old at the time of the marriage, and on his engagement to Mary he claimed to be in love with her.

Wilkes's treatment of Mary shows him in a most unpleasant light, and his behaviour was noted by her mother's friends. After the birth of their daughter – another Mary, known as Polly – Mary's relations could no longer stand Wilkes's behaviour towards her and drew up a deed of separation. Wilkes got custody of Polly, to whom he was devoted. Soon after their marriage Mary's family had granted Wilkes ownership of Prebendal House in Aylesbury. His sole ownership made him Squire of Aylesbury, and eligible for public office.[51] So Israel Wilkes achieved one of his aims: his son had become a gentleman and was set for a glittering career in public places. None of this would have been possible without Mary's money and property, and the influence of her family. He used them in the same way as he used Sir Francis Dashwood and the Friars – as stepping-stones to other offices and people.

Once he became squire of Aylesbury, he quickly became elevated to public office. First he became a churchwarden, feoffee of the Aylesbury Free Grammar School, and justice of the peace.[52] In London he became a member of the Sublime Company of Beefsteaks dining club, and in 1758 a governor of the Foundling Hospital, which opened a branch in Aylesbury. Wilkes had networked assiduously and efficiently to get these posts. He was made treasurer of the Foundling Hospital in Aylesbury, but due to his financial dishonesty, the branch was forced to close. Cash describes this as 'not dishonest but irresponsible'.[53] But what could be more dishonest than to appropriate hospital funds for his own use? Cash suggests that embezzlement is too harsh a term, but this is exactly what it was, and it was thanks only to the collusion of his fellow governors at Aylesbury in protecting him from London auditors that he managed to get away with it. This was not the only occasion on which he embezzled other people's money: he was given money to buy regalia for the Medmenham Friars, and this too disappeared into his own account.

In 1750 Wilkes met and became friends with the profligate son of an archbishop, Thomas Potter. Potter introduced Wilkes to Dashwood and the Friars, and it was Potter who suggested to Wilkes that entering Parliament would be a good way to make a living. Wilkes lost an election at Aylesbury in 1754, but was soon offered the seat of Berwick-upon-Tweed in a by-election. He lost that election too and then petitioned Parliament, claiming he had lost because of corruption. The petition was thrown out, but he was eventually elected for Aylesbury in 1757, and set about building a new network of contacts. Election expenses had left Wilkes in debt. In order to alleviate this he audaciously asked Mary to forgo her £200 alimony, and when she refused, he sued her in the civil court of the King's Bench. Mary refused to come to court, so Wilkes moved for a writ of habeas corpus to force her to appear.[54] This was an act of cruelty, given her reclusive nature (she probably suffered from what we would call agoraphobia). However, Wilkes's machinations were stopped abruptly in court, when he came face to face with the presiding judge Lord Mansfield, the Lord Chief Justice. Mansfield made an order preventing Wilkes from seizing or molesting Mary, thereby preventing any future attempts to invoke habeas corpus. He ordered Wilkes to pay her alimony as usual.

When Wilkes entered Parliament in December 1757 he was seen as a rising star, but he disappointed the chamber as he was no orator. Anxious to get a lucrative post to support his lavish lifestyle, he began to insinuate himself into ministerial circles. One of the contacts he cultivated was his near neighbour in Buckinghamshire, Lord Temple of Stowe, who had founded the Bucks Militia in 1759. Wilkes fostered his Buckinghamshire circle assiduously and was a popular companion.

He chose to attack his political opponents through his pen, and it was issue 45 of his pro-war journal the *North Briton* that ultimately led to the *Essay on Woman* affair. It was during this period that Wilkes made the speech at the Court of Common Pleas that was to make his name a synonym for liberty.

In this speech, Wilkes claimed that deprived of his liberty he stood as a symbol of 'all middling and inferior set of people, who stand most in need of protection'.[55] The cry of 'Wilkes and Liberty' was taken up and he became immensely popular with the lower classes. The damage done by *North Briton* 45 and his other treasonable activities would not go away. Injured in a duel, he fled abroad in December 1763, and in November 1764 was stripped of his parliamentary privileges and declared an outlaw. He slunk back to London secretly in February 1768 and in March asked the King for a pardon. His petition was returned unopened. Nevertheless, he offered to stand as one of the MPs for the city of London, and was nominated. He lost, but immediately announced he would stand for Middlesex. Here, where the electorate included shopkeepers and others of the middle classes, he was elected, with great rejoicing in London and Aylesbury as well as in Middlesex.[56] But he was still an outlaw. On 20 April he appeared before the King's Bench and was taken into custody. The mob was on his side, but this did not stop the government excluding him from the House of Commons. In the ensuing riot several people were shot dead. Wilkes was finally released and his outlaw status reversed in April 1770.

He then entered the establishment as an alderman in the city of London, and later became Lord Mayor. He founded the Bill of Rights Society with the aim of reforming the franchise and extending it to all adult males. However, the society collapsed leaving him heavily in debt. Elderly by this time, and losing his powers, he withdrew to a cottage on the Isle of Wight. He died on 17 October 1797, having lived to see what liberty produced in France.

Wilkes was a famous, or perhaps infamous, man and his private life often intruded on his public persona. His libertine behaviour and his treatment of his wife did not go unnoticed, and neither did the liaisons and affairs he indulged in. In 1762 he had an affair with Catherine Smith, who threatened to take him to court when he refused her an allowance. On legal advice Wilkes responded by making her his servant at a wage of £20 a year. In December 1762 she bore him a son, Jack. Wilkes paid for his education and sent him into the East India Company. Catherine, however, he abandoned. In 1793 she wrote to Wilkes asking if she could meet him, as he was her only friend. Wilkes sent Benjamin Perren to her with a half-guinea, and eventually agreed to settle an allowance of two guineas a quarter on her. Other mistresses were Mrs Grosvenor, and a lady who later became the wife of John Barnard, a city merchant. Wilkes gave her a house and servants at Greenwich, but no monetary settlement. She took him to court over this, but it ended the relationship.

Five years after the end of their relationship Wilkes and Mrs Barnard were to meet again, and the affair rekindled. By this time John Barnard was a wealthy man and could provide for his wife, so it was an ideal situation for Wilkes. She continued to see him after his imprisonment, but when he was freed he became friendly with her husband, so friendly that in fact John Barnard altered his will, leaving Wilkes £8,000 and a valuable collection of art. Perhaps out of pique or perhaps out of vindictiveness, Mrs Barnard then confessed her affair to her husband. Barnard wrote to Wilkes that he could forgive him for what had happened before he met his wife, but not for what happened after their marriage. He felt cruelly injured and hoped Wilkes would agree to a duel. Wilkes replied protesting his innocence, and went to Barnard to explain. Barnard was ill, and his wife was shut up in a room, weeping and claiming that the ghost of her dead daughter was haunting her, and the ghost had told her to confess. Wilkes denied every aspect of what she had told her husband and claimed it was the false imaginings of a distempered imagination, but when Barnard offered to call his wife down to accuse Wilkes to his face, Wilkes refused and left.[57] By this time he had learned of the legacy in Barnard's will. This would disappear if Mrs Barnard continued to accuse him and so he put it about that she was mad. He sent a friend to reason with the Barnards, without success, and then tried a different tack. He claimed that Mrs Barnard had once been a courtesan, who had attempted to get money out of him. Barnard was not convinced by this argument and wrote a new will leaving his wife an annuity and the rest of his fortune to his nephew.

None of this shows Wilkes in a good light. Even during his affair with Mrs Barnard he was making advances to a Mrs Otto who, sensibly, rejected him. In 1778 he started a new affair with Maria, the estranged wife of a William Stafford. At the same time as this he was involved with Amelia Arnold, whom he kept in an establishment at Bath. Maria returned to her husband, and Amelia bore him a child,

Harriet. In 1784 he moved Harriet and Amelia to Kensington, visited them as often as possible and entertained his friends there, although he kept his legitimate daughter apart from this establishment.[58]

It is interesting to note that Wilkes declared that if Maria Stafford had been single he would have married her, but he had no such ideas about Amelia, who came from the lower classes. She was a farmer's daughter, and Wilkes's 'kept woman'. While having these affairs Wilkes continued to visit brothels and to take advantage of chance encounters with attractive women.

Although Wilkes was separated from his wife and, in theory, a free man, there is something distasteful about his attitude to women. He was using them for entertainment, but once they asked for some independence and assurance for the future in the form of a financial settlement he resisted. When his friends and fellow members of the Friars of Medmenham stopped being useful to him, he dropped them. His much-vaunted speech on liberty meant liberty for him, and his ideas on the reform of the electoral franchise, which would have enfranchised adult males, would not have put bread in the mouths of the poor.

CONCLUSION

These four public men had chequered private lives that had no effect on their public standing. All were part of the Parliament that made the laws and upheld the established Church. Yet all of them acted against accepted social and moral norms with impunity. Parliamentary privilege helped to protect them and had they been of lower social standing undoubtedly the community would have subjected them to 'rough music' (the public shaming of immorality by neighbours, who loaded the guilty parties on to a donkey and led them through the streets to the sound of clashing saucepans and raucous bellowing). It was status, power and, perhaps more importantly, wealth that enabled them to have the leisure time to join clubs and societies; to take days out of the working week and to change from everyday clothes into the uniform of the Friars of Medmenham.

CHAPTER 8

Scotland and the Fires of Hell

'February 8th 1703   Mr Davison told that when Mr Andrew was at Aberdeen there was a club of profligate men, great mockers, who sent some of their men to hear Mr Andrew preach and to mock and ridicule him.' This evidence comes from Robert Wodrow who was born in Glasgow in 1679. After studying theology at the University of Glasgow he became a minister of the Church of Scotland, and an avid antiquarian and commentator on the affairs of the day. He is an important source of information on the Church of Scotland's attitudes to scepticism, superstition and those who challenged the Church's teaching. He thought that the safest way to deal with such people, as well as those who called themselves deists, was to state that miracles could only be performed by God, and not by Man. He was assiduous in recording all instances of witchcraft and demonic possession he came across, and was present at the 1693 executions of the Paisley witches.[1]

In the early eighteenth century the Kirk was the arbiter and controller of Scotland's morals, as embodied in the *First Book of Discipline*. In the later part of the century the strictness of the Kirk came into conflict with the ideas of the Scottish Enlightenment, and compromises were necessary.

Like London, Edinburgh and Glasgow had their own corpus of wild young men who flouted convention, as well as a full complement of taverns and coffee-houses where they could meet. Robert

Chambers described a number of clubs in eighteenth- and nineteenth-century Edinburgh. These included the Spendthrift Club, so called because its members refused to spend more than 4d. a night, the Boar Club of young fashionable gentlemen, who met in the Shakespeare Tavern to grunt at each other, and the Hell-Fire Club, 'a terrible and infamous association of wild young men who met at the beginning of the last [eighteenth] century in various places in Edinburgh'. Chambers had spoken to the 'last worn out members of the club who believed they had made a pact with the Prince of Darkness'.

Chambers said that many years after this another hell-fire club emerged: a 'set of persons associated with the purpose of purchasing goods condemned by the Court of the Exchequer, who called themselves the Hell-Fire Club, with a president called the devil Henry Mackenzie, an attorney of the Court of the Exchequer who said in his younger days that he knew the Devil'.[2] The members of the second Hell-Fire Club were respectable professional men by day, with good family names to preserve. There is little evidence of these two clubs, apart from Chambers's writing after the event.

In 1726 it was reported that secret or 'atheistical' clubs met in Edinburgh and that these were connected to the London Hell-Fire Club, which had come to Scotland when its activities became noticed in England. However, instead of propagating their foul wickedness in Scotland they went mad and died.[3] There is no hard evidence for this but there is ample evidence for the existence of other clubs in Scotland that come close to the twenty-first-century idea of what a hell-fire club was. The Beggar's Benison, the Wig Club and other clubs were concerned with sex, drink and gambling. The first of these, the Beggar's Benison, had an unusual beginning in a small town in Fife, but it had widespread influence in the continent and beyond; the second club involved Scotland's aristocracy. Like their English counterparts Scottish clubs were the haunt of the well-to-do rather than workers, but unusually the Beggar's

Benison's origins were firmly in the middle class of Scottish society. Their activities involved a mixture of prurience and scientific inquiry: viewing, but not touching, naked females, mutual masturbation and improving lectures. How far this peculiar mixture was connected to Scottish society in the eighteenth century will be discussed, starting with Scotland on the eve of Union, the Society for the Reformation of Manners in Edinburgh, and that ubiquitous Englishman, Daniel Defoe.

SCOTLAND ON THE EVE OF UNION AND THE
SOCIETY FOR THE REFORMATION OF MANNERS

The two kingdoms of England and Scotland had been united under one Crown since James VI of Scotland became James I of England, but Scotland still retained an independent Parliament and its own legal system. A real union would happen only when Scotland was brought under the parliamentary system in Westminster, paid the same tolls and taxes as the English and Welsh and, in return, received the same trade advantages; and when it was defended by the army and the Royal Navy.

On the eve of the Union Scotland was still an agrarian country. Farming methods were 'largely feudal and traditional', leases were rare, strip or run-rig farming was common, and oats, bere and coarse barley were the primary crops.[4] Fishing and linen weaving were the subsidiary occupations of farmers and their families. Trade in the royal burghs was still regulated by trade guilds, and there were few products that could be exported. Travellers left descriptions of a subsistence economy, and a population living in squalor and poverty.[5] How far these accounts were biased – written by pro-Unionists who wanted to show Scotland in its worst possible light, as a backward and undeveloped country – is still a matter of debate. The reliance of the Scottish diet on oatmeal was mocked by English observers, but it was the only practicable way of feeding the whole population. Cereal crops, however are dependent on outside and natural events, and Scotland entered the eighteenth century after a series of subsistence crises.

The transformation of the economy and improvement in agriculture did eventually follow the Union, but whether these were the result of it is not clear. Wasteland was enclosed, small farms were amalgamated into larger holdings, and production increased, meaning that the farmers with smallholdings lost their land and were forced on to the labour market and had to move to the towns. In the early eighteenth century Edinburgh and Glasgow were the main urban centres, and as the west coast coal, iron and tobacco industries developed so Glasgow took economic predominance. The Union opened up some new trade opportunities for Scotland, but the imposition of new taxes, such as the Salt Tax, led to increased amounts of smuggling. On the saltpans and in the coal pits a feudal system survived to the end of the eighteenth century. Salters and colliers were bound for life to the salt or coal masters, and if they absconded they could be retrieved and punished. In some places their children were automatically bound to the same master. C.A. Whatley argues that this system was not as harsh as it seems, and that bound salters and colliers were better off than freemen as their employment was guaranteed. He implies that accounts of its deplorable effects are the result of English and left-wing labour historians misinterpreting the evidence.[6] However, it cannot be denied that such a system existed in eighteenth-century Scotland, and it needed two Acts of Parliament to get rid of it.[7]

Later in the century Scotland produced two of its most prominent thinkers, David Hume and Adam Smith. Hume believed that society must channel human nature into constructive directions through laws and customs that turn destructive impulses into actions for the benefit of society. Liberty was good, but it had to be controlled. Adam Smith looked for instinctive goodness. He promoted capitalism and the division of labour and created the climate that made it possible for the tobacco lords of Glasgow and the professional men and merchants of Edinburgh to take their rightful place in society.

Moral backsliders were brought before the Kirk Sessions, but by the beginning of the eighteenth century in the cities of Edinburgh and Glasgow it was felt that this was not enough. Like their English counterparts, aggrieved members of the middle section of society formed Societies for the Reformation of Manners, and it was in this climate that Daniel Defoe arrived in Scotland.

THE EDINBURGH SOCIETY FOR THE REFORMATION OF MANNERS

Defoe was sent to Scotland as a government 'spy' to promote the Union with England by talking to men with political influence, and to this end he joined the Edinburgh Society for the Reformation of Manners. The society had its first meeting on 10 September 1700, and it met every Thursday from then on.[8]

The roll of members shows that they were ministers, merchants, craftsmen, professional men, and members of the military based in Edinburgh Castle. They aimed to enforce the Acts by King and Parliament to restrain vice and immorality, and to encourage others to form similar societies. They differed from the English societies in that they were not a vigilante group but instead aimed to influence the way in which Edinburgh was governed by petitioning the city council to appoint a judge to punish those who were guilty of immorality, and to appoint men of good sense as constables. They wanted to nominate one man in each parish as a censor, who would pass on information about wrongdoers to the local minister. By 29 October 1700 they had identified a bailie who was favourable to their aims and would put these forward to the council.[9] In December they resolved to apply to the magistrates and council to publish a proclamation against drunkenness and profanity of the Lord's Day, and to confirm that they would put the laws into operation and make innkeepers liable for their guests.[10]

In London, the neighbourhood Societies for the Reformation of Manners informed magistrates about Sabbath-breakers and prostitutes, but did not dictate to them what they should do. The Edinburgh society saw itself much more as a policy maker for the regulation of morals. But they did go out at night to accompany the constables, to see for themselves what was happening on the streets, and note down immoralities. It was during their street ramblings that they discovered a problem that was related to the hell-fire clubs, and one that the London societies failed to articulate: what should be done about persons of quality seen to be guilty of immorality? The Edinburgh society decided that any such persons should be dealt with by the minister of the parish in which they resided, and if they persisted they should be prosecuted according to the law.[11] On their night-time perambulations they observed another feature familiar to early hell-fire clubs, that of 'brothering', or clubs where excessive drinking took place, augmented by bands of vagabond 'boys' who were much given to swearing, thieving and wildness. They also found there was much drinking out of hours.

> In the house of Mistress Paterson in Canongate Road south side, they found several persons drinking and one swore horribly, and one Madam Skeen was very drunk ... And also on Saturday night about 12 hours one Captain Newlands was found very drunk ... At 12 hours there were drinking in the house of Mrs Pascall, my Lord Colhill, and others who were drinking and swearing horrible oaths. They should be prosecuted.[12]

In December 1701 the society asked the magistrates to proclaim against irregular marriages and penny bridals, and in January 1702 they targeted coffee and chocolate houses to stop gaming and blasphemy there.[13]

The work of the society came to the notice of other towns, a corresponding branch was set up, and in 1706 they sent an account of the Scottish societies to London. By that time the minutes show that there were fewer weekly meetings, and the society was turning away from petitions to the town council in favour of addressing the Scottish Parliament. This was on the eve of the Union and in March 1706 Bailie Duncan reported that he had spoken to Mr Defoe, who was a member of the English societies for the reformation of morals and desired to be admitted as a member of the Edinburgh Society for the Reformation of Manners. He was admitted to the society on 3 April 1706 when he signed the rules and agreed to abide by them.[14] On 29 April he led the prayers that opened each meeting. In his *History of the Union* he claimed (after the event) that he recommended that the society pray for the Union; however, this does not appear in the minutes. His last attendance at the society was in November 1706 when the immorality of the students at the College of Edinburgh was discussed. Defoe then disappeared from the society minutes and his name is crossed through in the list of members. Charles Burch suggests that this was because Defoe found the actions of the society distasteful in prosecuting the poor and helpless while the rich went free.[15] It is more likely that Defoe's mission was over and he no longer needed the backing of the society to support the Union with England, which took place on 15 January 1707.

The Union with England was not the instant success that Unionists had hoped. It did not suddenly transform Scottish society. The Scots' staple diet was still based on oatmeal. It still remained a rural nation with most of the population living in the countryside.

Local government before and after the Union was in the hands of bailies and burgesses of burghs, and the Kirk. The Kirk governed morals through a hierarchy of courts. The lowest and most local was the Kirk Session, the next court was the Presbytery, and the higher courts were the Synod and the General Assembly. Kirk sessions met after the Sunday sermon, the Presbytery at two-weekly intervals, the Synod twice a year, and the General Assembly once a year. It was the Kirk Session that regulated local behaviour. It dealt only with offences that could be proved, and relied on witnesses to report them. These offences could include misdemeanours towards the Church such as Sabbath-breaking, blasphemy and swearing in public, and social offences such as drunkenness, quarrelling, fighting with neighbours, adultery, fornication and pregnancies outside wedlock. Offenders brought before the Kirk Session could be fined, but the most effective method the Church had of regulating society was through humiliation: publicly naming and shaming the offender. A fornicator had to appear before the Kirk Session three times in the first instance, and six for a relapse. Girls pregnant without marriage appeared once, but adulterers of either sex had to appear in sackcloth for twenty-six consecutive weeks. Usually they were placed on a raised stool in full view of the whole congregation. Prosecution relied on informers, and therefore the eyes and ears of gossips in town and village were always open for scandal that they could present to the Kirk.[16]

Perhaps it was the social control of the Kirk and the fear of humiliation which led a group of gentlemen and merchants in the East Neuk of Fife to form a secret society, known as the Beggar's Benison. Why this particular, isolated corner of the northern shore of the Firth of Forth should have hosted such a society is a matter for speculation. Perhaps similar clubs existed elsewhere in rural Scotland. We know about this one because its records have survived and ended up in the library of St Andrews University.

ANSTRUTHER AND THE EAST NEUK OF FIFE

The East Neuk of Fife is the far north-eastern corner of the north coast of the Firth of Forth. Today, it is a picturesque mixture of coastal fishing villages and inland estates. Villages such as Pittenweem are home to artists' colonies, and the neighbouring Anstruthers are holiday and tourist destinations. In the eighteenth century the East Neuk presented a totally different picture, the coastal area dominated by coal pits and saltpans. Fishing provided other employment, often in conjunction with the manufacture of linen, and farming. Perhaps most relevant to this story was East Neuk's merchant fleet which traded with Norway, Sweden and the Baltic, leading to the establishment of a customs house at Anstruther Easter. This brought in customs and excise officers to mix with the burgh's merchants, traders and local gentry. It was this mix that coalesced to form the Beggar's Benison club.

The Anstruther family were the chief landowners in the area, but they were also coal and salt masters. The chief exports from the port were grain, herrings and malt, and the chief imports timber, iron, flax and linseed.[17]

Scottish politics were volatile in the eighteenth century, and there was some support for the Jacobites in the area. On 18 April 1744, '6 casks of gunpowder and 6 pennants' were brought to the notice of the watch by the commander of HM Row Boat *Patience* as being part of the cargo of the *Margaret and Christian of Pittenweem* incoming from Bergen, destined for Mrs Elizabeth Rolland, Alexander Walker and Charles Wightman.[18]

Elizabeth Rolland née Crawford of Anstruther was a merchant. It was claimed that she drank the Pretender's health in 1745 and sent a barrel of gunpowder to him. Charles Wightman, another Anstruther merchant, was also a Jacobite. He went with his wife to visit the Pretender, entertained the rebels to drinks, and sent a man at arms to join them at his own expense. He collected excise duty and gave it to the rebels, and was well known as a disaffected person.

In all, there were nineteen reputed Jacobites in the Anstruther area, some of whom were also members of the Beggar's Benison.

One David Ruel, or Row, described as a gentleman, had joined the rebels in arms and gone into England with them. In 1746 he was a prisoner in Carlisle Castle and was later hanged. The Earl of Kellie, of Carnbee House, had fought with the Jacobites at Preston in 1715, and was at Culloden in 1746. He went into hiding, or was reported as 'lurking in or about his own house'. The whereabouts of his cousin Thomas Erskine of Kilrenny was not known, but the rest of the suspected Jacobites were 'at home' in May 1746.[19] Despite the number of influential Jacobites in and around Anstruther in 1715, the Anstruther Kirk Session had a day of prayer for the preservation of George I, and following the 1745 rebellion, the town council resolved to support George II.

Thus in the eighteenth century the East Neuk of Fife was a provincial society, but one with strong international trading links, and in which the culture of Scottish society combined with a number of personalities to create a remarkable and long-lived club. It was in its time a radical and shocking organisation, and instead of meeting behind the eighteenth-century equivalent of the bike shed, the Beggars met in Castle Dreel in Anstruther Wester.

THE BEGGAR'S BENISON

The first meeting of the Beggar's Benison was probably held in 1732, as that is the date on the club seal, but the rules and institutions were not drawn up until 1739. The club's minutes, which are a copy of the originals destroyed in the nineteenth century, imply that between 1732 and 1738 the club met twice a year on St Andrew's Day and Candlemas.

When the relics and records of the Beggar's Benison came to light in the nineteenth century they were thought to be too shocking for public viewing. Some were destroyed, but a privately printed version of the minute book appeared in 1892. The surviving records and the relics ended up in St Andrews University. (The 1892 publication has been reissued in a facsimile edition.)[20]

The name Beggar's Benison comes from a tale about James V who travelled about Scotland disguised as a bagpiper. When he reached Anstruther he could not get across the Dreel Burn, which was in full spate at the time, until a buxom lass arrived, hitched up her skirts and carried him across on her back. On the other side of the burn the King gave her the fare, and she gave him the Beggar's Benison, or blessing:

> May your purse never be toom [empty]
> And your horn [penis] aye in bloom.

An abbreviated version of this became the club's motto: 'May your prick and your purse never fail you'. It appears on one side of the club's medals, along with an obscene female figure with legs apart pointing to the genitals of a male figure. On the reverse side is the biblical exhortation 'Be Fruitful and Multiply', with figures of Adam and Eve, and a resting lion. Other club seals show a phallus and a bag.[21] The medals are a mixture of the sacred and profane, which is in keeping with other eighteenth-century clubs such as the Medmenham Friars.

A bizarre typescript in St Andrews University Library has a different and probably fictitious origin for the club. After James V had been carried across the burn he gave the 'tinker's lass' a golden crown. She was so pleased with this she gave him the Beggar's Benison. He then revealed who he was, went into Castle Dreel and formed a body of knights called the Knights of the Beggar's Benison.[22]

The aims and rules of the club were written down in 1739 and signed by all the members present.

The Code of Institution

Be it known to all mankind by this present Constitution, that we whose names are hereunto annexed have deliberated, considered, that as it can give offence to none, and as it is not inconsistent with the municipal Law in any part of His Britannic Majesty's Dominions, or the General Law of Nations, to assume to ourselves, and those duly Qualified and admitted as Companions, as a collective body, the name and designation of the most Ancient and Puissant Order of the Beggar's Benison and Merryland, have resolved, covenanted, and agreed, to support, maintain, and defend each other in the protection of our most delightful territories of Merryland, and to extend the Fair Trade by National and Legal Entries, and to take all methods for the encouragement of good people who shall deal therein, and to prevent as much as possible a preposterous and Contraband Trade too frequently practised, which, by fatal experience, tends to the discouragement, and destruction of our loving subjects, the inhabitants of said Colonies, and for promoting the laudable purposes above mentioned which are founded on principles of universal Benevolence, Charity, and Humanity. It is expressly Decreed that no Person, or Persons whatsoever shall be invested with the Knighthood aforesaid unless he or they are really, actually, and truly possessed of those Qualities and are of undoubted worth, untainted honour, integrity, and candour, and detesting litigiosity; neither shall any person be capable of being admitted that is convicted of cowardice, or that is even suspected of being capable of ingratitude, malice, defamation, or other infamous thing or action. And that the business of our Order and Society be carried on and conducted with the greater decency and regularity . . .

It then listed the officers of the club, starting with the Sovereign Guardian who would call and preside at meetings, a deputy and a recorder.

> As also we have agreed that the four Royal Burrows [*sic*] lying next to that of Anstruther Easter, viz Anstruther Wester, Crail, Pittenweem, Kilrenny, as well as Anstruther Easter from which all Diplomas to be issued for the future shall be Dated, shall send a Commissioner, being a Knight to advise with annually, concerning the State of the Order, and Representatives shall be chosen annually at the Grand Festival of St Andrew by the Sovereign and Knights then present. Done at the Beggar's Benison Chamber, Anstruther Easter, upon this 14th day of the Month known by the Vulgar by the name of September and in the year of the Order 5739 and in that of the Christian era 1739.[23]

The Code of Institution contains some interesting statements. First, it claims it will give offence to none and will operate within the law, although its activities could be seen to give offence to the sensibilities of many. Secondly, there is the formal title of the club that includes the reference to Merryland. *Merryland* was one of the most influential erotic books of the eighteenth century, and had been through many editions by 1739. It is a description of the female anatomy couched in nautical terms, and we must assume that someone in this remote corner of Fife owned a copy of this book. The mention of the contraband trade could refer to the smuggling that was rife on the Fife coast, but it could, in this context, refer to illicit or perverted sex. The statement that the club's business should be carried on with 'greater decency and regularity' may refer to some of the activities that it got up to prior to 1739, which were not entirely 'decent'.

Thirty-two members signed the Code. They came from Anstruther Easter and Wester, Crail, Pittenweem and Kilrenny. Ten were involved in local government and were bailies and burgesses of their respective burghs, two members were part of the Customs and Excise Service, and others were representatives of the local landowners, the Anstruthers and the Earls of Kellie. The majority were merchants, shipowners and businessmen. Andrew Johnstone, for example, owned or was involved in ten trading vessels plying between Anstruther, Scandinavia and the Baltic. He shared one of these vessels with the Jacobite Charles Wightman. [24]

The Beggar's Benison did not include all men of equal social status in the area as members. There were at least twenty-seven men of similar standing in the royal burghs of the East Neuk of Fife; six of these were involved in business ventures with Benison members but were not invited to join the club. Neither do they appear on the list compiled by Stevenson from known recruits and extant diplomas.[25] Was this because they were deemed untrustworthy, or because once they heard about the club's activities they felt too squeamish to join?

Even the initiation ceremony may have put them off. This is described in detail in the records. The initiate was taken to the club-room and told to prepare an erection, and a 'testing platter' was placed on a high stool in the centre of the room. Four puffs were sounded on 'the breath horn'; the initiate was then ushered into the room and told to place his genitals on the test platter under a white cloth. All the other members touched his penis with theirs, and this was followed by the test of masturbation. The initiate had to fill a 'horn spoonful' to gain entry to the club. If he succeeded, his health was drunk and he was given a diploma and a sash and told to read an amorous passage from the Song of Solomon from a bible owned by the club and decorated with phallic symbols.[26]

This was not the only time that masturbation took place: '1734 Lammas. 18 assembled and frigged upon the Test Platter. The

Platter filled at seven, each Knight at an average did not benevolent [give] a horn spoonful'; '1735 St Andrew's Day. 24 present. Every penis exhibited and compared by jury.'[27]

Although masturbation proved that the prick would not fail, it was a direct contradiction of the other part of the club's motto: 'Be fruitful and multiply'. Was the group masturbation being done in the cause of scientific inquiry or as a way of uniting the brotherhood, an indecent version of the Masonic handshake? Was it bravado or retarded adolescence, or the result of repression and the fear of public humiliation if they actually fornicated with women other than their wives?

In an article on modernity and the self in the history of sexuality, H. Cocks states that masturbation was part of the secrecy of libertine clubs. It symbolised rejection of convention and in the case of the Beggar's Benison a rejection of the Union. Cocks suggests that the Beggar's membership came from the marginalised in society: the second rank of the urban elite, smugglers and Jacobites.[28] While it is true there were Jacobites among the Beggars, their place in burgh society, where they held important public offices, shows that they were not of the second rank; in fact James MacNaughton, the Beggar's first Sovereign, was a customs officer and a prominent member of society in Fife and Edinburgh.

Another activity that took place in the early days of the club was the hiring of local girls to come in and strip naked for them, and lie on a bed for them to examine, but not touch. In 1734, 'One of feminine gender aged 17 hired for one sovereign, fat and well developed. She stepped in the closet nude and was allowed to come in with her face half covered. She spread wide upon a sheet, first before and then behind: every Knight passed in turn and surveyed the Secrets of Nature.'[29] Girls were hired to exhibit themselves on St Andrews Day from 1734 to 1737. This may have been a genuine attempt to find out about the female anatomy, described symbolically in *Merryland*.[30]

Not all the early meetings were peaceful. At Candlemas 1735, nineteen members assembled, but one forgetful Knight had to be escorted out as he touched the girl on display rather than confining himself to looking. On Candlemas 1736 the minutes stated: 'Not a very Agreeable Assembly, owing to several Knights turning insubordinate.'[31]

At later meetings, after the Code of Institution, lectures and essays were read on subjects such as 'The Male Organs of Generation' or 'The Art of Generation'. [32] Club dinners were enlivened by toasts, poems, songs and riddles, all heavily laced with *double entendres*; for example, in 'The Sentiment of the Pittenweem Friar', friction comes 'because we all want Joys to the front Dormitory; for after saying I believe in God, we end for the night with the Resurrection of the Flesh!' This was given as a toast by David Anstruther, at the annual banquet in 1743.[33] Or as these riddles show, 'Question. Why is a woman like a mathematician? Answer Because she wishes to know the longitude.' Question. Why is Fanny M. . . . . . like a Sergeant at Arms? Answer Because she takes unruly members.'[34]

The diploma issued to members carried on the nautical theme of *Merryland*, giving the new member access to all 'the Harbours, Creeks, Havens and Commodious Inlets upon the Coasts of our Extensive Territories'.[35] It is, in fact, a parody of the naval licence and may have been designed by John McNactane or MacNaughton. He was born in 1688 or 1690, probably the son of the chief of Dunderewe Castle on Loch Fyne. John matriculated at Glasgow University in 1716. He next appears in 1718 as a tide waiter for the customs, he was a land waiter from 1720 to 1728, then inspector in charge of the port of Anstruther until 1761, when he became the joint inspector of the Out Ports until his retirement in October 1765.[36] A pillar of the Church, he attended the General Assembly of the Church of Scotland.[37] MacNaughton came from a Jacobite family, but he made an effort to distance the Beggar's Benison from the Jacobites, and in June 1746 offered membership to the hero of Culloden, the Duke of Cumberland.[38] In 1752 an Edinburgh branch of the Beggar's opened, which MacNaughton joined when he moved to Springfield in Leith. Stevenson suggests that there was a convergence of the social status of Edinburgh members and the original members, with gentry and royalty joining the Edinburgh branch, including the Honourable Nathanial Curzon; allegedly, the Prince Regent became a member in 1783. There is good evidence that the balloonist Vincenzo Lunardi became a member in 1785.[39] A branch opened in Glasgow in about 1765, and in that year Beggar's meetings were reported in newspapers.

By the nineteenth century social attitudes were changing. Erotica was no longer acceptable, and the middle ranks of society wanted to parade their respectability, and began to be ashamed of their sexual urges. The Anstruther Beggar's Benison was shut down in 1836.

Compared to the Medmenham Friars, the Beggar's Benison was crude and unsophisticated. Mutual masturbation and voyeurism were far removed from the watermen's outfits and the ceremonies of the Divans, Dilettanti and Friars. Politics, however, was also absent from the Beggar's. The members were Whigs, Jacobites and Tories who co-habited without disagreement. Neither were the Beggars blasphemous, and their members even included elders and ministers of the Kirk. What they had in common with similar societies was an interest in pornographic literature, and it is on this subject that another mystery surrounds the club.

THE BEGGAR'S BENISON AND *FANNY HILL*

It is clear that either the Beggar's as a club or one of the members owned a copy of the erotic book *Merryland*, and on St Andrew's Day 1737 the proceedings state 'Fanny Hill was read.'[40]

This book would have been a natural choice for the club to possess but *Fanny Hill* was not published in 1737, and even when it was, ten years later, it appeared as *Memoirs of a Woman of Pleasure*. *Fanny Hill* was the expurgated version published in 1749. Did the Beggars have a manuscript version that was in circulation before publication, and if so how did they get hold of it? Or is there some other explanation for this enigmatic entry?

John Cleland did not return from India until 1740. When prosecuted for publishing an obscene book he claimed that he had been given the manuscript by a young nobleman, and had merely added to it. There is some speculation that the unknown nobleman was a scion of a Scottish noble house, and a member of the Beggar's Benison. This may have been Sir Charles Carmichael, but Epstein suggests that it was a brother of Sir William Hanbury Williams, British envoy to Poland. This brother was the same age as Cleland and had been at Oxford at the same time as Cleland's brother.[41] But Cleland was in India when his brother was at Oxford. Sir Charles himself was known for writing bawdy verses and was involved with the early editions of *The Foundling Hospital for Wit*. In fact Cleland named Sir Charles himself as author of *Fanny Hill*, in a letter he wrote to Andrew Stone, Cleland's contemporary at Westminster School.[42]

Others have played on Cleland's links with Scotland and the customs service. *Fanny Hill* contains nautical and trade references, and it is argued that Cleland got these from his father who became a customs officer after meeting with financial difficulties, but how far this position was a sinecure and whether he ever went to sea is unknown. Furthermore, he may never have discussed his work with his son, who went to India at the age of eighteen.

Cleland senior was involved with the Scottish customs and excise, but his main residences were in Kingston upon Thames where John was born, and Twickenham where he moved later. His Scottish connections were minimal, although he was thought to be a member of the Lanarkshire Clelands. However, there were Clelands in the East Neuk of Fife, and one Robert was a member of Beggar's Benison in 1739.[43] Another branch of the Clelands lived in Pittenweem, where George Cleland was one of the keepers of the Pittenweem Sea Box in 1738–39,[44] but there is no evidence that John Cleland ever had any connection with this branch of the family. On his return from India John Cleland lived with his mother in St James's Place, before being thrown in the Fleet Prison for debt, where he allegedly wrote the *Memoirs*.

The nautical and trade references could have been copied from *Merryland*. After all, Cleland would have known that this was a bestseller, and he wanted to make money. It is possible that the link with the Beggar's Benison was not in Scotland or the customs service at all, but in India and the East India Company. There were strong links between the East India Company and the East Neuk of Fife: for example, three of the sons of Alexander Duncan of Crail were in the East India Company service and would have been Cleland's contemporaries, as were Thomas Carstairs of Anstruther and David Cleland.[45]

The East India Company was a trading venture where middle-class families and the gentry could honourably send their sons, and they went out to India as part of a public school fraternity, a club-bable set of men. They were usually young, separated from their families and from polite society, and in India they often led a bored and under-employed existence. The wealthier Company members took high-class native women, *bibis*, as their mistresses, and until the 1790s, when the missionaries stopped it, the Company encouraged intermarriage with the local population.[46] For the majority of young men, marriage or a mistress was not affordable, so they had to resort to prostitutes or sexual fantasy. The East India Company was ripe for clubs such as the Beggar's Benison, and it is probable that they existed on the subcontinent. It is equally probable that manuscripts such as that of *Fanny Hill* were circulated amongst Company employees and one copy was brought back to Scotland. The language of the book could have been the language of the empire builder penetrating into 'unfamiliar territory'.[47]

There remains the mystery of why the Beggar's referred to *Fanny Hill* rather than *Memoirs of a Woman of Pleasure*, its first title. The original proceedings of the Beggar's Benison were destroyed, so this is probably a later interpolation by someone who was familiar with *Fanny Hill*. Was there another book or manuscript current at this time known as *Fanny Hill*? If in fact 'Fanny Hill' was a slang term for the female pudenda, then this provides a likely explanation.

The real origin of what was read by the Beggar's Benison may never be known. But what this account does show is that the Beggar's Benison had a collection of erotic literature which was read out loud at meetings; probably to produce the desired result on the test platter (in the cause of scientific inquiry, of course).

BEGGAR'S ABROAD

The Beggar's Benison spread from the East Neuk of Fife to Edinburgh and Glasgow and further afield. There is good evidence to suggest that there was a branch in Russia. In the eighteenth century Britain had good contacts with Russia, partly through the Anglo-Russian Commercial Treaty of 1766, brokered by the Earl of Sandwich, and the activities of the Russia Company that had been in existence since the sixteenth century. The chief imports from Russia were bar iron, flax, hemp and timber.[48] These were all commodities that passed through the port of Anstruther, so that the Beggar's Sovereign John MacNaughton, as a customs officer, would have been known to merchants and skippers trading with Russia.

Evidence for the existence of the Beggar's in Russia comes from a Beggar's Benison medal, with the motto 'Be fruitful and multiply' on it, in the Hermitage Museum and from a commonplace book belonging to Alleyne Fitzherbert (1753–1839) now in the Derbyshire County Record Office.[49] Fitzherbert was British Envoy

Extraordinary to the Court of Catherine the Great from 1783 to 1787, and Ambassador to Alexander I in 1801.[50] A section of his commonplace book contains descriptions of the formalities of the Beggar's in Russia, and links it to the Scottish founders with a copy of a letter from John MacNaughton confirming Sir William Porter as Viceroy of the Province of Merryland. The letter ends with the Benison. There is a section on the admission of 'Knights'[51] in which the Chancellor declares that the candidate for admission is 'an upright man', and is admitted to the Viceroy by the Usher of the Pink Rod. The Chancellor declares that the requisite trials have been made (presumably the same as those in Scotland). The candidate was then addressed by the King at Arms, told that the Order's word is Uprightness and given its sign. This resembles a sock, and is presumably meant to be an erect penis. The order of the procession and a seating plan for supper follow, with a note on the toasts to be used.[52]

The Beggar's in Russia was probably founded under the initiative of Sir William Porter, who was admitted to the Russia Company in 1770.

The Beggar's was just one of several clubs for the British abroad, founded as a way of combating homesickness and keeping compatriots together. In the 1690s there was the Most Drunken Synod in Russia, a group of British and German gentlemen given to drunken carousing. There was also a Bung College and a British Monastery active in the 1720s and 1750s respectively, while Cross speculates that the 'Lodge of the Perfect Woman' found in Moscow in 1771 was a 'Hell-Fire Club'.[53]

Sir Francis Dashwood visited Russia, but his diary and account of his travels do not mention that he came across any clubs. As he was a man of great intellectual curiosity, they would have been something he would have searched out.[54]

Expatriate Scotsmen in Sweden were members of the Royal Bachelors Club of Gothenburg, founded by Thomas Erskine so that

Scottish bachelors living in Gothenburg had somewhere to play billiards, which was banned in public places in Sweden.[55] There is a link between the East Neuk of Fife and the Erskines, as Erskine was the family name of the earls of Kellie, members of the Beggar's Benison, and in 1799 this Thomas Erskine inherited the earldom, returned to Scotland to live in Carnbea House, joined the Beggar's and became its sovereign. The inventory of the Kellie estate taken after Erskine died in 1828 shows that he also had trading links with the East India Company.[56]

The Beggar's Benison spread beyond the shores of Scotland and embraced a large number of influential members, and towards the end of the nineteenth century it became something that the young nobleman aspired to join. However, there was an alternative club for young Scottish gentlemen: the Wig Club.

SCOTLAND'S ELITE AND THE WIG CLUB

The Wig Club is often bracketed with the Beggar's Benison, partly because the relics and records of both are in St Andrews University Library. However, the Wig Club always had a different class of member – peers, gentry and military men – and from the start most of its members came from Edinburgh. It was founded in 1775 and given the wig from which it took its name by the Earl of Moray. The wig was allegedly made from the pubic hair of royal mistresses of monarchs from Charles II to George IV. Stevenson suggests that pubic hair was believed to have magical properties in some societies, and the wig would have had the same properties.[57] However, if the wig was really made of pubic hair, then it was probably more in the character of a trophy of sexual prowess.

In February 1781 a letter to the *Edinburgh Courant* claimed that the wig had originally been a gift from Cleopatra to Mark Antony, that it was made of hairs from the heads of her handmaidens and was supposed to have recuperating properties. The article claimed that it had adorned the heads of Roman emperors until Constantine gave it to the Pope, and Pope Clement X gave it to Charles II. Eventually it had become part of the regalia of the Stuarts in exile, and Prince Charles Edward had lost it on the field of Culloden in 1746, which is how it came into the Earl of Moray's possession.[58] The letter turned out to be a hoax. As well as the wig the club also possessed an indecent drinking glass in the shape of a penis and a ballot box with a naked man on it.[59]

The club's first meeting was held in the Fortune Tavern in Edinburgh on 6 March 1775. Dinner was charged at 2s. 6d. per head, which was expensive, and indicated the wealth and status of the members. Each member had to kiss the wig or put it on during toasts.[60] In an age when wigs could harbour all sorts of infestations this was a sure way of passing lice, ticks and other unpleasant creatures between the members.

The club's general meeting was held each year on 'St Pego's Day'.[61] New members were elected at the general meeting. The club's rules, drawn up in 1827, stated that the club was to consist of seventy members, every member to pay two guineas as an entry fee. Meetings were to be held on the second Wednesday of the month, as well as on the day immediately following the regular meetings of the Caledonian Hunt, and the Tuesday of race week in Edinburgh.[62]

What happened at these meetings apart from balloting for members, dinner and drinking is not clear. However, there is some indication that gambling may have been the club's main preoccupation as one of the club's elected officers was a croupier.

By 1827 members included the earls of Dalhousie, Fife, Haddington and Moray, the marquesses of Queensberry and Tweeddale, and a covey of lords, gentry, military men and lawyers.[63] The club faded out in the 1830s as its members grew older and more respectable, and the Victorian age was ushered in when certain standards were expected from social leaders.

KNIGHTS OF THE MORTAR AND THE CAPE

Scotland was no stranger to indecent clubs, and it is clear that street gangs of young gentlemen such as the English Ballers and Mohocks flourished in Edinburgh. For example, in 1609 'The Society and Company of Boys' roamed the streets after dark committing acts of terrorism. One of their leaders, John Forbes, was executed for murder, and his henchman John Gordon fled to Germany. At the same time as the 'Boys' the Knights of the Mortar were also present in the streets of Edinburgh. They were a band of aggressive young men whose emblem, the mortar, represented the slang term for the vagina, while the pestle was the penis.[64]

A later club, the Knights of the Cape, was founded in 1764 and had some similarity to the Beggar's Benison. It had rules and regulations, diplomas signed by a sovereign were issued to members, and it had a processional mace. Its aims were to pass evenings socially in conversation and song washed down by beer and porter. Gaming was prohibited. Each member was known as a 'cape' and given a nickname. These included a John Cleland whose cape name was 'Cat-Hole'.[65] Another, John Lesley, was known as 'Disappointment', and other names surely indicate the members' situation or nature. Most members were clerks and professional men, although they included the comedian Thomas Lancashire. When one member, William Brodie, was hanged on 1 October 1788 for robbing an excise officer, his name was crossed through in the sederunt book and a gallows was drawn in the margin.[66] The ceremonial cape was made of red velvet and by 1770 the club regalia included a pendant medal and a crown. In their rituals the Sovereign carried two pokers, one large and one small. At the initiation ceremony the initiate took the larger one in his left hand, placed his hand on his heart and took the oath before the other knight, uncovered:

> I swear devoutly by this light
> To be a true and faithful knight
> With all my might, both day and night
> So help me poker.

He then kissed the large poker and the Sovereign intoned 'Concordia, Fraternitas, Decus' (harmony, brotherhood, honour), struck the initiate on the forehead and gave him his medal. The new knight then confessed to some adventure or misdeed. All members were sworn to secrecy.[67]

In 1773 one David Fleming established a Cape House in South Carolina, and there was a proposal for an English branch. Already there was a large Glasgow branch with eighty-eight members.[68] The Edinburgh club lasted until 1841 when the last four members handed in their records, documents and regalia to the Scottish Society of Antiquaries. McElroy suggests that the Cape Club rituals were a burlesque of those of the Masons.

There were other drinking clubs in Edinburgh and the Scottish provinces, such as the Whin Bush, the Club of Clydeside Gentlemen, the Sweating Club, the Ruffian Club and the Court of Equity, which McElroy suspects had similarities to the Medmenham Friars, but he does not provide any evidence for this suspicion. Robert Burns was the perpetual president of the Court of Equity, and the Court's favourite hero was Milton's Satan.[69] There were numerous other gentlemen's clubs in Scotland, and it was through these that many of the philosophical and practical treatises of the Scottish Enlightenment emerged.

All of these clubs were for men, although, as in the Medmenham Friars, women might be admitted as sexual partners, for exhibitions and as servants to cook the clubs' dinners. There were, however, some Scottish clubs for women.

THE JEZEBELS AND WOMEN'S CLUBS IN SCOTLAND

While some of the Scottish women's clubs mirrored those of their male counterparts, others had intellectual origins: The Fair Assembly for example, or The Fair Intellectuals' Club, founded in 1717 by three young women. This club had fifteen to twenty members, and its aim was to refute criticisms of women's intelligence made by men, to promote women's education, and to prevent the exploitation of women. As this was a controversial subject at the time, they met in secret.[70]

One of the ways in which women were exploited was through prostitution. All the members of the Jezebel Club were prostitutes. Stevenson suggests that the club was a fantasy created by a journalist, William Creech, for male titillation.[71] It is true that comical names have been given to the members, such as Lydia Harridan or Mrs Slammakin, but the descriptions of the meetings and the concerns of the club suggest to me that it may have been a prostitutes' co-operative which Creech, as a journalist, had been allowed to observe and that he had simply added false names to make the account more entertaining.[72] Proceedings of the meetings appear to involve an effort by the prostitutes to make their profession more acceptable to polite society. For example, a gala meeting held on a Sunday after evening service was used to discuss important business. Supper would not be on the table until after midnight so as to avoid the censure of the scrupulous for breaking the Sabbath, and no screaming would be permitted until the tenth bumper. Proposals put before the meeting included a suggestion to preserve friendly intercourse with a number of men's clubs. Letters of complaint were read out from parents and guardians about the corruption of youth; after a discussion it was decided that the fault lay at home and not with the club, but that club members should be careful to inculcate good manners in any young men they met. There was a proposal for the encouragement of circulating libraries, and schemes were put forward to defeat a proposal to build a new Bridewell, 'so shocking to female delicacy'. It was suggested that members who were intimate with MPs should persuade them to oppose this.

The route that evening walkers should take was detailed. For members with an established clientele the recommended route was from the Luckenbooth to the further end of the New North Bridge and along Princes Street. 'Mendicant' members, that is those plying for casual trade, were asked to keep to the 'low grounds' of Cowgate, Grassmarket and Blackfriars Wynd. They were also asked to modify their behaviour as several respectable inhabitants had complained that they could not visit the area with their wives and daughters without being blasted with gin and obscenity.

The club noted requests for patronage it had received from discharged footmen who wanted to set up as dancing masters, and the meeting decided that barbers should be taught how to enter a house with decorum and how to lead a conversation with their clients. The proceedings ended with a duet by Ned Hopeful and Bet Bouncer. Lydia Harridan was in the chair.[73]

All of this may have been a figment of Creech's imagination and journalistic flair, but it does illustrate some of the concerns of a prostitute trying to ply her trade in a way that was not offensive. She had to avoid upsetting potential clients and the public, and the club attempted to promote good behaviour on the streets. It also seems that the Jezebel Club was trying to preserve a monopoly for certain parts of the city. Creech may have been writing 'tongue in cheek', but I think he was aware of the problems faced by Edinburgh's prostitutes and this was a way of drawing attention to them. This is further illustrated by another piece he wrote dated 15 September 1783, describing a doctor's visit to a young female (a prostitute) dying of a disease. In a box by her bed were verses she wanted on her gravestone:

Covered with guilt, infection, debt and want
My home a brothel, and the street my haunt
For seven long years of infamy I pined
And fondled, balled and preyed upon mankind,
Till the full course of sin and vice gone through
My shattered fabric fail'd at twenty-two.[74]

At least Creech treated the prostitutes with some dignity. The attitudes of Edinburgh's gentlemen about town is perhaps more accurately displayed in *Ranger's Impartial List of the Ladies of Pleasure in Edinburgh* published in 1775. This lists prostitutes, where they could be found and their qualities. It describes the women in the terms a dealer would use to describe horses for sale, or cattle at market. For example, 'Miss Watt at Miss Adams, 21 years, middle size, light brown hair, good teeth but rather surly, especially after drink, a mistress of her profession.' Or, 'Miss Bruce at Miss Walkers 20 years, rather short, fair hair, good teeth, eyes and skin and good natured, but not a bad pennyworth for any gentleman.'[75]

Of course Edinburgh was not alone in publishing such lists. There were similar lists for London, such as Jack Harris's *List of Covent Garden Ladies* published in 1764, and undoubtedly gentlemen circulated information about the merit of certain brothels and prostitutes amongst themselves. Perhaps such lists shock the present-day reader, but they should not be taken out of the context of eighteenth-century society: where a married woman was her husband's property it is not surprising that prostitutes should be treated as cattle in a cattle market. It makes the Beggar's Benison's habit of hiring local girls in to strip for them seem almost civilised.

CONCLUSION

The Scottish clubs were not hell-fire clubs in the sense of being blasphemous or worshipping the Devil. But they were secret organisations, and in eighteenth-century Scotland secret societies were considered subversive. The Beggar's Benison could be seen as a cruder provincial version of the Medmenham Friars, and it should be remembered that the Beggar's pre-dates the Friars. It was probably not unique in eighteenth-century provincial Scotland, but it is the club that we know of, because its records and relics have survived. However, it is interesting that when the society of the East Neuk of Fife is examined in detail it appears that it was not so 'provincial' or isolated as it might seem and in fact had links to the Continent, to the Baltic and beyond.

The members of the Wig Club have more in common with the members of English clubs. They were upper-class gentlemen who lived on the rents from their estates (many Scottish noblemen exploited mineral resources such as coal on their estates – but that is another story). Apart from the hint of gaming there is no other indication in the Wig Club minutes of what they did at their meetings, but as their relics are overtly sexual, this would appear to be one of their main preoccupations. Perhaps we should not see this as prurience but as part of the world of scientific and social exploration of the Scottish Enlightenment.

CHAPTER 9

Beefsteaks, Demoniacs, Dalkey and Colonial America

JOURNEYS TO LONDON

A number of visitors to London in the late eighteenth century wrote down their impressions of the city. One of these, Monsieur Grosley from France, was in London in 1772, and another was William Hutton who visited London from Birmingham in 1785. Both described street life, and their descriptions show that little had changed since the Mohocks roamed the streets.

Grosley found London a sad and gloomy place. He noted that management of the police was in the hands of the justices. There were no troops on the streets at night; instead they were guarded 'by old men with a lanthorn and a pole, who cry the hour as the clock strikes, and who proclaim good or bad weather in the morning, and whom it is customary for young rakes to beat and use ill, when they come reeling from the taverns in the morning, where they have spent the night',[1] just as in the days of the Mohocks. Grosley suggested that the women of the town were more numerous than those of Paris, but did not give the magistrates any trouble, and he praised the liberty of the press shown by the publication of *North Briton* 45.[2]

Clubs, wrote Grosley, were part of the English character, made up of friends with interests forged in early life. Regular clubs met in coffee-houses and taverns on fixed days, when wine and beer were drunk and pipes of tobacco smoked. Some clubs were held in private houses: members to these usually had to be elected. One feature of English clubs was that 'Women could never gain admittance . . . but have private coteries of their own.' Grosley observed the members' custom of drinking each other's health in clubs, and suggested that it had its origin in asking the person whose health was being drunk to guard you while you drank.[3]

William Hutton went to London in 1785 because he was subpoenaed to attend the King's Bench. Like Grosley, he observed the 'girls of the town' who importuned passers-by. He wanted to believe that the many streetwalkers were destitute of protection, but decided that 'the principle [*sic*] cause is idleness. It is not the man they want, but the money, which they spend on gin.' On closer examination he saw that their clothes were in disrepair and those he spoke to were not natives of London.[4] This coincides with Hogarth's *Harlot's Progress*, Cleland's *Fanny Hill* and the ladies of pleasure described in Ranger's list for Edinburgh. At the Pantheon Hutton saw Lunardi's balloon, surrounded by 'beautiful ladies'.[5]

These are two of several descriptions of the condition of London's streets at the end of the eighteenth century, and show that the voluntary watch was still the main enforcer of law and order in the capital.

THE SUBLIME SOCIETY OF BEEFSTEAKS

The Beefsteaks was a patriotic society and, during the American War of Independence, extremely anti-American. The club's motto was 'Beef and Liberty', and beef became their symbol of England. This is illustrated in William Hogarth's painting of *The Gates of Calais*, and Hogarth was himself a founder member of the Beefsteaks. The society was founded in 1735 by John Rich, theatre manager and pantomimist. At first the membership was limited to twenty-four, and spaces were filled as they became available. John

Wilkes was elected to the society in 1754, and the Earl of Sandwich in 1761. More illustrious members included the Prince Regent, elected in 1785; the Duke of York, who joined in 1790; and William Gladstone, who became a member in 1864.[6]

The society soon acquired the paraphernalia of an eighteenth-century club, a hierarchy of officers, rules and uniforms. Early members wore a blue coat and buff waistcoat with brass buttons impressed with a gridiron used for grilling steaks, and the club motto. At first the club met in the Covent Garden Theatre. When it burned down they transferred to the Bedford Coffee House, until that too burned down and they ended up at the Lyceum in the Strand.[7] How far these conflagrations were due to the society's cooking exploits is not recorded, but they could have been a factor. The beefsteaks were placed on a gridiron over an open fire, and passed directly from the gridiron to the members. There would have been a great deal of fat spitting about. The steaks were accompanied by baked potatoes, Spanish onions raw and fried, beetroot and chopped shallots. The meal ended with toasted cheese and porter, port, punch and whisky toddies. Smoking was permitted after the dinner when the cook came round to collect the money for the dinners on a pewter plate. Edward Henderson, the society's cook for many years, retired in 1832 and the Song of the Day was dedicated to him.

The club's officers were the President of the Day, the Vice-President, the Bishop, the Recorder who kept the minutes and a 'boots', who was the equivalent of a public school 'fag', required to fetch and carry for the other members. The president had two hats to wear, a tricorn and a Beefeater hat, which had to be worn when putting resolutions to the club. His most important task was to perform the Song of the Day,[8] and music played an important part in the society's life, with members composing songs for special events and on the issues of the day.

The Club Song of the Day written by Theodorus Forrest

> No more shall Fame expand her wings
> To sound of heroes, states and kings;
> A nobler flight the Goddess takes
> To praise our British Beef in steaks,
> *A joyful theme for Britons free*
> *Happy in Beef and Liberty.*

The last two lines were the chorus and all members joined hands for the final chorus.[9] The 'Jubilee Song' is a hymn to the Enlightenment, and the lines about the expiry of priestcraft suggest that some members may have been atheists or deists. Debates within the society were not recorded, but it is probable that the religious as well as the political issues of the day were discussed. Like many of the other Beefsteak songs, the 'Jubilee Song' has a patriotic tone, as it declares that Britain and its beef are the best:

> In British breasts the Spirit sprung
> For Freedom's preservation,
> But British beef their sinews strung
> Who save this freeborn nation.

> When Reason loosed the shackled mind,
> And Priestcraft's might expired,
> Her Science her rude works refin'd
> Here learning's sons retired.
> 'Twas here Newton pierced the skies
> With bold unerring flight sir;
> 'Twas here the world saw Shakespeare rise,
> It's a wonder and delight sir.[10]

The current anti-American feeling was demonstrated in a song by C.W. Halkett, to be sung to the tune of 'Yankee Doodle', a verse of which is shown below:

> Yankee Doodle borrows cash,
> Yankee Doodle spends it,
> And then he snaps his fingers at
> The Jolly Flat [Britain] who lent it.
> Ask him when he means to pay,
> He shows no hesitation,
> But says he'll take the shortest way,
> And that's Revolution.[11]

Other songs were more light-hearted, such as 'The Toper's Apology', 'The Catalogue of All the Women' the song-writer had known, 'Laugh While You May' and a satire on history that foreshadowed *1066 and All That*.

> But Stephen here, at fearful risk,
> Fought Richard for his right,
> And freely shed at Bannockburn
> Their Royal Blood in Fight.
> Then Stephen, by a cunning plan,
> Got Richard in his power,
> And famed Wat Tyler, smothered him
> With onions in the Tower.

The author of this ditty was William Bolland, Esq.[12]

Was this society anything more than a dining club where men met to talk, sing and make wagers? The initiation ceremony suggests that they parodied the Masons. At the initiation the Recorder withdrew with the initiate and plied him with port and punch. He was then blindfolded and, accompanied by the Bishop in a mitre and another member with a sword of state, brought before the president to take the oath of allegiance. The rules of the society were read out to him and he was reminded of the Horatian motto:

> Let none beyond this threshold bear away
> What friend to friend in confidence may say.

In the oath he promised to attend the society regularly, vote impartially on resolutions, support its dignity, recognise its rules and promote its welfare: 'Beef and Liberty' would be his reward. He then kissed either the rulebook or a beef bone.[13] Although the initiate agreed to secrecy this was not a secret society as one of the rules allowed members to introduce guests on ordinary club nights.

The Beefsteaks earn a place on the periphery of a discussion of the hell-fire clubs, because of their association in the mid-eighteenth century with the Medmenham Friars. However, by the nineteenth century the membership had changed from the old Georgian rakes to politicians who used the club as a place where they could relax.

CRAZY CASTLE AND THE DEMONIACS

> There is a castle in the north
> Seated upon a swampy clay,
> At present but of little worth,
> In former times it had its day,
> This ancient castle is called Crazy . . .[14]

Crazy Castle is Skelton Castle in Cleveland, renamed 'Crazy' by its owner John Hall-Stevenson. It was here he collected together the local squires and gentry who were dubbed the Demoniacs.

John Hall-Stevenson (1718–85) was born John Hall, the son of an army colonel. He became the owner of Skelton Castle through his wife Ann Stevenson, and added her surname name to his own. He was educated at Jesus College, Cambridge, where he was a contemporary and friend of the novelist Laurence Sterne, who later became a member of the Demoniacs. Hall-Stevenson was a classical scholar, poet and eccentric hypochondriac who refused to leave his bed if the east wind was blowing. He was also a contemporary of the Medmenham Friars and an acquaintance of Sir Francis Dashwood. He visited the Friars in 1762, but wrote to a friend that he had left 'without believing anything miraculous in the Shrine of St Francis'.[15] Anyway, he did not need to lease a ruined abbey as he had a ruined castle of his own. In view of the scurrilous poem he wrote on Sir Francis, discussed in the chapter on the Friars, his member-ship may have been refused, or the poem may have been the result of Dashwood expelling John Wilkes from the Friars, as Hall-Stevenson idolised Wilkes, and supported him in his quarrel with the earls of Bute and Sandwich. He poured more scorn on Medmenham in the introduction to *Makarony Fables*, published in 1768.[16]

Skelton Castle stood on a wooded eminence above the River Tees, with a distant view of the sea. It was built in about 1140, was defended by a moat and outworks and possessed a ruined ivy-clad tower as well as habitable apartments. John Hall-Stevenson consid-ered remodelling it into an even more mysterious and ruined site, but the architect hired for this thought the site perfect as it was and refused to touch it.[17]

Hall-Stevenson's poem on the castle describes its walls as moul-dering, and the moat as full of 'appalling frogs . . . water rats, dead cats and dogs', the whole thing ready to tumble down. Surrounded by rooks

> That foul and darken all the sky,
> With wood the castle is surrounded,
> Except opening to a peak,
> Where the beholder stands confounded,
> At such a scene of mountains bleak.[18]

Sterne first visited the castle in 1741.[19] Other Demoniacs included neighbouring Yorkshire squires and clerics, and Andrew Irvine, a schoolmaster. They took on pseudonyms such as Panty/Pantagruel from Rabelais, alias Henry Lascelles; the Blackbird, who may have been Sterne; and Captain Shadow, or Don Pringello, who was the architect hired by Hall-Stevenson to remodel the castle.[20]

Apart from letters from Laurence Sterne to Hall-Stevenson in 1761 there is little evidence about the Demoniacs. Sterne asks Hall-Stevenson to send greetings to his fellow Demoniacs,[21] but it is not clear whether they referred to themselves by this title, or whether Sterne is using it in a general sense to refer to all those who met up at Skelton. In another letter he describes a quarrel with Panty, claiming that Panty had lost his temper with Sterne because he would not fall down and worship the brazen image of learning and eloquence that Panty had set up. 'I sat down upon his altar and whistled in the time of his divine service and kicked his incense pot to the Devil.' Jones alleges that Sterne had suggested it was the Benediction of St Paul that was being parodied.[22] But surely this is an assault on Panty/Lascelles's intellectual pretensions rather than a hint that blasphemy and black rituals were conducted at Crazy Castle.

So what did the Demoniacs do at Crazy Castle? The introduction to Hall-Stevenson's *Crazy Tales* (1765) describes them:

> Some fell to fiddling, some to fluting,
> Some to shooting, some to fishing,
> Others to pishing and disputing,
> Or to computing by vain wishing,

And on the evening, when they met
To think on't always does me good
There never was a jollier set.[23]

They probably sat around telling stories that John Hall-Stevenson
put into verse and published. Or he may have made the tales up
himself. *Crazy Tales* suggests that the Demoniacs were more
Decameron than demons. The tales are, like other works by Hall-
Stevenson, mildly pornographic, and owe much to Chaucer's
Canterbury Tales. (The exception was the poem on Sir Francis and
Lady M., which was downright indecent.)

The tales tend to dwell on young girls, nuns and monks. For
example, *The Author's Tale, or The Boarding School Tale* is about Lucy
who

> . . . was not like other lasses,
> From twelve her breasts swelled in a trice,
> First they were like two cupping-glasses,
> Then two peaches made of ice.

Lucy has swimming eyes and golden locks and she has to struggle
to keep her virtue intact. [24]

Tale III, *Captain Shadow's Tale*, is about Miss Molly aged fourteen
and her cousin Dick who spies on her through the keyhole as she
undresses. Nuns appear in *Panty's Tale*, which is about a nun who
seduces a monk, and *Don Pringello's Tale* concerns two nuns in
Ghent who fall out over a priest. To end the disputation he tells
them:

> I'll set my back against that gate,
> And there produce, erect and straight,
> The cause of all your altercation,
> But first you both shall hooded be,

> Both so effectually blinded,
> 'Twill be impossible to find it
> Except by chance or sympathy.[25]

There was no evidence of anything sexual at Crazy Castle, and Jones says that this was not a pale imitation of Medmenham but a meeting of men who enjoyed company and an indecorous yarn after dinner.[26]

We could perhaps see the Demoniacs as the Whig equivalent of Dashwood's Tory Friars. Many of the Demoniacs supported Wilkes and were against what the Earl of Sandwich and Dashwood represented. One Demoniac may have been a politician who appears in *The Privy Councillor's Tale*. Cash suggests that this was Edwin Lascelles, although there have been suggestions that it was Bubb Dodington or Sir Francis Dashwood; this seems unlikely given the enmity towards that set by some of the Demoniacs.[27]

John Hall-Stevenson's work gives us some idea of the activities of the Demoniacs. It was not a blasphemous group questioning the established Church, and neither was it dedicated to sex; indeed, women seem to have been absent from the proceedings. It was a group of gentlemen who enjoyed healthy exercise, good company and telling tales. This was a watered-down hell-fire club.

THE KINGDOM OF DALKEY

Ireland was no stranger to hell-fire clubs. Geoffrey Ashe claims that in 1771 there was a revival of the Dublin Hell-Fire Club, which had branches throughout Ireland and was known for its blasphemous toasts to the Devil and damnation to everyone. The club was also known as the Holy Fathers.[28] The *Freeman's Journal* of 12 March 1771 suggested that the founder of this new manifestation of the Irish hell-fire clubs was Thomas 'Buck' Whaley, an Irish Protestant with a penchant for burning down Catholic places of worship. He

is alleged to have revived the old Hell-Fire Club's meeting place on
Mont Pelier Hill, where reputedly Satanic and homosexual rites
were performed, and where allegedly he caught, killed and ate a
farmer's daughter! He was also said to have killed several of his
fellow members by pouring brandy over them and setting fire to it.[29]

How did these stories get attached to Whaley and the Hell-Fire
Club? The answer probably lies in the religious composition of late
eighteenth-century Ireland, where 80 per cent of the population
were Catholic, but the Protestant 20 per cent were the 'Ascendancy'
or elite. The Hell-Fire Club members were young wealthy
Protestant gentlemen with little to do and too much time on their
hands. The Catholics saw the Protestant Ascendancy as Saxons or
Huns and 'black, horned, foreign, a hate-crested crew'.[30] From there
it was but a short step to seeing these wild young men as murderers,
Devil-worshippers and cannibals. The modified version of their
activities suggests that they set fire to their clubroom in a drunken
orgy. They mocked religion, Protestant as well as Catholic, and
blasphemed freely.

One branch of these clubs called 'The Pink Dandies' cut an inch
off the scabbard of their swords so that they could creep up and stab
people without bystanders noticing. The Tigers and the Chalkers
take us back to the Mohocks, as they went through the street
attacking people, or 'chalking' or maiming strangers' faces, or
scrawling graffiti on their houses.[31]

Ireland in these years was a powder keg of tension waiting to
explode. It was still a poor country, badly affected by bad harvests.
The inheritance system meant that farms were divided and subdi-
vided until they became too poor to support a family. It was only in
the north that there was any industry to take up the labour surplus,
and farming incomes could be supplemented by spinning for the
northern mills. Much of the land was owned by Protestant landlords, many of whom were absent for part of the year and who
looked to their Irish estates to provide them with an income to

enable them to live like the gentlemen they were.[32] There were wide divisions between rich and poor, as well as between Protestants and Catholics. The clamour for Catholic representation in Parliament and the right for Catholics to vote became a tumult, while the high rents exacted by landlords drove peasants into abject poverty and fuelled resentment. There were riots against enclosure and high rents in the 1760s and 1770s, and against paying tithes to the Church of Ireland. (This concerned not only the Catholics but also the Presbyterians in the north of Ireland.) The American and the French revolutions inspired those trying to gain equal political and civil rights for all of the Irish people, for they showed that non-violence would not work. Political societies were formed, such as the United Irishmen and the Sons of Irish Liberty, dedicated to freeing Ireland from the British Crown and turning it into a republic.

The United Irishmen was founded in Belfast in 1791 by Dr William Drennan. Its aims were independence and a republic for Ireland and it had revolutionary and treasonable aims based on Tom Paine's *The Rights of Man* (1791–92):

1. Men are born free and equal.
2. The rights of men are liberty, property and the right to oppression.
3. The nation is the source of sovereignty and not the sovereign.[33]

During the Napoleonic wars, contact was made with the French, who were offered support for an invasion of England through Ireland. Some French troops were landed in Ireland, but withdrawn to another theatre of war. However, Ireland had another Protestant secret society, the Orange Society, which was founded in 1795. This Protestant body armed its supporters and atrocities were committed by both Protestants and Catholics, with the result – in what was an eerie foretaste of what would happen in the twentieth century – that the military were sent in. Rebellion and civil war followed, but this did not involve the whole country, and many of the insurrectionists were rounded up and hanged, including the United Irishmen's charismatic leader, Wolfe Tone.[34] In 1800 the Act of Union removed the Irish Parliament and declared that, like Scotland, Ireland was to be governed from Westminster.

Where did the Kingdom of Dalkey fit into the Irish social and political scene? In an era of sedition and plotting it was not surprising that the authorities should be suspicious of it, but they still allowed it to meet until at least 1797.

Dalkey Island was described by Gaskin in the nineteenth century as 'a beautiful picturesque spot and a fashionable watering place', but by Jones in the twentieth century as 'a barren island'.[35] (There is no evidence that Jones actually visited the island.) Dalkey lies a quarter of a mile off the coast at the southernmost entrance to Dublin Bay, and is about 239 acres in size. In 1763 it boasted a tavern and eight large houses, and it was to Dalkey Island that the inhabitants of Dublin fled in the time of plague and other epidemics.[36] It was also a place to which they could retire in summer; Dalkey was a summer kingdom.

The kingdom was founded by a bookseller, Stephen Armitage, and his friends, and Stephen became Stephen I. It was not a secret society as it published its own newspaper, the *Dalkey Gazette*, that advertised the date of its 'summer reunion', which encouraged hundreds to sail to the island to join in the revels. On its last meeting in August 1797 it is claimed that over 20,000 people were on the island.

The revels started with a 'royal' procession from the 'Palace', that is Armitage's bookshop on Fownes Street, Dublin, to the harbour. On reaching the island King Stephen preached a sermon. In 1797 this took the text, 'To everything there is a season and a time to every purpose under the heaven.' The sermon was followed by a 'Parliament' with proceedings and debates being published in a later edition of the *Gazette*, entitled 'House of Nobs, Dies Stephani'.

'Their Wigships being assembled in their best bibs and tuckers the King entered ushered in by the Cross-Poddle, King-at-arms, and was seated on the Great Stool.'[37] Officers of the kingdom were appointed by the King and included Grand-Duke Bullock and Lord Mayor Laughable. The solemnities being over, the assembly feasted and danced into the evening, taking as their toast 'Equal liberty, political and religious to all sons of Adam'.[38] These were sentiments which were surely borrowed from the United Irishmen and the radical writer Tom Paine.

While on the island, the company held mock trials of government officials who had transgressed, such as Sir James Parnell who embezzled £20,000 of public money, or Chancellor Fitzgerald who declared meetings in support of Catholic Emancipation illegal.[39]

The trials of public officials suggest that there was a political element to the Kingdom of Dalkey, as well as a blasphemous taint in the voice of King Stephen, an unordained man preaching a sermon. This is borne out by the odes declaimed by the kingdom's resident poetess, Mrs Henrietta Battier.

> How much unlike those untold realms,
> Where wicked statesmen guide the helm,
> Here no first-rate vessels taking,
> Here no property is shaking,
> Here no shameful peace is making,
> Here we snap no apt occasions,
> On the pretext of invasion,
> Here informers get no pension,
> To requite their foul invention,
> Here no secret dark committee,
> Speaks corruption through the city,
> No placemen or pensioners here are haranguing,
> No soldiers are shooting or sailors hanging,

No mutiny reigns in the army or fleet,
For our orders are just and our commanders discreet.[40]

The date of this ode is not clear but it contains a number of political references which can be dated and which suggest that it was declaimed in 1797 at the last meeting, when the situation in Ireland was at boiling point. In 1794 habeas corpus had been suspended in Ireland, and in 1795 the Treasonable and Seditious Meetings Act was passed, forbidding public meetings. The kingdom was blatantly breaking this Act. The 'sailors hanging' is a reference to the 1797 mutinies at Spithead and the Nore. Pitt was the wicked statesman, people like Sir James Parnell were symbolic of the corruption in Dublin, and the city magistrates and national government used informers to report on wrongdoers and to infiltrate secret societies. The shameful peace is more difficult. Is it Versailles in 1783, which recognised American Independence, or the 1796 failure of peace proposals between Britain and France?

Was the Kingdom of Dalkey a front for revolutionary activities, or simply an excuse for a good day out? Stephen Armitage may have been connected to the United Irishmen, as he frequented the Devil's Head Tavern in George Street, Dublin, where they were known to meet. It was here, in 1792, that he founded the Druids, a secret organisation about which nothing is known.[41] Proclaiming himself King, preaching a sermon and holding mock trials of public officials were in themselves treason, blasphemy and sedition, but Armitage escaped prosecution, and the overall picture of the Kingdom of Dalkey is one of good companionship and merriment, without the dark overtones of what was happening on the mainland of Ireland. It was a chance for the population of Dublin to escape for one day a year, and to indulge in carnivalesque inversion and pleasure; the difference between the kingdom and the hell-fire clubs was that the kingdom was inclusive. Anyone who could afford the boat fare could go to the kingdom, so that it remained true to its toast of liberty to all sons of Adam.

Before we leave late eighteenth-century Ireland there is one more club to discuss, which may have had connections to the Scottish Beggar's Benison. We know about this club from the *Memoirs of Mrs Leeson*, published in 1795–97. These were written to provide her with an income and perhaps to extort money from her previous clients, as she was the madam of a brothel in Pitt Street, Dublin, which was patronised by the elite, including the Lord-Lieutenant of Ireland.[42] Through her clients Mrs Leeson was connected to the States of Castle Kelly, and the Story Batter, which between them had about 500 members. She and her 'nymphs' were given the freedom of the Batter Commonwealth, a club dedicated to stories and pleasure. This was confirmed by a 'parchment enclosed in a beautiful silver box which had on it the emblem of the beggar's benison handsomely carved and inside a delectable poem called the Guide to Joy or pleasures of the imagination . . .' In return for this Mrs Leeson gave the Batters the freedom of her house and appointed 'Sappho fat and fair to a seat in the enclave, with all the adults in my female menagerie'.[43] The poem is not included in the memoirs, but Mrs Leeson claimed that it was worse than Rochester's poems and *Fanny Hill*.

It is not surprising that the Beggar's Benison should have connections with Ireland, especially after a Glasgow branch had been founded with its connections westward, and it is clear that Mrs Leeson had come across it before she was presented with the casket as she was able to identify the symbol on it. Another connection between Mrs Leeson and the Beggar's, was, as she claimed, that the poem in the silver box was written by 'the amiable Mrs H, now of Drumcobra, the once happy favourite of that prince of good fellows'.[44] Mrs H has been identified as Maria Fitzherbert, the Catholic morganatic wife of the Prince Regent, and the Prince Regent was allegedly a member of the Edinburgh branch of the Beggar's Benison. Thus do the threads of history intertwine, but did they also stretch across the Atlantic into colonial North America?

HELL-FIRE AND COLONIAL AMERICA

Wherever Englishmen gathered together in the eighteenth century, drink, conversation and club life followed. Peter Clark suggests that the early clubs in colonial America were religious, Masonic or based on ethnic groups, such as the Irish. He claims that in early eighteenth-century Boston 20 per cent of adult males belonged to a club.[45] Club life also flourished in New York, Philadelphia, Charleston and Annapolis.[46] In fact in Rye, to the north of New York, there was a so-called Hell-Fire Club known as the Bold Robin Hood's Men.[47]

Dr Alexander Hamilton, who emigrated from Edinburgh to Annapolis in 1739, came from a background rooted in club life. When he decided to take a tour of his new country before settling down to work he contacted clubs in the towns he visited and dined with them. In Boston he dined at Withered's Club, whose president was a pot-bellied Scotsman who lent money. He also dined with the Physical Club, which met in the Sun Tavern where the members drank punch, smoked and talked of sundry matters. The Scots Quarterly Society also met in the Sun Tavern, although this was a charitable society which gave relief to the poor.[48]

At Tradeaway, a tavern at a trading post in Maryland, he was accosted by a drunken club 'just dismissing and unable to sit straight on their horses'. Oaths and God-damns followed them into the night, and Hamilton dismissed them as 'disorderly fellows'.[49] This might put us in mind of some of the street gangs of early eighteenth-century London, while the Hungarian Club in New York, which Hamilton described as 'bumper men who talk bawdy and make puns', might also remind us of some British clubs.[50]

On his return to Annapolis Hamilton founded his own club, the Tuesday Club. This club had fifteen members at a time, and was dedicated to toasts to the Ladies, the King and the Deluge, and to making coarse jokes and playing pranks.[51] Despite similarities with British drinking clubs, none observed by Hamilton were from the hell-fire genre. But it is clear that alcohol fuelled much of colonial America's life. Tavern culture was strong, even in the Quaker city of Philadelphia, where there were 101 licensed premises by 1751. In Massachusetts there were more public houses than any other kind of public building,[52] and the same must have been true for other British colonies.

Some effort was made to regulate behaviour in the taverns and to curtail the hours of drinking. Philadelphia drew up regulations for the ordering of taverns in 1688.[53] However, it was recognised by authorities that the tavern was a place where a workman could go to sit in the warmth with his fellows after a hard day's labour, a place where the merchant could meet his peers and discuss business, and where gentlemen could gather over a bowl of wine and discuss the affairs of the day. It was not long before taverns began to supply different rooms for different groups to use, and club life was born. The first Masonic lodge in Philadelphia met at the Tun and Indian King tavern, and the second, known as St John's Lodge, at the Royal Standard. A branch of the Sublime Society of Beefsteaks also used the Tun.[54] In Boston there was a hierarchy of clubs, depending on the clientele and whereabouts in the city the tavern was situated (an early example of city zoning).[55]

In most colonial towns the tavern was the only large covered space apart from the church, and because of this the local court and other official bodies usually met there. News and rumours were disseminated through the tavern network and, of course, discussed and chewed over by the drinkers. Rumours that started in taverns could run like wildfire through the streets and cause panic amongst the inhabitants. Political clubs met in taverns, and some taverns were known for illicit gaming, cockfighting, and bare-knuckle boxing matches; these events often resulted in fights and riots that upset the peace and local order. Competitive drinking also took place, and there were taverns that allowed sexual perversions on their premises. In 1701 two men dressed in women's clothes were found in John Simes's Tavern in Philadelphia, and in 1770 Samuel Coates disowned a schoolfellow for paying £50 to young girls to strip naked for him in the private room of a tavern.[56]

This incident brings us closer to the Beggar's Benison, but overall it can be seen that in colonial America the tavern could be an instrument for subversion, where plotters could meet and political bargains could be made; it was also a place where the local peace was disturbed and illicit gaming went on. It is no accident that many historians see the tavern as a crucial element of the American Revolution. But was the blasphemous hell-fire club also imported to America?

A glass of English manufacture which was part of the Philadelphia bequest of George Barford Lorimer suggests that this may have been the case. The glass is dated to about 1770 and is inscribed with the images of the Hell-Fire Club and the legend 'Joseph M—— Master of the Revels'.[57] Joseph M has not been identified; neither has the hell-fire club of which he was the Master of the Revels, so we do not know if this was a group of deists and a blasphemous organisation, or a group of young gentlemen aping the British clubs in order to be daring. However, there were some in colonial America who thought that the mere act of toasting someone's health was blasphemous as it imitated the transubstantiation that transformed Christ's blood into wine; and eventually state laws tried to suppress the habit of toasting.[58]

A key figure and someone who could have been a link between British hell-fire clubs and colonial America was Benjamin Franklin. Franklin was intimate with Sir Francis Dashwood and other Medmenham Friars in England, and an attack on Cotton Mather in 1721 by Benjamin's brother James in his newspaper the *New England Courant* had resulted in Mather calling the Franklins and their friends a 'Hell-Fire Club'.[59]

The date is significant, as this is the year that the Duke of Wharton's alleged Hell-Fire Club was in operation. We know that the Franklin was aware of this club as on 6 May 1721 the *New England Courant* had published an account of the London club taken from *Applebee's Journal*, which, being sensational news of blasphemy and supposed sexual orgies, boosted the circulation of Franklin's paper considerably. News of the Hell-Fire Club and the King's proclamation against scandalous clubs was also published in Boston. Tavern rumour suggested that Boston had its own Hell-Fire Club, of which James Franklin was alleged to be a prominent member.[60]

Other reports show that New England was aware of the Mohock scare in London as well. This was not surprising as there was a continuous flow of ships passing between the American colonies and Britain, bringing with them news, scandal, rumour and emigrants.

The Franklins were early emigrants to New England. Benjamin was born in Boston in 1706, the son of a candle and soap maker. He gained some education at a grammar school before being withdrawn and apprenticed to a candle-maker. This noisome occupation did not please him, and he left the tallow trade to become apprenticed to a printer. But his ambition was to become a writer, and he modelled his early pieces on the *Spectator*, imported from London.[61] He first visited England in 1724 to work as a printer, and stayed for two years.[62]

This was the time of Edmund Curll and the start of the publication of erotic literature and pamphlets questioning the existence and nature of God. Morgan suggests that, although Franklin never doubted that God existed, he was a deist who rejected a vengeful God, and believed that sin was wrong not because it offended God, but because it harmed other people. Franklin kept a list of virtues by him; these were all practical utilitarian virtues,[63] for Franklin was a practical man, a perfect child of the Enlightenment with an insatiable curiosity about nature and how things worked. His inventions and his exploration into the nature of static electricity demonstrate this. He was also a good eighteenth-century clubbable man. He started a club called the Junto where young men could meet to debate politics, drink together and make music. He belonged to the Philadelphia Masons, and to the Club of Honest Whigs, as well as being a member of the Royal Society and the Académie Française.

He probably met Sir Francis Dashwood on his second visit to England in 1757. This time he came as official agent for Pennsylvania and was accompanied by his illegitimate son William. Together they travelled round Britain, meeting David Hume in St Andrews, and other luminaries of the Enlightenment.[64]

While in London, Franklin regularly attended a Monday Club at the George and Vulture whose members were city and business types, and the Club of Honest Whigs at the Mitre Tavern, his Thursday club. The Honest Whigs were dissenters, Scottish academicians and schoolmasters, and they included Joseph Priestley, who like Franklin was interested in electricity. They discussed politics and experimental science.[65] No hint of blasphemy, hell-fire sulphur or sexual misbehaviour was connected to this club, but Franklin belonged to it at the time when John Wilkes exposed the Medmenham Friars. Even if Franklin was not a Friar he must have known about them, yet despite this he stayed at West Wycombe with Sir Francis Dashwood and sent home glowing accounts of its magnificence.

It was at West Wycombe that Franklin and Dashwood worked on their revision of the Book of Common Prayer. They did this with the aim of shortening the services. Franklin was given the task of abbreviating the Psalms and the catechism. The revised version of the Prayer Book was published in 1773, but raised little interest.[66] There is no evidence that it was even adopted by Dashwood's own newly remodelled modern church at West Wycombe, which it might have been designed for in the first place: a modern service to match a modern and fashionable church.

Franklin and Dashwood were extremely presumptuous and arrogant in taking on the role of ordained clergymen and revising the liturgy. Their motives may have been practical – the hope that shorter services would attract more people to attend the Church of England, and stem the growing tide of dissent – but even though Franklin had rejected organised religion he came from a dissenting background. Was this an attempt to unite dissent with the established Church? We do not know. The revised Prayer Book faded into obscurity in England, although Ashe suggests it was used widely in American churches.[67]

Undoubtedly British subversive, anti-religious clubs dedicated to sex and gaming spread to the American colonies, even if the evidence is sparse. This type of club was also probably found in the West Indies, where there were Masonic and dining clubs in ports and government towns.[68] Wherever young British gentlemen went throughout the Empire they took their club culture with them. It was a way of keeping in touch with compatriots and maintaining a semblance of the life they had left behind.

WILLIAM HICKEY

William Hickey provides us with a bridge between the eighteenth and nineteenth centuries. Born in 1749, he died in 1830 and his memoirs demonstrate a change in attitude towards leisure that reflects changes in wider society. Hickey was the son of an Irish attorney living in London. As a child he was introduced to Simon Luttrell of the Irish Hell-Fire Club, and if the memoirs are to be believed, he knew Charles Churchill, Wilkes's friend and a Medmenham Friar, and the Vansittart brothers, who were also members of the Friars. Had he been older he might well have been a Friar himself, but he was of the next generation, aged only twelve in 1761.

His brother Henry displayed characteristics similar to those of the Earl of Rochester. In 1770, in a drunken riot that issued from Mrs Harrington's bagnio at Charing Cross, Henry killed a man. He fled to Paris and was eventually sent off to Madras with the East India Company, but was drowned on the way. William was already on his way to India by this time, having been sent there after embezzling money from the family firm. But he disliked India so much that he returned to England on the ship that had taken him out.[69]

In London he was an *habitué* of low life, and he recounts many amorous adventures in his memoirs, including seducing maid-servants, going to brothels and picking up women in the streets. He belonged to a club that met at the Red House in Battersea dedicated to eating, drinking and billiards, and he was a member of a group of young men full of wine who issued from a den called Wetherby's in Little Russell Street to assault passers-by.[70]

In 1775 he was sent to Jamaica after another unfortunate affair with someone else's money. Nominally he went to the island as an attorney, but he does not seem to have done any work there, and returned to England in 1776. The following year he was sent back to India, this time to Bengal. Again he showed a marked reluctance to do any of the work he was sent to do, and when asked to attend court went down with a headache. However, when transferred to Calcutta he was made to work, and 'no man laboured harder'.[71]

Hickey's memoirs are a mixture of events designed to shock and show him as a libertine and swindler, interspersed with bouts of repentance and self-righteousness. It is this awareness that what he was doing was often both immoral and illegal that marks him out from earlier libertines. After the death of his common law wife he became a reformed character, and a symbol of the age of reform of the 1830s.

Another figure who bridged the centuries, and surely an obvious candidate for becoming a member of a hell-fire club, was George Gordon, Lord Byron (1788–1824). Ashe claims in *Do What You Will* that Byron tried to revive Devil worship at Newstead Abbey in 1809 after leaving Cambridge, but moderates this, presenting Byron as 'flirting with hell-fire', in his later book, *Hell-Fire Clubs*.[72]

Strangely enough, hell-fire and Devil worship is one of the accusations that cannot be proved against Byron. In fact during his stay at Newstead Abbey he seems to have been extremely subdued; although he did get a servant pregnant, he also published his first major poem while he was there, before departing on a Grand Tour. As the anonymous editor of the Wordsworth edition of Byron writes, 'the Byronic myth is persistent and seductive'. His reputation was so scandalous that he was refused burial in St Paul's or Westminster Abbey, but this was as much for his morals as for his lack of belief in God. If he was anything, he could be called a pagan who believed in life rather than a Devil-worshipper.[73]

Conclusion

We started this book with a young peer who had been accused of being a member of the Hell-Fire Club; we end it with another young nobleman suspected of Devil worship. So had anything changed?

As the eighteenth century drew to a close, so the old libertine way of life started to die with it. The Napoleonic wars distracted minds from dressing up, and from secret clubs and societies, and concentrated them on defending the country and preventing invasion. The bucolic roistering aristocracy began to transform into sober and responsible leaders of men, while the respectable God-fearing middle classes, professionals, mill-owners, businessmen and entrepreneurs helped to change the moral economy and social attitudes of the ruling classes. The seeds for change and the Victorian age were sown in the 1780s, and the great reforming movements of the 1830s took root in that decade. A new evangelism appeared, symbolised by William Wilberforce and the campaign to abolish the British slave trade, and Wilberforce was firmly rooted in the middle class, as were many of his supporters.

Social, economic and political reform was very necessary. The end of the Napoleonic wars in 1815 brought poverty and depression to Britain. There were riots in town and country, and in 1819 the yeomanry charged an unarmed meeting of political reformers in St Peter's Fields, Manchester, killing and injuring scores of people in what became known as the Peterloo Massacre. Britain seemed to teeter on the edge of revolution, but the revolution never happened.[1] The reason for this may have been the silent majority of the middle class, but it could have been related to localism: each disorderly district had its own aims, the protests were mostly economic and only a minority sought to change distress at poor conditions into a revolution.

One result was a change in the way in which public order was administered. Peel's London police force was formed in 1829, and the County Police Act came into force ten years later. Law and order was no longer in the hands of volunteers; now professionals patrolled the streets. The parish constable, so long a figure of fun and target for attack, was gone. The 1832 Reform Act abolished rotten boroughs and started to extend the franchise (a process which would take nearly a century to complete), and in 1834 the New Poor Law changed the way in which poor relief was given and established the workhouse. A year later the Municipal Corporations Act started the reform of local government. When civil registration was established in 1837, the vital events of life – birth, marriage and death – were no longer the monopoly of the established Church. The 1840s saw the great series of Royal Commissions and social inquiries into the state of the nation, and especially the state of the labouring classes. The result of these was a change in the lives of working men and women.

The development of the railway improved communications and meant that Britain was no longer a series of isolated regions. The Great Exhibition of 1851 saw the nation and the Empire come together. The Britain of the 1830s and 1840s was totally different to the Britain of the 1730s and 1740s. By 1840 an increased popula-tion lived mainly in towns and worked for wages in mills, factories and service industries. Modern Britain was being established, and there was no room in it for hell-fire clubs, as this was a society more family orientated, and much more commercial than in the eighteenth century.

Of course gentlemen's clubs survived. The imposing buildings in Pall Mall, London, are evidence of this. Brooks's and White's, descendants of eighteenth-century gaming clubs, took on a political tinge, while the Reform Club and the Carlton Club were openly political. But other types of clubs emerged in the nineteenth century – clubs that involved classes other than the leisured gentleman; mechanics' institutes, philosophical and literary societies, and savings clubs, for example, were the preserve of the middle and working classes. Self-improvement and self-help were enthusiastically embraced by many working men and women, and encouraged by the middle and upper classes as engines to regulate public disorder.

London and other towns were being rebuilt, and the extension of suburbs moved the middle class out of the town centre, divorced home and the workplace, and created a society of commuters. In middle- and upper-class society the gap between the genders widened. Women became domesticated figures, angels in the house, close to the role that eighteenth-century moralists had wanted for them, obedient, respectable and chaste and increasingly confined to the private space of the home. A series of Acts of Parliament passed in the 1840s went some way towards creating this ideal in the working class as well. Gradually women were removed from working in the mines, and their hours of work in mills and factories were regulated.

There was, of course, still a large underbelly of society. Prostitution in Britain's towns and cities was a cause for concern, and visible on the streets for all to see. To combat this the Society for the Suppression of Vice, a moral purity campaign, was started in the early nineteenth century, and in towns such as Cambridge female refuges were founded to give shelter to women who had fallen from virtue. However, some of the nobility still kept mistresses, while the hidden world of the country house had erotic books in its library and erotic statuary in its gardens. There was still the potential for hell-fire clubs to flourish, but they did not.

One reason for this was Romanticism, which examined the relationship between man and nature. Planned classical landscapes were replaced by a preference for rugged mountains and rocky eminences. Associations of friends were abandoned in favour of Wordsworthian solitude, in direct contradiction to the Enlightenment tenet that sociability was a key to happiness.

Notes

INTRODUCTION

1. *The Parliamentary History of England*, compiled by W. Cobbett and J. Wright, Vol. III *AD 1714–1722*, 894.
2. R. Porter, *Enlightenment*, 2000, 258.
3. G. Ashe, *The Hell-Fire Clubs: Sex, Rakes and Libertines in Eighteenth-century Europe*, xii–xiii, 221–53, 272.
4. Betty Kemp ignored the goings-on at Medmenham in her political biography of Sir Francis Dashwood; D.P. Mannix accused Medmenham of specialising in sex. B. Kemp, *Sir Francis Dashwood*, 1967; D.P. Mannix, *The Hell-Fire Club*, 1978.
5. See for example J. Peakman, *Lascivious Bodies*, 2004.
6. Ashe, xi–xiv.
7. R. Porter, *Flesh in the Age of Reason*, 2003, 22.
8. R. Porter, 'England', in A.C. Kors, *Encyclopaedia of the Enlightenment*, Vol. I, 414.
9. J.W. Yolton, *The Blackwell Companion to the Enlightenment*, 1991, 1–3.
10. Porter, *Enlightenment*, 5. This book is recommended to readers who would like a more detailed analysis of the British Enlightenment and its effect on society. Michel Foucault reversed the Enlightenment view that knowledge creates power, claiming that power creates knowledge. A Foucauldian exploration of the hell-fire clubs has yet to be written, and is beyond the remit of this book.
11. Quoted in P. Gay, *The Enlightenment: an interpretation of the rise of modern paganism*, 1967, 20.
12. J. Locke, *An Essay Concerning Human Understanding*, ed. P. Nidditch, 1975, 46.
13. How far the introduction of street lighting in the late eighteenth century contributed to a fall in crime figures and drove street gangs and clubs indoors is still to be explored.
14. G. Pearson, *Hooligan*, 1983, 188.
15. *OED*, Vol. XIII, 1989, 146.

16. See for example Peakman, xv.
17. R. Porter, *English Society in the 18th Century*, 1990, 259.
18. I am a cynic when it comes to suggesting that the eighteenth century was the high point of sexual liberation. Chaucer's *Canterbury Tales*, for example, shows a healthy concern for sex, as do the *Decameron*, John Donne's poems to his lover, and so on.
19. Porter, *English Society*, 260; R. Shoemaker, 'Male Honour and the Decline of Public Violence in Eighteenth-century London', *Social History*, 26, No. 2, 2001, 190–1.
20. P. Carter, 'Men about Town: representations of foppery and masculinity in early 18th century England', in H. Baker and E. Chahis, *Gender in Eighteenth-Century England*, 1997, 33; For an up-to-date discussion on eighteenth-century sexuality see E. Mackie, 'Boys will be Boys: masculinity, conviviality and the Restoration rake', *The Eighteenth Century*, 46, No. 2, 2005, 129–49; H. Cocks, 'Modernity and the Self in the History of Sexuality', *Historical Journal*, 49, No. 4, 2006, 1211–27.
21. B. Southgate, *History: What & Why*, 1996, 8, 129.

CHAPTER 1 – PRELUDE TO THE FIRES OF HELL

1. J. Bruce ed., *The Diary of John Manningham 1602–1603*, 1868, 142–3.
2. This information comes from the *Calendar of State Papers, 1623–1625* (1859), 125, 130.
3. The witness statement is quoted in T.S. Graves, 'Some Pre-Mohock Clansmen', *Studies in Philology*, 20, 1923, 401–2.
4. '*Tityre tu patulae recubans sans tegmine fagi*', quoted in Pearson, *Hooligan*, 188.
5. 'Chevy Chase' is a ubiquitous folk tune which lends itself to any form.
6. L. Normand and G. Roberts, *Witchcraft in Early Modern Scotland*, 2000, 327, 332. The full text of *Demonology* is reproduced on pp. 353–425 of this book.
7. A.R. Braunmuller and M. Hattaway, *The Cambridge Guide to English Renaissance Drama*, 1999, 431.
8. F. Laroque, *Shakespeare: Court, Crowd and Playgoer*, 1999, 62–3.
9. Braunmuller and Hattaway, 106–7.
10. 'Lord Rochester against his Whore Pipe', quoted in H. Blyth, *The Rakes*, 1971, 39.
11. E. De Beer ed., *The Diary of John Evelyn*, Vol. III, 2000, 246.
12. D.M. Vieth, *The Works of the Earl of Rochester*, 1995, 'To the Postboy', 131.
13. Ibid., 'A Translation from Seneca's 'Troades', Act II, Chorus', 151.
14. V. De Sola Pinto, *Enthuisastic Wit. A portrait of John Wilmot, Earl of Rochester*, 1962, 83–5. The original manuscript for the Dr Bendo episode is University of Nottingham, MS 1489.
15. H. Blyth, *The Rakes*, New York, Doubleday Press, 1971.
16. Edward Hyde, Earl of Clarendon, *Life of Edward, Earl of Clarendon, written by Himself*, 1857 edn, 307.

17. G. Burnet, *Some Passages of the Life and Death of the Right Honourable John, Earl of Rochester*, 1680; sources for Rochester's life can be found in J. Aubrey, *Brief Lives*, 1898 edn; A. Wood, *Athenae Oxon*, 1885–1921 (but written in the seventeenth century).

18. D.M. Vieth, 'Sir Charles Sedley and the Ballers Oath', *The Scriblerian*, 12, no. 1, Autumn 1979, 47–8. The poem is in the Bodleian Library, MS Wood, 19 (2) fol. 11ʳ.

19. BL Harl. MS 7003 f. 296.

20. BL Harl. MS 7317 f. 68.

21. J. Woodward, *An Account of the Progress of the Reformation of Manners in England and Ireland*, 1701, 16.

22. Ibid., 35, 69, 71.

23. T. Curtis and W. Speck, 'Societies for the Reformation of Manners', *Literature and History*, 3, 1976, 46–7.

24. J. Barry and K. Morgan eds, *Reformation and Revival in Eighteenth Century Bristol*, 1994, 3–6. The manuscript is Bristol Reference Library, MS 10162.

25. Barry and Morgan, 18–19, 22.

26. Woodward, 18.

CHAPTER 2 – GENTLEMEN'S CLUBS, JOURNALISTIC HACKS, THE MOHOCKS AND CHANGE

1. P. Clark, *British Clubs and Societies, 1580–1800*, 2000, 10.

2. Ibid., 194.

3. R. Porter, 'England', in Kors, Vol. I, 414.

4. Clark, 9.

5. J.M. Roberts, *The Mythology of Secret Societies*, 1972, 17.

6. R.J. Morris, 'Clubs, Societies and Associations', in F.M.L. Thompson ed., *The Cambridge Social History of Britain, 1750–1950*, 1990, 395–443.

7. Clark, 145.

8. Ibid., 142.

9. Ibid., 85.

10. V. Gatrell, *The City of Laughter*, 2006, 118–19.

11. N. Ward, *The Secret History of Clubs, particularly the Kit-Kat Club etc.*, 1709, 1–2.

12. Ibid., 26–33.

13. Ibid., 36–45, 94.

14. Ibid., 112–15. Is this one of the earliest references to Yorkshire people as 'tykes', and of their disdain for the south?

15. Ibid., 284, 362, 374. Portraits of the Kit-Kat Club members are in the National Portrait Gallery.

16. There is some corroboration of the existence of the Calves' Head Club in journals such as the *Female Tatler*.

17. Ward, 56–7, 103–4.

18. E.A. Wrigley, 'A Simple Model of London's Importance in a Changing English Society and Economy, 1650–1750', *Past and Present*, 37, 1967, 44–70; P. Earle, *A City Full of People. Men and women of London 1650–1750*, 1994, 38–9.

19. J. Strype, *A Survey of the Cities of London and Westminster*, 1720, 229.

20. Many English Jacobite plots of the late seventeenth and early eighteenth centuries started with meetings in Covent Garden. See E. Lord, *The Stuarts' Secret Army*, 2004.

21. J. Beattie, *Policing and Punishment in London, 1660–1750*, 2001, 150.

22. H.M. Quarrel and M. More eds, *London in 1710 from the Travels of Zacharias Conrad von Uffenbach*, 1934, 130, 146.

23. P. Roberts ed., *The Diary of David Hamilton, 1709–1714*, 1975, 41.

24. The watch were the keepers of the Queen's peace. An insult to them was an insult to the Queen and could be accounted as treason.

25. It was when searching the statutes as recommended by the Queen that the magistrates came across the Damned Crew and other seventeenth-century clubs.

26. *London Gazette*, 15–18 March 1712, no pagination.

27. J. Gay, *The Mohocks*, 1712, 204.

28. J. Gay, *Trivia, or The Art of Walking in the Streets of London*, 1716, 52. The Scourers also appeared in a play by Thomas Shadwell.

29. *Spectator*, 12 March 1712, 13–16.

30. H. Williams ed., Jonathan Swift's *Journal to Stella*, 1974, 508–9, 515.

31. J. Cartwright ed., *The Wentworth Papers 1705–1739*, 1883, 277–8.

32. P. Smith ed., *The Letters of Thomas Burnet to George Duckett, 1712–1722*, 1914, 209, 215.

33. Sources for the 'Mohock' arrests, their bail and subsequent appearance in court can be found in the Greater London Record Office, Middlesex Session Book, and the *London Gazette*.

34. *London Gazette*, 17–19 April 1712.

35. *Spectator*, 8 April 1712, speculated as to whether the Mohocks were 'bull-beggars' invented to deter wives and daughters from going out at night, suggesting that the women should not have been there in the first place.

36. Visit any town centre on a weekend evening and there are groups of young men fuelled up by alcohol and ready for a fight. Are they asserting their masculinity? Or is it the effect of conviviality and alcohol on the senses? Could it be said that in this case 'boys will be boys'?

37. T. Jones and G. Holmes eds, *The London Diaries of William Nicolson, Bishop of Carlisle, 1702–1718*, 1895, 595.

38. *Plot upon Plot* (1712), a ballad to be sung to the tune of 'Heigh-Ho Boys Up We Go'. The smoking ministry refers to the letter bomb.

39. N. Guthrie, 'No Truth or Very Little in the Whole Story? A reassessment of the Mohock scare of 1712', *Eighteenth Century Life*, 20, no. 37, New Series, May 1996. This is a reply to D. Stott, 'The Case of the Mohocks: rake violence in London', *Social History*, 20, no. 2, 1995.

40. *Spectator*, 8 April 1712.

41. R.J. Allan, *The Clubs of Augustan London*, Harvard Studies in English, VII, 1933, 113–16.

42. Swift, 511.

43. *Spectator*, 27 April 1711.

44. J. Axtell, *The European and the Indian*, 1981, 41, 45, 56.

45. Quoted in the *OED* definition of Mohock.

46. P. Quennell ed., *Memoirs of William Hickey*, 1960, 158–9.

47. Hickey, 159–61, 167.

48. Shoemaker, 198–9.

49. Lord, 44–8.

50. B. Bekker, *The World Bewitched*, 1696.

51. In *Four Centuries of Witch Beliefs* (1947) R.T. Davies suggested that the Pilgrim Fathers set sail not for theological freedom, but because the government was too lax in its treatment of witches.

52. *Spectator*, 17 July 1711.

53. *A Full and Impartial Account of the Discovery of Sorcery and Witchcraft practised by Jane Wenham of Walkern, Hertfordshire*, 3rd edn, 1712, preface, 15–16.

54. F. Bragge, *A Defence of the Proceedings against Jane Wenham*, 1712; F. Bragge, *The Case of the Hertfordshire Witch Considered*, 1712, v.

55. *A Full Confutation of Witchcraft More Particularly of the Full Deposition against Jane Wenham lately tried at Hertford*, 1712, 4–6.

56. *OED*, Vol. XIV, 115. Is Ariel in *The Tempest* a spirit of the elements, controlled by the Rosicrucian Prospero?

57. R. Hutton, *The Druids*, 2007, 12–14.

58. Ibid., 93,102; for a discussion on antiquarians see R. Sweet, *Antiquaries*, 2004.

59. M.C. Jacobs, *The Radical Enlightenment: pantheists, Freemasons and republicans*, 1981, 154–5, 267–8.

CHAPTER 3 – THE HELL-FIRE CLUBS

1. *Journal of the House of Lords*, Vol. XXI, 1721, 510–11.

2. *London Gazette*, 28 April 1721, no pagination.

3. Ibid.

4. Quoted in R.M. Baine, *Daniel Defoe and the Supernatural*, 1968, 71.

5. D. Defoe, *A System of Magic*, 1728, 242–3.

6. GLRO Middlesex Session Book, 1721, fols 118–20.

7. *Journal of the House of Lords*, Vol. XXI, 1721, 894.

8. *The Parliamentary History of England*, Vol. II AD 1714–1727, 1806, 894.

9. J. Redwood, *Reason, Ridicule and Religion: the Age of Enlightenment in England 1660–1750*, 1976, 169, 175.

10. *The Life and Writings of Philip, Late Duke of Wharton*, 1732, Vol. I, 1, 4.

11. Ibid., 4; W. Graham ed., *Letters of Joseph Addison*, 1941.

12. Wharton, 7.

13. *Calendar of State Papers in the Stuart Mss in Windsor Castle*, 1906, 312.

14. M. Blackett-Ord, *Hell-Fire Duke*, 1982, 44–57.
15. Allan, 121.
16. *Applebee's Journal*, 6 May 1721.
17. *The Hell-Fire Club: Kept by a Society of Blasphemers*, 1721.
18. 'The Diary of Thomas Smith Esquire', *Wiltshire Archaeological and Natural History Magazine*, 11, 1869, 91.
19. J. Puckle, *The Club or Grey Cap for a Green Head*, 1723, 1, 76.
20. *Memoirs of the Life and Writings of Mr William Whiston*, 1753, 135.
21. Mary Granville, *The Autobiography and Correspondence of Mary Granville, Mrs Delaney*, ed. Lady Llanover, 2nd series, Vol. III, 162–3.
22. B.B. Schnorrenburg, 'Mary Delany', *DNB*, 2004, Vol. XV, 711–12.
23. This is one of the acknowledged problems when using oral history as a source.
24. Halsband, R. ed. *The Complete Letters of Lady Mary Wortley Montagu*, 1965–67, 38–40.
25. F. Bickley ed., *Report on the Hastings Mss of the late Rawdon Hastings Esq.*, 1934, Vol. III, 1.
26. *Daily Post*, September 1724.
27. Wharton, 19.
28. Both Blackett-Ord and the *DNB* mention this incident, but neither gives a clear reference to which source it comes from.
29. Wharton, 38.
30. *Epistles to Several Persons (Moral Essays)*, ed. F.W. Bateson, Methuen, 1951, 29–31.
31. For further information on Ireland in the eighteenth century see for example T.W. Moody and W.E. Vaughan eds, *A New History of Ireland*, IV, 1986.
32. W.D. Handcock, *History and Antiquities of Tallaght*, 1877, 74–6.
33. A.C. Elias, 'Laetitia Pilkington', *DNB*, 2004, Vol. XLIV, 321–3.
34. A.C. Elias ed., *The Memoirs of Laetitia Pilkington*, 1997, xxxix.
35. N. Gormley, 'The Trials of James Cotter and Henry, Baron of Santry; two case studies of the administration of criminal justice in early eighteenth-century Ireland', *Irish Historical Studies*, 21, May 1999, 325–42.
36. C. Jenkinson, *Life, History and Remarkable Pedigree of the Right Honourable Simon, Lord Luttrell*, 1769, 22.
37. This story is part of oral tradition, but appeared in print in *Notes and Queries*, 5, series 2, 330.
38. A. Cash, *John Wilkes: The Scandalous Father of Civil Liberty*, 2006, 253, 336.
39. L.C. Jones, *The Clubs of the Georgian Rakes*, 1942, 51, 77–8.
40. C. Rawcliffe and R. Wilson eds, *Norwich since 1550*, 2005, 154, 181.
41. P.D. Hayes, 'Politics in Norfolk, 1750–1832', Ph.D. thesis, 1957, 55, 78, 165, 410.
42. E. Bellamy, *James Wheatley and Norwich Methodism in the 1750s*, 1994, 32, 34.
43. Ibid., 25–8.
44. Ibid., 35.
45. Ibid., 38–9.
46. Lord, 226–7.

47. Jones, 53.
48. Ibid., 54–5.
49. G. Midgley, *University Life in Eighteenth Century Oxford*, 1996, 64–5.
50. Ashe, *The Hell-Fire Clubs*, 66–7.
51. A. Gray and F. Brittain eds, *A History of Jesus College, Cambridge*, 1979, 194, 197.
52. J. and J.A. Venn, *Alumni Cantabrigiensis*, 1922, Part I, 129–30.
53. W.B. Whitaker, *The Eighteenth Century Sunday*, 1940, 62.
54. G.V. Portus, *Caritas Anglicana*, 1912, 114–16, 146, 154, 178.

CHAPTER 4 – INTERLUDE ABROAD: THE GRAND TOUR, DILETTANTI AND DIVANS

1. For a bibliography of travel writing by Grand Tourists to Italy see R.S. Pine-Coffin, *Biblioteca di bibliografia italiana*, 1974.
2. The model for many books on the Grand Tour is W.E. Mead's publication of 1914, *The Grand Tour in the Eighteenth Century*, which sets out the agenda that other authors have followed. It starts with the hazards of crossing the English Channel and deals with the exigencies of travel and foreign inns, the cost of living, destinations and the experience of tourists abroad. Excellent as such books are, they do tend to dwell on the practical side of the Grand Tour. Later works which use Mead's model include J. Black, *The British Abroad: The Grand Tour in the Eighteenth Century*, 1992, and *The British and the Grand Tour*, 1985; C. Hibbert, *The Grand Tour*, 1969.
3. F. Bacon, *Essays*, ed. M.J. Hawkins, 1994 (1st edn 1612), 47–8.
4. Pine-Coffin, 4–5.
5. J. Spence, *Letters from the Grand Tour*, ed. S. Klei, 1975 (1st edn 1766), 419–26.
6. L. Sterne, *A Sentimental Journey through France and Italy*, 1926 edn, 22.
7. Quoted in E. Cheney, *The Evolution of the Grand Tour. Anglo-Italian cultural relations since the Renaissance*, 1998, 134, 314.
8. Sterne, 23–35.
9. D. Garrick, *Lethe*, 1740.
10. R. Hurd, *A Dialogue on the Uses of Foreign Travel*, 1764, 1, 8, 10, 15, 31, 43, 51.
11. Ibid., 9, 12, 14, 18, 21, 25, 55, 73, 81, 83, 123, 142.
12. Pine-Coffin, 25.
13. Ibid., 27.
14. W. Bromley, *Remarks on the Grand Tour of France and Italy*, 1705, 94–5, 106.
15. Cambridgeshire Record Office, 588/O15.
16. JRULM, Cornwall-Legh Collection, High Legh II, Box 15, Papers concerning prints and pictures brought by George John Legh in Italy and Switzerland.

17. In the earlier part of the eighteenth century there was little appreciation of Greek classical culture. It was thought that many Greek statues and temples had in fact been built by the Romans.

18. Spence, 115.

19. J. Addison, *Remarks on Several Parts of Italy in the Years, 1701, 1702, 1703*, 1705, Preface, no pagination.

20. Pine-Coffin, 1–20, 47.

21. For histories of eighteenth-century Italy in English see for example D. Carparetto, and G. Ricuperati, *Italy in the Age of Reason*, trans. C. Higget, 1982; or J.A. Mario, *Early Modern Italy*, 2002.

22. Spence, 80.

23. Mario, 123, 192–3.

24. Carparetto and Ricuperati, 81–2, 131.

25. Bromley, 36–8; John Howard the prison reformer visited Italy to investigate Italian prison reforms.

26. Pine-Coffin, 45–6.

27. Mario, 229.

28. G. Berkeley, *Essay towards Preventing the Ruin of Great Britain*, quoted in Cheney, 342.

29. P. Ayres, *Classical Culture and the Idea of Rome*, 1997, 81–3.

30. C. Middleton, *A Letter from Rome Shewing Conformity between Popery and Paganism*, 5th edn, 1742, viii, 131, 143–8, 160–1.

31. It was not until William Stukeley's drawings of Stonehenge in the 1720s that it was realised that Britain had its own pagan sites.

32. J. Burke, 'The Grand Tour and the Rule of Taste', in *Studies in the Eighteenth Century*, ed. R.F. Brissenden, Canberra: Australian National University Press, 1968, 231–50.

33. Ayres, 13, 79–83.

34. Of course we do not know whether Sir Francis Dashwood consciously planned his garden to mock those at Stowe. However, Lord Temple of Stowe was a political rival.

35. E. Towers, *Dashwood. The man and the myth*, 1986, 31–9.

36. H. Walpole, *Memoirs of George II*, ed. J. Brooke, 1985, Vol. I, 114; Walpole, *Letters*, 1, 343.

37. The manuscript of this diary is in the Bodleian Library, but there is a printed version edited by B. Kemp in the *Slavonic Review*, 38, 1959–60, 195–222.

38. Walpole, *Memoirs*, Vol. I, 82–3.

39. Lady Mary Wortley Montagu, *Letters*, 1906, 304, 362.

40. Spence, 243.

41. *A Voyage Performed by the Late Earl of Sandwich around the Mediterranean in the years 1738 and 1739 written by himself*, 2nd edn, 1807, lii.

42. Spence, 243–4, 258.

43. *A Voyage . . . Sandwich*, 137–69.

44. F. Dashwood, *The Dashwoods of West Wycombe*, 1987, 22.

45. Quoted ibid., 23. No source given.

46. Ibid.; Towers, 63. No source given.

47. R. Fuller, *Hell-Fire Francis*, 1939, 65; Towers, 64.
48. R. Cust, *History of the Society of Dilettanti*, 1892, 4.
49. Horace Walpole, *Correspondence*, ed. P. Cunningham, 1891, 1340, Walpole to Mann, 14 April 1743.
50. Cust, 7–8.
51. Ibid., 24–9.
52. Ibid., 28–30.
53. Ibid., 36–7.
54. C. Harcourt-Smith, *The Society of Dilettanti, its Regalia and Pictures*, 1937, 23–8.
55. S. West, 'Libertinism and the Ideology of Male Friendship in the Portraits of the Society of Dilettanti', *Eighteenth Century Life*, Vol. 16 New series 2, May 1992, 80, 86.
56. Walpole, *Memoirs of George II, 1751–1754*, Vol. I, 113–14.
57. West, 86.
58. Cust, 49–53, 71, 78–99; Harcourt Smith, 8.

CHAPTER 5 – THE MEDMENHAM FRIARS

1. J. Almon, *The New Foundling Hospital for Wit being a collection in prose and verse*, 1784, Book III, 105–7.
2. C. Johnstone, *Chrysal, or The Adventures of a Guinea*, 1908 edn, 387.
3. H. Walpole, *Journal of Visits to Country Seats*, 1982 edn, 50–1.
4. T. Langley, *The History and Antiquities of the Hundred of Desborough and Deanery of Wycombe*, 1797, 343–4.
5. Walpole, *Journal*, 51.
6. Dashwood, 35–8. The cellar books and letters from members are still in the possession of the Dashwood family.
7. E. Weatherley ed., *The Correspondence of John Wilkes and Charles Churchill*, 1954, 3. The ghost refers to one of Churchill's poems.
8. Dashwood, 26.
9. Ibid., 20.
10. Ibid., 36.
11. D. McCormick, *The Hell Fire Club*, 1958, 197. There are no references or supporting evidence in this book.
12. J. Laver ed., *The Poems of Charles Churchill*, 1933, 382–3.
13. Johnstone, 388–9.
14. L. Carswell and J. Dralle eds, *The Political Journal of George Bubb Dodington*, 1965, xii–xiv.
15. L. Namier and J. Brooke, *The History of Parliament 1754–1790*, 1985, 32–3.
16. Ibid., 302.
17. Ibid., 640.
18. Ibid., 243.
19. Ibid., 441–2.
20. Ibid., 38.

21. Dashwood, 38.
22. Jones, *Clubs*, 203–5.
23. Ibid., 110.
24. Dashwood, 38–9.
25. *Nocturnal Revels. The History of the King's Place and other modern nunneries . . . by a member of the Order of St Francis*, 1774. 'Nun' was an eighteenth-century slang word for prostitute, and a nunnery was a brothel.
26. J. Hall-Stevenson, *The Works*, 1795, Vol. III, 269–79.
27. F.A. Pottle ed., *Boswell's London Journal 1762–1763*, 1985, 14.
28. Kemp, *Sir Francis Dashwood*, 152.

CHAPTER 6 – *ESSAY ON WOMAN*: THE FRIARS EXPOSED

1. Cash, *Wilkes*, 68.
2. This showed a certain hypocrisy on Wilkes's part, as had the peace not been signed he would not have been able to go to France.
3. Thomas suggests 1754 for the *Essay on Woman* and gives as evidence a letter in BL Add. MS 39867 fol. 103: P. Thomas, *John Wilkes*, 1996, 4; Cash gives 1759 as the date of the poem: A. Cash ed., *The Essay on Woman*, 2006, vii.
4. Cash, *Essay on Woman*, 16, 18, 19, 25.
5. Ibid., 23.
6. Ibid., 33.
7. Ibid., 85.
8. Ibid., 128.
9. Ibid., 151.
10. Ibid., 96, 101.
11. Ibid., 101, 125–6.
12. *Journal of the House of Lords, 1760–1764*, 414.
13. H. Walpole, *Memoirs of the Reign of King George III*, ed. D. Jarrett, 2005, 205.
14. Ibid., 247–8.
15. Cash, *Wilkes*, 153.
16. *Parliamentary History of England, 1760–1764*, 1813, 414.
17. G. Martelli, *Jemmy Twitcher. A life of the fourth Earl of Sandwich*, 1962, 63–4.
18. Ibid., 60.
19. *Journal of the House of Lords*, 429.
20. Cash, *Wilkes*, 165.
21. A.P. Harvey, *Sex in Georgian England*, 1994, 12–13.
22. P. Wagner, *Eros Revived*, 1988, 47–8.
23. J. Foxon, *Libertine Literature in England 1660–1745*, 1964, 5–6.
24. Ibid., 3, 12, 39.
25. Wagner, 56, quoting from *The Secrets of the Convent*, which was published in 1765, shortly after the Medmenham Friars were exposed.
26. Wagner, 65.
27. *The Rule of Taste, or The Elegant Debauchee. A True Story*, 1760.

28. Harvey, 40. Early feminists such as Mary Astell and Mary Wollstonecraft tried to raise women's consciousness, and Astell wrote that marriage was a form of slavery.
29. R. D. Altick, *The English Common Reader*, 1957, 30.
30. Dissenters were barred from Oxford and Cambridge, but not from the Scottish universities, and the University of Edinburgh ran a distance learning course for dissenters who wished to become physicians.
31. Altick, 35.
32. Ibid., 52.
33. Ashe, *Hell-Fire Club*, 38. Ashe's source for this information is Horace Walpole, who cannot be relied upon to give the absolute truth.

CHAPTER 7 – PUBLIC MEN AND PRIVATE VICES

1. Dashwood, 14–15.
2. K.G. Davies, *The Royal African Company*, 1957, 4, 45, 64–6, 380–90.
3. E. Hatton, *A New View of London*, 1708, Vol. II, 593.
4. Kemp, *Sir Francis Dashwood*, 9.
5. For a full discussion on whether English landed society was open to newcomers see L. Stone, *An Open Elite?*, 1986.
6. R. Sedgwick, *The History of Parliament, The House of Commons 1715–1754*, 1970, Vol. I, 604.
7. Ibid., 604–5.
8. Walpole, *Memoirs of George II*, 7.
9. Ibid., 82.
10. Ibid., 117.
11. Ibid., 215–16.
12. Cash, *Wilkes*, 98.
13. Walpole, *Memoirs of George III*, 113.
14. Fuller, 210.
15. B. Kemp ed., 'Sir Francis Dashwood's Diary of his Visit in St Petersburg in 1733', *Slavonic Review*, 38, 1959–60, 205.
16. Ibid., 119.
17. Dashwood, 194–5.
18. Ibid., 192.
19. Ibid. However, Pevsner describes this as a Palladian double loggia: N. Pevsner, E. Williams and K. Brandwood, *Buildings of England: Buckinghamshire*, 2nd edn, 1994, 730.
20. Dashwood, 196, 213, 216; Pevsner et al., 732.
21. W. Pearson, 'Digging for Victory', *The National Trust Magazine*, 2006.
22. C. Fabricant, 'Binding and Dressing Nature's Loose Tresses: the ideology of Augustan landscape design', *Studies in Eighteenth Century Culture*, 8, 1979, 131.
23. S. Ross, *What Gardens Mean*, 1998, 67.

24. L. Moor, 'Queer Gardens: Mary Delaney's *Flowers and Friendship*', *Eighteenth Century Studies*, 39, issue 1, 2006, 57–8; Ross, 68; see also J.G. Turner, 'The Sexual Politics of Landscape: images of Venus in eighteenth century poetry and landscape gardening', in *Studies in Eighteenth Century Culture*, Vol. II, 343–66.
25. National Monuments Record, Buckinghamshire (NMR), Number SU 89 SW 54, SU 89 SW 337.
26. National Monuments Record, SU 89 SW 55, SU 89 SW 51, SU 89 SW43, SU 89 SW 49.
27. The house and park at West Wycombe are in the hands of the National Trust, although the Dashwood family still live in the house and have restored it at their own expense. The caves are still privately owned.
28. Kemp, *Sir Francis Dashwood*, 120–1.
29. Ibid., 108–9.
30. Ashe suggests Weymouth, Dorset, instead of Herefordshire: Ashe, *Hell-Fire Club*, 90.
31. Carswell and Dralle eds, *Dodington*, x–xiii.
32. Ibid., xiii.
33. Ibid., xiv.
34. Ibid., 96.
35. Ibid., xiv.
36. Ibid., 82, 225.
37. Ibid., xv–xvii.
38. Ibid., 109, 113, 326.
39. N.A.M. Rodger, *The Insatiable Earl*, 1962, 2.
40. Martelli, 26.
41. Rodger, 70–2.
42. Ibid., 75.
43. Ibid., 143, 170, 173.
44. Martelli, 90, 96.
45. Rodger, 123; Martelli, 174.
46. Quoted in Martelli, 85.
47. The most recent and comprehensive biography of Wilkes is A. Cash, *John Wilkes. The Scandalous Father of Liberty*, 2006.
48. Ibid., 89–9, 20.
49. Ibid., 17; Thomas, 4.
50. Cash, 18.
51. Ibid., 20.
52. Ibid., 26–7.
53. Ibid., 28.
54. Ibid., 46.
55. Ibid., 115.
56. See ibid., for a full account of this election.
57. Ibid., 326.
58. Ibid., 378.

CHAPTER 8 – SCOTLAND AND THE FIRES OF HELL

1. R. Wodrow, *Analecta or Materials for a History of Remarkable Providence mostly relating to the Scotch Ministers and Christian Elders*, 1842, x, xxviii, 40, 325.
2. R. Chambers, *Traditions of Edinburgh*, 1868, 150–1, 153–4.
3. M. McElroy, *A Century of Scottish Clubs 1700–1800*, 1969, quoting from Wodrow, *Analecta*, 309.
4. G.S. Pryde, *Social Life in Scotland since 1707*, 1934, 3–4.
5. Ibid., 4.
6. C.A. Whatley, 'The Dark Side of the Enlightenment: sorting out serfdom', in T.M. Devine and J.R. Young, *Eighteenth-Century Scotland: New Perspectives*, 1999, 259–74.
7. E. Lord, 'Slavery in Scotland?', *The Local Historian*, 37, no. 4, November 2007, 233–44.
8. Edinburgh University Library, Special Collections, Laing MS 339, Register of the Resolutions and Proceedings of the Society for the Reformation of Manners.
9. Ibid., 1–3, 6–7.
10. Ibid., 16.
11. Ibid., 20.
12. Ibid., 22–3.
13. Ibid., 25.
14. Ibid., 8–9.
15. G.E. Burch, 'Defoe and the Edinburgh Society for the Reformation of Manners', *Review of English Studies*, 16, no. 63, July 1940, 306–12.
16. For a full discussion on social control in Scotland see L. Leneman and R. Mitchison, *Sin in the City: sexuality and social control in urban Scotland 1660–1780*, 1998.
17. Scottish National Archives (SNA), E/5043/1 Anstruther Customs Accounts 1742–1748.
18. Ibid.
19. *A List of Persons concerned in the Rebellion transmitted to the Commissioners of Excise by Several Supervisors in Scotland*, ed. W. MacLeod, Scottish Historical Society, Vol. VIII, 1890, 62–9. The list was sent to the government on 7 May 1746.
20. *Records of the Most Ancient and Puissant Order of the Beggar's Benison and Merryland of Anstruther*, facsimile edn, 1982.
21. There are Beggar's Benison medals in the British Museum and the Royal Museum of Scotland. David Stevenson has traced evidence of the saying 'prick and purse' as being used by the criminal underworld in London in 1732: D. Stevenson, *The Beggar's Benison*, 2001, 12–13.
22. St Andrews University Library, MS 38351, The Knights of the Beggar's Benison at the Wig Club, 1827. This document reads as follows: 'On the 20th day of the month known to the vulgar as September in the third year of my Sovereignty and that of the Order 5923'. Using the date given in the Beggar's Benison Code of Institution 5923 = 1923.

23. *Records of . . . the Beggar's Benison*, 2–5.
24. Evidence from SNA E/5043/1.
25. Stevenson, 151–2.
26. *Records of . . . the Beggar's Benison*, 9–10.
27. Ibid., Supplement, 14.
28. Cocks, 1218–19.
29. *Records of . . . the Beggar's Benison*, Supplement, 13–14.
30. For a full discussion on Scottish attitudes towards sex in the past see R. Mitchison and L. Leneman, *Sexuality and Social Control, Scotland 1660–1780*, 1981.
31. *Records of . . . the Beggar's Benison*, Supplement, 14–15.
32. Ibid., 33, 45.
33. Ibid., 19.
34. Ibid., 84–5.
35. *Records of . . . the Beggar's Benison*, 6–8.
36. D. McNaughton, 'John MacNaughton and the Beggar's Benison', *Scottish Genealogist*, 14, no. 3, November 1967, 55–8.
37. Stevenson, 136.
38. SNA GD26/11/84 quoted in Stevenson, 149–50.
39. W. Creech ed., *Edinburgh Fugitive Pieces*, 1791.
40. *Records of . . . the Beggar's Benison*, 10.
41. W.H. Epstein, *John Cleland*, 1974, 68–71.
42. Ibid., 69.
43. *List of Persons*, 62–3.
44. St Andrews University Library, Mss 133/7/4 Minutes of the Pittenweem Sea Box, 1633–1757.
45. V.C.P. Hodson, *List of the Officers of the Bengal Army*, 1927. It is probable that civil lists would show more examples, and the relationship between Pittenweem and the East India Company in the nineteenth century is described by D.Affleck in 'Reality History? A heritage story told in drama', *Scottish Local History*, 63, Spring 2005, 34–6.
46. R. Hyams, *Empire and Sexuality. The British experience*, 1990, 46, 88, 115–16.
47. J. De Groot, 'Sex and Race: the construct of language and image in the nineteenth century', in C. Hall ed., *The Culture of Empire*, 2000, 53.
48. H.H. Kapland, *Russian Overseas Commerce with Great Britain in the Reign of Catherine the Great*, 1995, 36, 39.
49. A.G. Cross, 'The Order of the Beggars Benison in Russia: an unknown episode in Scoto-Russian relations in the eighteenth century', *Scottish Slavonic Review*, 3, Autumn 1984, 45–63.
50. Ibid., 49.
51. The use of the word 'knight' for members does not appear in the Scottish evidence, but one of the nineteenth-century speculations on the origin of the Beggar's suggests that James V created an order of Knights of the Beggar's Benison.
52. The manuscript reference is Derbyshire Record Office, D239M/0478. The relevant documents have been transcribed and printed by Cross.

53. Cross, 51–2.
54. A Beggar's Benison punchbowl at Kedleston Hall in Derbyshire suggests that Sir Nathanial Curzon was a member.
55. J. Berg and B. Lagercrantz, *Scots in Sweden*, 1962, 65.
56. J.G. Duncan, 'Scottish Trading Links with Sweden', *Scottish Local History*, 23, 1991, 13.
57. Stevenson, 193, 198, 253.
58. 'An Account of the Friday Club written by Lord Cockburn together with notes on certain other social clubs in Edinburgh', in *The Book of the Old Edinburgh Club*, Vol. III, 1910, 135–6.
59. Ibid., 138.
60. Ibid., 139.
61. Small Red Book of the Wig Club, 15 April 1807.
62. Ibid.
63. Ibid., 4–7.
64. D. Stevenson, 'What was the Quest of the Knights of the Mortar? An indelicate suggestion', *Scottish Historical Review*, 68, no. 2, October 1989, 182–4.
65. National Library of Scotland, MS 2004, *The Sederunt Book of the Knights of the Cape*, 3–14.
66. Ibid., 19, 21, 37.
67. M.D. McElroy, *Scotland's Age of Improvement*, 1969, 147–52.
68. *Sederunt Book*, 91–3.
69. McElroy, 280.
70. J. Ramsay, *Scotland and Scotsmen of the Eighteenth Century*, 1888, 42–4.
71. Stevenson, 223–4.
72. Creech ed., *Edinburgh Fugitive Pieces*.
73. Ibid., 48–52.
74. Ibid., 59–62.
75. *Ranger's Impartial List of the Ladies of Pleasure in Edinburgh*, 1775; facsimile edn Scolar Press, 1978, no pagination.

CHAPTER 9 – BEEFSTEAKS, DEMONIACS, DALKEY AND COLONIAL AMERICA

1. M. Grosley, *A Tour to London*, 1772, Vol. I, 49, 52.
2. Ibid., 59–60.
3. Ibid., 160–7.
4. W. Hutton, *A Journey from Birmingham to London*, 1785, 5, 75–80.
5. Ibid., 98.
6. W. Arnold, *The Life and Death of the Sublime Society of Beefsteaks*, 1871, xiii, xix–xxx, 3.
7. Ibid., 4–5.
8. Ibid., 7–8.
9. Ibid., 45.

10. Ibid., 47–8.
11. Ibid., 105–7.
12. Ibid., 51, 56, 59, 133.
13. Ibid., 9–10.
14. J. Walker Ord, *The History and Antiquities of Cleveland*, 1849; facsimile edn Patrick & Shelton, 1972, 245.
15. Jones, 155.
16. Hall-Stevenson, Vol. I, 187.
17. Walker Ord, 253; Hall-Stevenson, Vol. III, 149.
18. Walker Ord, 254.
19. A.H. Cash, *Laurence Sterne. The Early and Middle Years*, 1975, 181.
20. Jones, 159; Hall-Stevenson, Vol. III, 44, 133, 149.
21. Cash, *Sterne*, 193.
22. Ibid.; Jones, 156.
23. Hall-Stevenson, Vol. III, 15.
24. Ibid., 17–21.
25. Ibid., 44–51, 150.
26. Jones, 156.
27. Cash, *Sterne*, 188.
28. Ashe, *Hell-Fire Club*, 207–8.
29. G. Ashe, *Do What You Will: a history of anti-morality*, 1974, 185.
30. *An Duanaire, Poems of the Dispossessed*, quoted in G. Holmes and D. Szechi, *The Age of Oligarchy. Pre-Industrial Britain 1722–1783*, 1993, 234.
31. J.J. Gaskin, *Varieties of Irish History*, 1869, 410–19.
32. Moody and Vaughan, 160–1.
33. J. Killen ed., *The Decade of the United Irishmen*, 1997, 1–2.
34. Ibid., 5–7.
35. Gaskin, 1; Jones, 165.
36. Gaskin, 35–6.
37. Ibid., 267.
38. Ibid., 255.
39. Jones, 172.
40. Ibid., 170.
41. Gaskin, 222.
42. M. Lyons ed., *The Memoirs of Mrs Leeson*, 1995, vii.
43. Ibid., 169–70.
44. Ibid., 169.
45. Clark, 389.
46. Ibid., 390–2.
47. Ibid., 393. Unfortunately it is not clear which primary source reference refers to this club.
48. C. Bridenbaugh ed., *Gentleman's Progress. The itinerarum of Dr Alexander Hamilton*, 1948, xii, 108, 115, 133.
49. Ibid., 6.
50. Ibid., 46, 88.
51. Ibid., xviii–xxi.

52. P. Thompson, *Rum Punch and Revolution*, 2005, 2; D.W. Conroy, *In Public Houses: drink and the revolution of authority in colonial Massachusetts*, 1995, 2.
53. Thompson, 9.
54. Ibid., 63, 86.
55. Conroy, 7.
56. Thompson, 43, 92, 102, 104.
57. Thompson, 101, has an illustration of the glass.
58. Conroy, 25.
59. C.A. Lopez and E.W. Herbert, *The Private Franklin*, 1975, 12.
60. J.A.L. Leman, *The Life of Benjamin Franklin*, Vol. I: *1706–1730*, 2005, 110–11, 133.
61. G.S. Wood, *The Americanisation of Benjamin Franklin*, 2004, 17–19.
62. E.S. Morgan, *Benjamin Franklin*, 2002, 1.
63. Ibid., 21–2.
64. Ibid., 105–8, 115.
65. V.W. Crane, 'The Club of Honest Whigs: friends of science and liberty', *William and Mary Quarterly* , 3rd series, 23, no. 2, April 1966, 16–18, 22, 25.
66. Dashwood, 67–9.
67. Ashe, *Hell-Fire Club*, 195.
68. Clark, 420–1.
69. Quennell ed., 10–12, 24, 27, 30–1.
70. Ibid., 58, 63.
71. Ibid., 181, 221, 234, 237, 240.
72. Ashe, *Do What You Will*, 185; *Hell-Fire Club*, 256.
73. *The Works of Lord Byron*, Wordsworth edn, 1994, v–viii.

CONCLUSION

1. For a full discussion on this topic see E. Royle, *Revolutionary Britannia?*, 2000.

Bibliography

Unless otherwise stated, place of publication is London.

PRIMARY SOURCES: MANUSCRIPTS

Cambridgeshire Record Office 588/015

British Library

Add. MS 39867 fol. 103
Harl. MS 7003; Harl. MS 7317

Edinburgh University Library, Special Collections

Laing MS 339: Register of the Resolutions and Proceedings of the Society for the Reformation of Manners

Greater London Record Office (GLRO)

Middlesex Session Book 1721

John Rylands University Library of Manchester (JRULM)

Cornwall-Legh Collection, High Legh II, Box 15, Papers concerning prints and pictures bought by George John Legh in Italy and Switzerland

Scottish National Archives

E/5043/1: Anstruther Customs Accounts 1742–1748
GD 50/214: Beggar's Benison Diploma for James Stewart 7 August 1770

National Library of Scotland

MS 2004: The Sederunt Book of the Knights of the Cape

National Monuments Records, English Heritage

SU 89 SW 54
SU 89 SW 337
SU 89 SW 55
SU 89 SW 57
SU 89 SW 43
SU 89 SW 49

St Andrews University Library, Special Collections

MS 133/7/4: Minutes of the Pittenweem Sea Box, 1622–1757
MS 38351: The Knights of the Beggar's Benison at the Wig Club, 1827

PRIMARY SOURCES: PRINTED

Addison, J., *Remarks on Several Parts of Italy in the Years 1701, 1702, 1703*, 1705
Almon, J., *The New Foundling Hospital for Wit, Being a collection of curious pieces in verse and prose*, J. Debrett, 1784
Aubrey, J., *Brief Lives*, Oxford: OUP, 1898
Bacon, F., *Essays,* ed. M.J. Hawkins, Everyman, 1994
Barry, J. and K. Morgan, *Reformation and Revival in Eighteenth Century Bristol*, Bristol Record Society, No. 45, 1994
Becker, B., *The World Bewitched*, 1696
Bickley, F. ed., *Report on the Hastings Mss of the Late Rawdon Hastings Esq.*, Historical Manuscripts Commission, 1934
Bragge, F., *The Case of the Hertfordshire Witch Considered*, 1712
Bragge, F., *A Defence of the Proceedings against Jane Wenham*, 1712
Bridenbaugh, C. ed., *Gentleman's Progress. The itinerarum of Dr Alexander Hamilton*, Williamsburg: Institute of Early American History and Culture, 1948
Bromley, W., *Remarks on the Grand Tour of France and Italy*, 1705
Bruce, J. ed., *The Diary of John Manningham 1602–1603*, Camden Society, 1868
Burnet, G., *Some Passages of the Life and Death of the Right Honourable John, Earl of Rochester*, 1680
Byron, G., *The Works of Lord Byron*, Wordsworth Editions, 1994
Calendar of State Papers 1623–1625, Longman, Brown & Green, 1859
Calendar of State Papers in the Stuart Mss in Windsor Castle, HMSO, 1906
Carswell, J. and L. Dralle eds, *The Political Journal of George Bubb Dodington*, Oxford: Clarendon Press, 1965
Cartwright, J. ed., *The Wentworth Papers 1705–1739*, Wyman & Sons, 1883
Creech, W. ed., *Edinburgh Fugitive Pieces*, Edinburgh, 1791
De Beer, E. ed., *The Diary of John Evelyn*, Oxford: OUP, 2000
Defoe, D., *The History of the Devil*, 1726
Defoe, D., *A System of Magic*, 1728
The Diaboliciad, 1777

Doble, C.E. ed., *Remarks and Collections of Thomas Hearne*, Volume III, Oxford Historical Society, 1889

Elias, A.C. ed., *Memoirs of Laetitia Pilkington*, Athens, Georgia: University of Georgia Press, 1997

A Full Confutation of Witchcraft More Particularly of the Full Depositions against Jane Wenham, tried at Hertford, 1712

A Full and Impartial Account of the Discovery of Sorcery and Witchcraft practised by Jane Wenham of Walkern, Hertfordshire, 3rd edn, 1712

A Further and Particular Account of the Hell Fire Sulphur Club, Edinburgh, 1721

Garrick, D., *Lethe*, 1740

Gay, J., *The Mohocks*, 1712

Gay, J., *Trivia, or The Art of Walking the Streets of London*, 1716

Graham, W. ed., *Letters of Joseph Addison*, Oxford: Clarendon Press, 1941

Granville, Mary, *The Autobiography and Correspondence of Mary Granville, Mrs Delaney*, ed. Lady Llanover, R. Bentley & Son, 1862

Grosley, M., *A Tour to London*, translated from the French by T. Nugent, Dublin, 1772

Hall-Stevenson, J., *The Works*, 1795

Halsband, R. ed., *The Complete Letters of Lady Mary Wortley Montagu*, Oxford: Clarendon Press, 1965–7

Hatton, E., *A New View of London*, 1708

Hawkes, W. ed., *The Diaries of Sanderson Miller of Radway*, Warwick: Dugdale Society, 2005

The Hell-Fire Club kept by a Society of Blasphemers, 1721

Historical Manuscripts Commission, *The Calendar of State Papers in the Stuart Mss. in the Possession of HM the King at Windsor*, HMSO, 1906

Hurd, R., *A Dialogue on the Uses of Foreign Travel*, 1764

Hutton, W., *A Journey from Birmingham to London*, 1785

Hyde, E., *Life of Edward, Earl of Clarendon, written by Himself*, Oxford: OUP, 1857

Jenkinson, C., *Life, History and Remarkable Pedigree of the Right Honourable Simon, Lord Luttrell*, 1769

Johnstone, C., *Chrysal, or The Adventures of a Guinea*, 1721, Routledge, 1908 edn

Jones, T. and G. Holmes eds, *The London Diaries of William Nicolson, Bishop of Carlisle 1702–1718*, Oxford: Clarendon Press, 1985

Journal of the House of Lords, 1760–64

Langley, T., *The History and Antiquities of the Hundred of Desborough and Deanery of Wycombe*, 1797

Laver, J. ed., *The Poems of Charles Churchill*, Eyre & Spottiswoode, 1933

A List of Persons concerned in the Rebellion, transmitted to the Commissioners of Excise by Several Supervisors in Scotland, ed. W. MacLeod, Edinburgh: Scottish Historical Society, Volume VIII, 1890

Locke, J., *An Essay Concerning Human Understanding*, ed. P. Nidditch, Oxford: OUP, 1975

Lyons, M. ed., *The Memoirs of Mrs Leeson 1727–1797*, Dublin: The Lilliput Press (1795–7), 1995

Middleton, C., *A Letter from Rome Shewing Conformity between Popery and Paganism* (1729), 5th edn, 1742

Nocturnal Revels. The history of the King's Place and Other modern nunneries . . . by a member of the Order of St Francis, 1779

Oldmixon, J., *History of England*, 1731

The Parliamentary History of England, Vol. III AD *1714–1722*, compiled by W. Cobbett and J. Wright, Longman, 1811

Plot upon Plot. A ballad to be sung to the tune of Heigh-Ho Boys Up We Go, 1712

Pope, A., *Epistle to Several Persons (Moral Essays)*, ed. F.W. Bateson, Methuen, 1951

Pottle, F.A. ed., *Boswell's London Journal, 1762–1763*, The Folio Society, 1985

Puckle, J., *The Club, or Grey Cap for a Green Head*, 1723

Quarrel, W.H. and M. More, *London in 1710 from the Travels of Zacharias Conrad von Uffenbach*, Faber & Faber, 1934

Quennell, P. ed., *Memoirs of William Hickey*, Hutchinson, 1960

Ranger's Impartial List of the Ladies of Pleasure in Edinburgh, Edinburgh, 1775; facsimile edn, Scolar Press, 1978

Records of the Most Ancient and Puissant Order of the Beggar's Benison and Merryland of Anstruther, facsimile edn, Edinburgh: Paul Harris, 1982

Roberts, P. ed., *The Diary of David Hamilton, 1709–1714*, Oxford: Clarendon Press, 1975

The Rule of Taste, or The Elegant Debauchee. A True Story, 1760

Smith, P. ed., *The Letters of Thomas Burnet to George Duckett, 1712–1722*, The Roxburghe Club, 1914

Smith, T., 'The Diary of Thomas Smith Esq', *Wiltshire Archaeological and Natural History Magazine*, 11, 1869

Spence, J., *Letters from the Grand Tour* (1741), ed. S. Klei, Montreal: McGill–Queen's University, 1975

Sterne, L., *A Sentimental Journey through France and Italy*, New York: Liverright, 1926

Strype, J., *A Survey of the Cities of London and Westminster by John Stow*. Corrected, improved and enlarged, 1720

Swift, J., *Journal to Stella*, ed. H. Williams, Oxford: Blackwell, 1974

Treglown, E.J. ed., *The Letters of John Wilmot, Earl of Rochester*, Oxford: Blackwell, 1980

Vieth, D.M. ed., *The Works of the Earl of Rochester*, Wordsworth Poetry Library, 1995

A Voyage Performed by the Late Earl of Sandwich around the Mediterranean in the Years 1738 and 1739, written by himself, 2nd edn, 1807

Walpole, H., *Correspondence*, ed. P. Cunningham, R. Bentley & Son, 1891

Walpole, H., *Journal of a Visit to Country Seats*, 1982 edn, New York: Gould taken from the 16th volume of the Walpole Society's Publications

Walpole, H., *Memoirs of George II, 1751–1754*, ed. J. Brooke, Yale University Press, 1985

Walpole, H., *Memoirs of the Reign of King George III*, ed. D. Jarrett, Yale University Press, 1999

Ward, N., *The Secret History of Clubs*, 1709

Weatherley, E. ed., *The Correspondence of John Wilkes and Charles Churchill*, New York: Columbia University Press, 1954

Wharton, P., *The Life and Writings of Philip, late Duke of Wharton*, 1732

Whiston, W., *Memoirs of the Life and Writings of Mr William Whiston*, 1753

Wodrow, R., *Analecta, or Materials for a history of Remarkable Providence, mostly relating to the Scotch Ministers and Christian Elders*, Edinburgh: Maitland Club, 1842

Wood, A., *Athenae Oxon*, Oxford, 1885–1921

Woodward, J., *An Account of the Progress of the Reformation of Manners in England and Ireland*, 1701

Wortley Montagu, Lady M., *Letters*, Everyman Library, 1906

PRIMARY SOURCES: JOURNAL AND NEWSPAPERS

Applebee's Journal
The Connoisseur
The Daily Post
The London Gazette
Mist's Weekly Journal
Notes and Queries
The Spectator

SECONDARY SOURCES: BOOKS

Allan, R.G., *The Clubs of Georgian London*, Harvard Studies in English VII, Cambridge, Massachusetts: Harvard University Press, 1933

Altick, R.D., *The English Common Reader*, Chicago: University of Chicago Press, 1957

Arnold, W., *The Life and Death of the Sublime Society of Beefsteaks*, Bradling, Evans, 1871

Ashe, G., *Do What You Will: a history of anti-morality*, W.H. Allen, 1974

Ashe, G., *The Hell-Fire Club: Sex, Rakes and Libertines in Eighteenth-century Europe*, Stroud: Sutton, 2005

Axtell, J., *The European and the Indian*, Oxford: OUP, 1981

Ayres, P., *Classical Culture and the Idea of Rome*, 1997

Bailey, B. and P.D. Morgan, *Strangers within the Realm: cultural margins of the first British Empire*, Chapel Hill: University of North Carolina Press, 1992

Baine, R.M., *Daniel Defoe and the Supernatural*, Athens, Georgia: University of Georgia Press, 1968

Barrett Botsford, J., *English society in the eighteenth century as influenced from overseas*, Macmillan, 1924

Beattie, J.M., *Policing and Punishment in London, 1660–1750*, Oxford: OUP, 2001

Bellamy, E., *James Wheatley and Norwich Methodism in the 1750s*, Peterborough: WHHS Publications, 1994

Berg, J. and B. Lagercrantz, *Scots in Sweden*, Stockholm: The Swedish Institute, 1962

Black, J., *The British and the Grand Tour*, Croom Helm, 1985

Black, J., *The British Abroad: The Grand Tour in the eighteenth century*, Stroud: Alan Sutton, 1992

Blackett-Ord, M., *The Hell-Fire Duke*, The Kensal Press, 1982

Blyth, H., *The Rakes*, New York: Dial Press, 1971

Bond, P., *Queen Anne's American Kings*, Oxford: Clarendon Press, 1952

Bostridge, I., *Witchcraft and its Transformations 1650–1750*, Oxford: OUP, 1997

Braunmuller, A.R. and M. Hattaway, *The Cambridge Guide to Renaissance Drama*, Cambridge: CUP, 1999

Brissenden, R.F. ed., *Studies in the Eighteenth Century*, Canberra: Australian National University Press, 1968

Carparetto, D. and G. Ricuperati, *Italy in the Age of Reason*, transl. by C. Higget, Longman, 1982

Cash, A. ed., *The Essay on Woman*, New York: ANS Press, 2000

Cash, A., *John Wilkes: the scandalous father of civil liberty*, New Haven, Connecticut: Yale University Press, 2006

Cash, A., *Laurence Sterne. The Early and Middle Years*, Methuen, 1975

Chambers, R., *Traditions of Edinburgh*, Edinburgh: W. & R. Chambers, 1868

Cheney, E., *The Evolution of the Grand Tour*, Frank Cass, 1998

Clark, P., *British Clubs and Societies, 1580–1800* (2000), Oxford: OUP, 2007 edn

Cooper, C.H., *Annals of Cambridge*, Cambridge: CUP, 1852

Cust, R., *History of the Society of Dilettanti*, Macmillan, 1892

Dashwood, F., *The Dashwoods of West Wycombe*, Aurun Press, 1987

Davies, K.G., *The Royal African Company*, Longman, 1957

Davies, R.T., *Four Centuries of Witch Belief*, Methuen, 1947

Devine, T.M. and J.R. Young eds, *Eighteenth Century Scotland: New Perspectives*, East Linton Tuckwell Press, 1999

Earl, P., *A City Full of People. Men and women of London 1650–1750*, Methuen, 1994

Epstein, W.H., *John Cleland*, New York: Columbia University Press, 1974

Foxon, J., *Libertine Literature in England 1660–1745*, The Book Collector, 1964

Fuller, R., *Hell-Fire Francis*, Chatto & Windus, 1939

Gaskin, J.J., *Varieties of Irish History*, Dublin: W.B. Kelly, 1869

Gatrell, V., *The City of Laughter*, Atlantic Books, 2006

Gay, P., *The Enlightenment: an interpretation of the rise of modern paganism*, Weidenfeld & Nicolson, 1967

Hall, C. ed., *The Culture of Empire*, Manchester: Manchester University Press, 2000

Handcock, W.D., *History and Antiquities of Tallaght*, Dublin: Foster & Figgis, 1877

Harcourt-Smith, C., *The Society of Dilettanti, its Regalia and Pictures*, Macmillan, 1937

Harvey, A.P., *Sex in Georgian England*, Duckworth, 1994

Hibbert, C., *The Grand Tour*, Weidenfeld & Nicolson, 1969

Hodson, V.C.P., *List of the Officers of the Bengal Army*, Constable, 1927

Holmes, G. and Szechi, D., *The Age of Oligarchy*, Longman, 1993

Hutton, R., *The Druids*, Hambledon, 2007

Hyams, R., *Empire and Sexuality. The British experience*, Manchester: Manchester University Press, 1990

Jacobs, M.C., *The Radical Enlightenment: pantheists, Freemasons and republicans*, Allen & Unwin, 1981

Jones, L.C., *The Clubs of the Georgian Rakes*, New York: Columbia University Press, 1942

Kaplan, H.H., *Russian Overseas: commerce with Great Britain in the reign of Catherine the Great*, Philadelphia, Pennyslvania: American Philosophical Society, 1995

Kemp, B., *Sir Francis Dashwood: an eighteenth-century independent*, Macmillan, 1967

Killen, J., *The Decade of the United Irishmen*, Belfast: Blackstaff Press, 1997

Knox, T., *West Wycombe Park*, The National Trust, 2001

Kors, A.C. ed., *Encyclopaedia of the Enlightenment*, Oxford: OUP, 2003

Laroque, F., *Shakespeare: court, crowd and playgoer*, Thames & Hudson, 1999

Lea, H.C., *Minor Historical Writings*, Philadelphia: University of Pennsylvania Press, 1942

Leneman, L. and R. Mitchison, *Sin in the City: sexuality and social control in urban Scotland, 1660–1780*, Edinburgh: Scottish Cultural Press, 1998

Lord, E., *The Stuarts' Secret Army. English Jacobites 1689–1752*, Pearson, 2004

McCormick, D., *The Hell-Fire Club*, Jarrold, 1958

McElroy, D.D., *Scotland's Age of Improvement*, Edinburgh, 1969

Mannix, D.P., *The Hell-Fire Club*, New English Library, 1978

Mario, J.A., *Early Modern Italy*, Oxford: OUP, 2002

Marshall, P.J. and G. Williams, *The Great Map of Mankind: British perceptions of the world in the Age of Enlightenment*, J.M. Dent & Sons, 1982

Martelli, G., *Jemmy Twitcher. A life of the fourth Earl of Sandwich*, Jonathan Cape, 1962

Mead, W., *The Grand Tour in the Eighteenth Century*, Boston, Massachusetts: Houghton Mifflin, 1914

Meek, R.L., *Social Science and the Ignoble Savage*, Cambridge: CUP, 1970

Midgley, G., *University Life in Eighteenth-Century Oxford*, New Haven, Connecticut: Yale University Press, 1996

Mitchison, R. and L. Leneman, *Sexuality and Social Control: Scotland 1660–1780*, Oxford: Blackwell, 1981

Moody, T.W. and W.E. Vaughan eds, *A New History of Ireland, IV: Eighteenth Century*, Oxford: Clarendon Press, 1986

Morgan, E.S., *Benjamin Franklin*, New Haven, Connecticut: Yale University Press, 2002

Namier, L. and J. Brooke eds, *The History of Parliament 1754–1790*, The History of Parliament Trust, 1985

Normand, L. and G. Roberts, *Witchcraft in Early Modern Scotland*, Exeter: University of Exeter Press, 2000

Oxford English Dictionary, Oxford: Clarendon Press, 1989, 2nd edn

Peakman, J., *Lascivious Bodies: A sexual history of the eighteenth century*, Atlantic Books, 2004

Pearson, G., *Hooligan. A history of respectable fears*, Macmillan, 1983

Pevsner, N., E. Williams and K. Brandwood, *Buildings of England: Buckinghamshire*, Penguin, 2nd edn 1994

Pine-Coffin, R.S., *Biblioteca di bibliografia italiana*, Florence: Leo S. Olschki, 1974

Pinto, V. De Sola, *Enthusiastic Wit. A portrait of John Wilmot, Earl of Rochester*, Routledge, 1962

Porter, R., *Enlightenment*, Penguin, 2000

Porter, R., *Flesh in the Age of Reason*, Penguin, 2003

Pryde, G.S., *Social Life in Scotland since 1707*, The Historical Association, 1934

Ramsay, J., *Scotland and Scotsmen of the Eighteenth Century*, Edinburgh, 1888

Redwood, J., *Reason, Ridicule and Religion: the Age of Enlightenment in England 1660–1750*, Thames & Hudson, 1976

Roberts, J.M., *The Mythology of Secret Societies*, Secker & Warburg, 1972

Rodger, N.A.M., *The Insatiable Earl*, HarperCollins, 1962

Ross, S., *What Gardens Mean*, Chicago: University of Chicago Press, 1998

Royle, E., *Revolutionary Britannia?*, Manchester: Manchester University Press, 2000

Sedgwick, R., *The History of Parliament. The House of Commons 1715–1754*, The History of Parliament Trust, 1970

Stevenson, D., *The Beggar's Benison*, East Linton: Tuckwell Press, 2001

Stone, L., *An Open Elite?*, Oxford: OUP, 1986

Thomas, P., *John Wilkes: a friend to liberty*, Oxford: Clarendon, 1996

Thompson, P., *Rum Punch and Revolution*, Philadelphia: University of Pennsylvania Press, 2005

Towers, E., *Dashwood. The man and the myth*, Crucible Press, 1986

Venn, J. and J.E., *Alumni Cantabrigiensis*, CUP, 1922

Wagner, P., *Eros Revived*, Secker & Warburg, 1988

Walker Ord, J., *The History and Antiquities of Cleveland*, 1849; facsimile edn, Patrick & Shelton, 1972

Wood, G.S., *The Americanisation of Benjamin Franklin*, New York: Penguin Press, 2004

Yolton, J.W., *The Blackwell Companion to the Enlightenment*, Oxford: Blackwell, 1991

SECONDARY SOURCES: ARTICLES

Affleck, D., 'Reality History? A heritage story told in drama', *Scottish Local History*, 63, Spring 2005

Bolton, A., 'Country Houses and Gardens Old and New. West Wycombe, Buckinghamshire, I and II', *Country Life*, 1 and 8 January, 1916

Burch, G.E., 'Defoe and the Edinburgh Society for the Reformation of Manners', *Review of English Studies*, 16, no. 63, July 1940

Cockburn, H. 'An Account of the Friday Club together with Other Notes on Certain Other Social Clubs in Edinburgh', in *The Book of the Old Edinburgh Club*, Volume III, 1910

Cocks, V.W., 'Modernity and the Self in the History of Sexuality', *Historical Journal*, 49, no. 4, 2006

Crane, V.W., 'The Club of Honest Whigs: friends of science and liberty', *William and Mary Quarterly*, 3rd series, 23, no. 2, April 1966

Cross, A.G., 'The Order of the Beggar's Benison in Russia', *Scottish Slavonic Review*, 3, Autumn 1984

Curtis, T. and W. Speck, 'Societies for the Reformation of Manners', *Literature and History*, 3, 1976

Duncan, J.G., 'Scottish Trading Links with Sweden', *Scottish Local History*, 23, 1991

Fabricant, C., 'Binding and Dressing Nature's Loose Tresses: the ideology of Augustan landscape design', *Studies in Eighteenth Century Culture*, 8, 1979

Gormley, N., 'The Trials of James Cotter and Henry, Baron Barry of Santry: two case studies of the administration of criminal justice in early eighteenth-century Ireland', *Irish Historical Studies*, 21, May 1999

Graves, T.S., 'Some Pre-Mohock Clansmen', *Studies in Philology*, 20, 1923

Guthrie, N., 'No Truth or Very Little in the Whole Story? A reassessment of the Mohock scare of 1712', *Eighteenth-Century Life*, 20, no. 37, New Series, May 1996

Kemp, B., 'Sir Francis Dashwood's Russian Diary', *Slavonic Review*, 38, 1959–60

Klein, L.E., 'Politeness and the Interpretation of the British Eighteenth Century', *Historical Journal*, 45, no. 4, 2002

Lord, E., 'Slavery in Scotland?', *The Local Historian*, 37, no. 4, November 2007

Mackie, E., 'Boys will be Boys: masculinity, conviviality and the Restoration rakes', *Eighteenth Century*, 46, no. 2, Summer 2005

McNaughton, D., 'John MacNaughton and the Beggar's Benison', *Scottish Genealogist*, 14, no. 3, November 1967

Moor, L., 'Queer Gardens: Mary Delany's *Flowers and Friendship*', *Eighteenth Century Studies*, 39, issue 1, 2006

Pearson, W., 'Digging for Victory', *The National Trust Magazine*, 2006

Shoemaker, R., 'Male Honour and the Decline of Public Violence in Eighteenth-century London', *Social History*, 26, no. 2, 2001

Stevenson, D., 'What was the Quest of the Knights of the Mortar? An indelicate suggestion', *Scottish Historical Review*, 68, no. 2, October 1989

Stott, D., 'The Case of the Mohocks: rake violence in London', *Social History*, 20, no. 2, 1995

Turner, J.G., 'The Sexual Politics of Landscape: images of Venus in eighteenth century poetry and landscape gardening', in *Studies in Eighteenth Century Culture*, Vol. II, 1982

Vieth, D.M., 'Sir Charles Sedley and the Ballers' Oath', *Scriblerian*, 12, no. 1, Autumn 1979

West, S., 'Libertinism and the Ideology of Male Friendship in the Portraits of the Dilettanti', *Eighteenth Century Life*, 16, New Series, 2, May 1992

Wrigley, E.A., 'A Simple Model of London's Importance in a Changing English Society and Economy, 1650–1750', *Past and Present*, 37, 1967

UNPUBLISHED THESES

Hayes, P.D., 'Politics in Norfolk 1750–1832', Ph.D. thesis, University of Cambridge, 1957

McElroy, M., 'A Century of Scottish Clubs 1700–1800', Ph.D. thesis, University of Edinburgh, 1969

Index

Addison, Joseph 82
Admiralty 81, 106, 107, 144–6
Alleyne, Tim 30, 35
Almon, John 98, 105, 117
America 34–6, 203, 205
  Annapolis 203, 204
  Boston 206
  Maryland 203
  New England 206
  New York 203
  Pennsylvania 109, 110
  Philadelphia 203–5
American Sublime Society of Beefsteaks
  204
American War of Independence 37, 65,
  77, 188, 191, 201
Anne, Queen 27, 28, 33, 35, 38, 77
Anstruther, Fife 125, 164–70, 172, 175,
  177
Applebee's Journal 53, 206
Armitage, Stephen 199–201
Ashe, Geoffrey xviii–xx, 69, 70, 208, 210
Aubrey, Sir John 106, 107
Aylesbury 150–2

Ballers 12–14, 72
Baltic 165, 170, 185
Beggar's Benison xx, xxi, 158, 164–78,
  184, 185, 202, 203, 205
blasphemy 46, 52, 48, 99, 106, 118, 119,
  196, 205
Bold Bucks 52, 53
Book of Common Prayer 109, 112, 207,
  208
Bristol Society for Reformation and
  Revival, 16

brothels 12, 49, 51, 124, 126, 151, 154,
  202
Buckinghamshire 87, 97 106–9, 118, 136
Bugle Boys 1, 3–5
Burnet, Bishop Gilbert 12, 14, 30, 31,
  77
Bute, Lord 104, 116, 117, 135, 193
Byron, Lord George Gordon 210

Cambridge 69, 78, 85, 89, 90, 143, 210,
  213
  Jesus College 70, 71, 193
Castle Dreel 166, 167
Catholicism 2, 4, 51, 75, 78, 80, 81, 83–5,
  88, 112, 124
Charles II 7, 14, 107
Chrysal 87, 97, 99, 100
Church of England xxvii, xviii, xx, 7, 9, 12,
  46, 47, 59, 61, 124, 154, 207
Church of Scotland 157, 163, 164
Churchill, Charles 102, 104, 108, 112,
  208
Churchill, Edward 32
Civil War 4, 77, 107
class xx, xxvii, 38, 128, 133, 134, 155, 158,
  178
Cleland, David 175
Cleland, John xxvi, 125, 126, 174, 180
Cleland, Robert 174
clubs xviii, xxi, xxv, 3, 5, 19–21
  Atheistical Club 24
  Boar Club 158
  Broken Shopkeepers' Club 23
  Calves' Head Club 23
  Club of Honest Whigs 207
  Clydeside Gentleman's Club 181

clubs (*cont.*)
  Fair Intellectuals Club 182
  Farting Club 22
  Hungarian Club 203
  Kit-Kat Club 23, 93
  Man Hunters Club 24
  Man Killing Club 24
  Mollies Club 23
  Monday Club 207
  No Nose Club 22
  Physical Club 203
  Royal Bachelor's Club 177, 178
  Ruffian Club 181
  Spendthrift Club 158
  Sweating Club 181
  Tuesday Club 204
  Whin Bush Club 181
  Withered's Club 203
  Yorkshire Club 23
Commonwealth xxv, 6, 7, 39
Crazy Castle 84, 192, 194, 196
Crazy Tales, 194–5
Creech, William, 182–4
Curll, Edmund 40, 124, 206

Dalkey Island 199
Damned Crew 1, 2
Dashwood, Sir Francis xix, 78, 98, 99, 100,
    102–6, 110, 111, 119, 123, 136, 138,
    139, 142–4, 150, 193, 205, 207
  Book of Common Prayer 109, 207, 208
  Catholicism 81, 88, 112, 113
  Chancellor of the Exchequer 104, 135
  Dilettanti Society 90, 92–5, 132, 136,
      137
  Divan Club 90, 91, 105, 132
  family 132, 133
  Grand Tour 78, 79, 81, 85–7, 132, 134
  Jacobitism 81, 112, 134
  Medmenham Abbey 85, 95, 98
  Medmenham Friars 85, 92, 95, 101, 131
  as Member of Parliament 107, 134, 135
  politics 134–6
  Russia 88, 89, 177
  Turkey 19, 89, 90
  West Wycombe 85, 86, 97, 136,
      137–40
Defoe, Daniel 40, 47, 122, 159, 161, 163
deists 42, 47, 109, 194
Delany, Mrs 56, 57, 63
Demoniacs 193, 194, 196

Devil xviii, 4, 9, 10, 14, 17, 27, 39, 41, 43,
    62–4, 69, 94, 100, 105, 158, 194, 210
Divan Club 90–3, 100, 105, 113, 132, 144,
    147, 173
Dodington, Bubb 92, 103, 106, 107, 109,
    131, 137, 140–3
Dublin 61–4, 196, 199, 201, 202
duelling 9, 121, 152

Edinburgh 157–62, 173, 176, 202, 203
Edinburgh Society for the Reformation of
    Manners 159, 161–3
Elizabeth I, Queen of England 1, 2, 4
Enlightenment xviii, xxi–xxiii, 19, 20, 39,
    85, 122, 207, 214
Essay on Woman 69, 115, 117, 118, 120,
    121, 126, 146, 151
Evelyn, John 7, 10

Fanny Hill, xxvi, 125, 126, 173–6, 188
Franklin, Benjamin, 109, 110, 205–8

Gay, John 28, 29
George I xvii, 33, 38, 59
George II 134, 142
Glasgow 157, 160, 161, 173, 176, 202
Grand Tour xxvi, 8, 50, 75–86, 90, 132–4,
    136, 143, 210
Grosley, Monsieur, 187, 188
Gunpowder Plot 1, 2

Hall-Stevenson, John 108–11, 192–4
Hamilton, Dr Alexander 203–4
Hectors 5, 6
Hell-Fire Club xvii, xviii, xxv, xxvii, 24, 39,
    42, 44–6, 48, 49, 51–7, 69–72, 94, 95,
    97, 102, 158, 162, 177, 185, 196, 201,
    203, 205, 206, 211, 212
Hickey, William 36, 37, 208
Hillsborough, Viscount, 52, 57, 58
Hinchingbrooke House 144, 147
Hinchingbrooke, Lord Edward 31, 32
Hogarth, William xxv, 108, 122, 126, 188
Holland 13, 37, 43, 44, 50, 75, 108
House of Commons 107, 134
House of Lords xvii, 45, 47, 51, 61, 120,
    134, 144
Hume, David 160
Huntingdon 144, 146, 147
Hurd, Richard 79, 80
Hutton, William, 187–8

India 108, 125, 132, 152, 174, 175, 208
Ireland 61, 62, 196–8
Irish Catholics 196–8
Irish Hell-Fire Club 61–6, 92, 109, 196, 197
Irish Protestants 61, 197–9
Iroquois 28, 35
Italy 3, 79–84, 89, 90
  Rome 2, 76, 79, 80, 83, 87, 88

Jacobites 33, 38–40, 50, 51, 53, 58, 60, 61,
  67–9, 78, 81, 94, 107, 112, 134, 143,
  145, 165, 170, 172, 173
James V of Scotland 167
James VI of Scotland and I of England,
  1–5, 139
  Demonology 4
Jezebel Club, 182–3
Johnson, Samuel xxi, 19
Johnstone, Charles, 87, 97, 99, 100
justices *see* magistrates

Kidgell, Reverend John 69, 119
Killigrew, Henry 8
Kingdom of Dalkey 196, 199–201
Knights
  Knights Errant 5
  Knights of St Francis *see* Medmenham
    Friars
  Knights of the Blue 5
  Knights of the Cape 180, 181
  Knights of the Golden Fleece 22, 23
  Knights of the Jubilation 43
  Knights of the Mortar 180

Leeson, Mrs 202
Locke, John xxii, xxiii, 79, 80, 132
London xxiii, xxv, xxvi, 1, 2, 4, 5, 8, 10, 15,
  16, 22–8, 31, 33, 36–8, 43, 49, 50, 55,
  83, 102, 103, 132, 137, 148, 152, 162,
  184, 187, 188, 209, 212, 213
London Journal 53, 111
Low Countries *see* Holland
Luttrell, Lord Simon 62, 64, 65, 92, 109,
  208

MacNaughton, John 172, 173, 176, 177
Magistrates 2, 15, 26, 47, 48, 131, 162
Mary II 15–17
masculinity xxvii, 9, 32
Masons xxi, 58, 61, 103, 112, 171, 191,
  203, 204

masturbation 112, 125, 170, 171, 173
Medmenham Abbey xix, 85, 87, 92, 95,
  98–104, 109–13, 116, 131
Medmenham Friars xxi, xxvi, 14, 84, 85,
  92, 94, 95, 97, 99–112, 115–17, 119,
  121, 122, 127, 129, 131–3, 136, 140,
  142, 143, 145, 147, 150, 154, 155,
  167, 173, 181, 185, 193, 196, 205,
  207–9
Memoirs of a Woman of Pleasure xxvi, 125,
  174, 176
Merryland 125, 127, 168, 169, 171–3, 175,
  177
Methodists 67, 68, 127, 128
Middleton, Conyers 85, 86
Mist's Weekly Journal 52, 53, 59
Mohocks xxi, 27–38, 72, 180, 187, 197, 206
Murray, Fanny 91, 102, 118, 147

Netherlands *see* Holland
North Briton 115, 117, 119, 121, 151, 187
Norwich 67, 68
Norwich Hell-Fire Club 67–9

Ottoman Empire *see* Turkey
Oxford 69, 77, 78, 108
  Brasenose College 69
  Exeter College 141
  Magdalen College 108
  Phoenix Club 70
  Wadham College 8

Paris 7, 9, 59, 116
parish constables 11, 26
Parliament xvii, xxi, xxiii, 16, 17, 19, 71,
  101, 106, 107, 117, 119, 121, 127,
  131, 134, 141, 150, 151, 154
penis xxv, 99, 118, 119, 167, 170, 171–2,
  180
Pepys, Samuel 10, 123
Pilkington, Laetitia 63
Pitt, William the elder 116, 143
Pittenweem, Fife 165, 170, 175
Pope, Alexander 60, 118, 119
  Essay on Man 118, 119
Potter, Thomas 108, 117, 118, 150
Presbyterians 7, 149, 198
Prince Regent 173, 202
Proclamation Society, 127
prostitution 12, 18, 51, 182, 183, 188,
  213

Rabelais xix, 98, 100, 111
rake-hells xxiii, xxiv, 15–17, 55
Ray, Martha, 147, 148
Rochester, John Wilmot, Earl of 7, 10, 11,
    131 89, 144, 209
  Ballers 13
  death 9, 12, 77
  as Doctor Alexander Bendo 10
  duelling 9
  friends 8, 9, 12–14
  Grand Tour 89, 144
  marriage 10
  mistresses 12
  poems 6–8, 10, 123 6–14, 17, 77, 89,
      123, 131, 144, 208
Royal Africa Company, 132
Royal Proclamations xviii, 27, 45, 47,
    127
Russia 88, 89, 137, 176, 177

Sandwich, John Montague, 4th Earl of,
    129, 132, 143, 193
  admiralty 87, 105, 144–6, 148
  cricket 147
  Divan Club 91, 105, 144, 147
  education 89, 143
  finances 145
  gambling 147
  Grand Tour 87, 90, 143, 144
  House of Lords, 144
  as Jeremy Twitcher 120, 121, 148
  and John Wilkes 100, 105, 116,
      119–121, 146
  marriage, 145
  Medmenham Friars 99, 100, 104, 105,
      116, 145
  mistresses 147, 148
  music 147
  politics 144–6
  Society of Dilettanti 90, 92, 93, 105,
      144, 147
Santry, Harry Barry, Lord 62, 64, 65
Savile, Henry 8, 9, 13
Schemers 58, 103
Scottish Enlightenment 157, 185
Scotland xx, 1, 4, 43, 125, 157–61, 164
Sedley, Charles 8, 12, 13
Seven Years War 77, 115
sex xxiv, 87, 99, 102, 113, 122, 158
sexuality xxiv, 99, 102, 122, 158, 173
Shaftesbury, Lord 78–80

Skelton Castle 84, 192, 193
Smith, Adam 160
Societies for the Reformation of Manners
    England 14–16, 71
    Ireland 66, 67
Society for the Suppression of Vice 127,
    213
Society of Dilettanti 79, 90, 92–5, 101,
    105, 113, 132, 136, 137, 144, 147,
    173
Spectator, The 29, 30, 35, 40, 206
St Andrews University 164, 167, 178
Sterne, Laurence 78, 79, 94
Stourhead 82
Stowe 82, 86, 139, 151
street theatre 5, 38
Sublime Company of Beefsteaks 150,
    188–92
Sweden 177, 178

theatre 4–6, 26, 89
Tityre Tues 2–5
Toland, John 42, 43
Tories 23, 34, 38, 39, 40, 41, 58, 60, 61,
    94, 173, 196
True Briton 58
Turkey 2, 90, 91, 132, 144
  Constantinople 91, 92

Union with Scotland 159–63, 171
United Irishmen 198, 200–1

Vansittart, Arthur 106
Vansittart, Henry 105, 108
Vansittart, Robert senior 13
Vansittart, Robert junior 106, 108, 208
Vaux, Edward Lord 2, 3
Venus 98
  de Medici 94
  School of 123, 126, 127
  Temple of 139

Walcot, Mary 91, 102
Wales, Frederick Prince of 109, 136, 142
Walpole, Horace 79, 87–9, 92, 94, 95, 100,
    101, 105, 134, 135
Walpole, Sir Robert 59, 134, 144
Warburton, William Bishop of Gloucester
    118, 119
Ward, Ned 21–4

West Wycombe xix, xxvi, 82, 85, 86, 103, 104, 106, 107, 110, 132, 136–40, 142, 207, 208

Wharton, Philip Duke of 39, 49, 61, 75, 131
  death 60
  debts 57–9
  education 49
  estates 49, 50, 61, 62
  father 49–50
  Freemasons, 58
  Grand Tour 50, 75, 79
  Hell-Fire Club xvii, xxvi, 48, 57, 206
  Jacobitism 50, 51, 58, 81, 107
  Madrid 59
  marriage 49–51, 59
  Spanish army 59, 60
  treason 59, 60

whigs xxii, 23, 33, 34, 38, 40, 41, 49, 51, 58, 60, 61, 72, 94, 134, 173, 196

Whitehead, Paul 103, 104, 123, 133

Wig Club 158, 178, 179, 185

Wilkes, Israel 148

Wilkes, Jack 152

Wilkes, John 65, 132, 133
  Aylesbury, Squire of 150
  Bucks Militia 151
  daughter 149, 151
  death 152
  debts 151
  duel 152
  and Earl of Sandwich 100, 116, 121–1, 129, 146
  Essay on Woman 69, 117, 120, 121, 151
  Governor of Foundling Hospital 150
  illegitimate Son 152
  Lord Mayor of London 152
  marriage 133, 159, 150
  Medmenham Abbey 116
  Medmenham Friars 97–9, 102, 103, 105, 106, 110, 137, 150, 207
  Member of Parliament 115, 135, 150–2
  mistresses 152–4
  North Briton 115, 117
  Parliament 119, 151
  politics 116
  prosecution 126
  Sublime Company of Beefsteaks, 189
  wife 149, 151
  West Wycombe 139,

Wilkes, Mary 148, 149, 151

Wilkes, Polly 149

William III of England 15–18, 49, 77

witchcraft 4, 39–42, 157

Wodrow, Robert 157

Wodrow Collection 53

women xxiv, 10, 19, 84, 91, 102, 103, 110, 123, 126, 127, 147, 181, 182, 184

Worsdale, James, 62, 63

Wortley Montagu, Lady Mary 57, 58, 89, 91, 92